Praise for
The Constitution in Jeopardy

"Only a small number of Americans know what an Article V constitutional convention is. That needs to change—and fast. Feingold and Prindiville expose the underbelly of a national movement to overhaul the United States Constitution and radically change the nature of our democracy. Secrecy is their best friend, so patriotic citizens who want our Republic to survive *must* read this book."

—Larry Sabato, professor and director of the center for politics,
University of Virginia

"A well-crafted book about the history, relevance, challenges, and future of the Constitution's amendment process. This book is for all citizens who want to better understand our Constitution and why it is the core and soul of our democracy."

—Senator Chuck Hagel, former secretary of defense

"This book masterfully and accessibly canvases history, portrays current events, and sketches out a variety of possible futures for this nation's basic law—and thus for the United States itself. I would call it artistic but fear that it might then be hung on a wall—far better and more important that the book should become a major practical means of civic education, widely read, and debated among the engaged citizenry generally."

—Joseph D. Kearney, dean and professor of law,
Marquette University Law School

"This book is essential reading for two quite different reasons. One is its acuity in examining the lack of clarity in the Constitution's amendment procedure and its convention route. The other, though, is its equal acuity in noting that the country very much needs a long-overdue conversation about the adequacy of the Constitution for our twenty-first-century realities and that an all-important first step is to confront the problems of the amendment procedure itself, including the stumbling blocks it presents to adoption of needed changes."

—Sanford Levinson, professor of law and political science, University of Texas, and coauthor (with Cynthia Levinson) of *Fault Lines in the Constitution*

"Feingold and Prindiville have thrown a bright spotlight on a fascinating question that's going to explode into the national consciousness."

—Sai Prakash, professor, University of Virginia School of Law

"In their fascinating, historically rich volume, Feingold and Prindiville offer both an urgent warning against the current right-wing movement for a new constitutional convention and a constructive framework for revising the amendment process itself to give 'We, the People' direct constitutional amendment power through processes designed to mitigate factionalism in the pursuit of constitutional change."

—Peter Shane, professor, Ohio State University Moritz College of Law

"This is an important book about a subject that we need to pay more attention to, Article V of the U.S. Constitution, which governs the process by which the Constitution can be amended. Feingold and Prindiville explain how the framers of the Constitution saw the amendment process as the best way for the people of the United States to ensure the document and the country's continuing vitality. George Washington, for example, saw Article V as the middle way between the havoc of constant change and the danger of stagnation. The authors also discuss in detail some of the vital changes that constitutional amendments have brought about, such as the abolition of slavery, the establishment of an income tax, and the progress toward racial and gender equality.

At the same time, however, they alert us to two dangers relating to Article V, the first involving efforts by far-right activists to awaken its convention mechanism and capitalize on its ill-defined procedure, and the second, the possibility that, because of the difficulty of the amendment process and the fact that only twenty-seven amendments have been ratified in over two centuries, people will conclude that it is useless to even contemplate amending the Constitution. The authors also explain the defects in Article V itself. Ultimately, however, Feingold and Prindiville make clear that it is necessary not to succumb to passivity but rather to engage in a robust national conversation about Article V and the critical issues that it presents."

—Hon. Lynn Adelman, United States district judge

THE
CONSTITUTION
IN
JEOPARDY

THE
CONSTITUTION
IN
JEOPARDY

An Unprecedented Effort to Rewrite Our
Fundamental Law and What We Can Do About It

RUSS FEINGOLD
AND
PETER PRINDIVILLE

PUBLICAFFAIRS
New York

PublicAffairs
Hachette Book Group
1290 Avenue of the Americas, New York, NY 10104
www.publicaffairsbooks.com
@Public_Affairs

Printed in the United States of America

First Edition: August 2022

Published by PublicAffairs, an imprint of Perseus Books, LLC, a subsidiary of Hachette
Book Group, Inc. The PublicAffairs name and logo is a trademark of the Hachette Book
Group.

The Hachette Speakers Bureau provides a wide range of authors for speaking events.
To find out more, go to www.hachettespeakersbureau.com or call (866) 376-6591.

The publisher is not responsible for websites (or their content) that are not owned by the
publisher.

Library of Congress Control Number: 2022939558

ISBNs: 9781541701526 (hardcover), 9781541701540 (ebook)

LSC-C

Printing 1, 2022

For our parents—

Leon and Sylvia Feingold
of blessed memory

Mary Ellen and Jim Prindiville

This book is typeset in Adobe Caslon Pro, a modern reproduction of the typeface designed by William Caslon in 1734. Type from Caslon's foundry was common in British North America and was used in the first printings of the Declaration of Independence in 1776 and the Constitution in 1787.

CONTENTS

We the People of the United States, in Order to form a more perfect Union, establish Justice, insure domestic Tranquility, provide for the common defence, promote the general Welfare, and secure the Blessings of Liberty to ourselves and our Posterity, do ordain and establish this Constitution for the United States of America.

United States Constitution, Preamble

The Congress, whenever two thirds of both Houses shall deem it necessary, shall propose Amendments to this Constitution, or, on the Application of the Legislatures of two thirds of the several States, shall call a Convention for proposing Amendments, which, in either Case, shall be valid to all Intents and Purposes, as Part of this Constitution, when ratified by the Legislatures of three fourths of the several States, or by Conventions in three fourths thereof, as the one or the other Mode of Ratification may be proposed by the Congress; Provided that no Amendment which may be made prior to the Year One thousand eight hundred and eight shall in any Manner affect the first and fourth Clauses in the Ninth Section of the first Article [provisions relating to slavery and direct taxation]; and that no State, without its Consent, shall be deprived of its equal Suffrage in the Senate.

United States Constitution, Article V

PROLOGUE

J ANUARY 29, 2019, was a light workday in the Arkansas State Senate. The twenty-five Republicans and nine Democrats approved a resolution congratulating the state football champions, altered prison disciplinary grievance procedures (passed 32–2), changed rules regarding safe deposit boxes (34–0), raised the maximum borrowing limit for certain state-issued loans (34–0), and altered the procedure for confirming new highway commissioners (34–0). All told, the Senate adjourned in under two hours—an hour earlier than planned. Observers in the gallery might have been forgiven for remarking that not much important had happened. But slipped between these small-bore votes was an uncommon item, complete with a peculiar name: an application to Congress for an Article V convention.[1]

State Senator Gary Stubblefield, a Republican dairy farmer from western Arkansas, introduced the vote. "They give these speeches in Washington, D.C., and talk about the interests of the American people. You know what it's really about in Washington, D.C.? It's about maintaining power. . . . Congress has known this all along," he remarked.[2] What the country needed, he continued, was radical constitutional change—curtailing the national budget, diminishing federal regulatory power, and other proposals "to limit the power and jurisdiction of the federal government." The states needed to neuter the federal government. Congress could not be trusted to do that on its own.

Article V—the Constitution's oft-forgotten amendment provision— was created by the Framers for this very moment, Stubblefield argued. If two-thirds of the states apply for a convention, he explained, then one must be held. Congress has no say in the matter. It would be the first time such a convention had ever convened, but if not now, when? "This Article V is not a Democrat or Republican issue, it's an American issue," Stubble-field told his colleagues.[3]

Senator Joyce Elliott, a Democrat from Little Rock, took the floor to counter. "We have become so lazy about our democracy we look for short-cuts, and this is one of them. . . . I'm just as uncomfortable thinking about some kind of re-write in the Constitution because . . . we do not know what will happen at this convention."[4]

Senator Linda Chesterfield, a Democrat also from Little Rock, agreed. "I fear that as we go down this road willy-nilly, we are putting together a convention that might not look like me, might not care about me, might not care about the diversity of America. . . . What will we do about making sure that this constitutional convention reflects the diversity that really is America? . . . I would say leave things alone."[5]

But most of Elliot and Chesterfield's colleagues brushed aside their concerns, voting 19–13 to submit Arkansas's application to Congress. Four Republicans joined all Democrats in opposition.[6]

The vote in Montana two years later on February 10, 2021, was not so smooth. A convention advocacy organization had wined and dined Republican state senators, hoping to grease the skids before the legislature considered the application in public, reported Theresa Manzella, a Repub-lican state senator from western Montana. As she later remarked, "By the time it got to the committee for the hearing, [convention advocates] had already developed a lot of support for the issue."[7] But when the application reached the state senate floor for a vote, tensions ran high.[8]

Manzella had sparked the drama. She had been an early supporter of a twenty-first-century constitutional convention, attending an Article V war game held in 2016. "I got there, it was really well done, and I got kinda excited," she remarked.[9] But now swayed by the opposition of the ultraconservative John Birch Society and the far-right militia group the Oath Keepers, Manzella decided to pull her support.[10] A constitutional convention could run away, she believed, meaning it could become uncon-trollable and propose radical changes to our constitutional system.

"Show me where it says that the states will control a convention," she emphatically asked her colleagues on the senate floor. "Show me where it says [that] in Article V."[11] Even convention proponents are "conflicted in the information they've put out," she argued. "They're making the rules up as they go."[12]

In retaliation for her stance, a convention advocacy organization run by the founder of the Tea Party Patriots, Mark Meckler, launched an aggressive smear campaign to silence her. "I have been targeted by them," Manzella remarked on the senate floor.[13] "They have cherry-picked my quotes, they have taken them out of context and they have compared me to Hillary Clinton and George Soros."[14]

Manzella, continuing, revealed that she had written a letter resigning from the legislature the night before the vote because of the harassment, unsure whether she would feel moved to submit it. "I think you need to know that," she told her colleagues on the senate floor, many avoiding eye contact with her.[15] "I have never felt more disrespected as a committee member and a human being than I have felt in association with this bill."[16]

After her speech, the application was voted down twenty-six to twenty-four, with six other Republicans and all Democrats joining Manzella in opposition.[17] Reflecting on the vote, Manzella later remarked, "Their approach has been to sicken the people against you. . . . Sadly many of them are aggressive and hateful and that's sad. That's really sad. I feel betrayed by the people that promote [a convention]."[18]

Activists issued a chilling statement following the loss: "The 26–24 defeat is a setback for our team in Montana, but we are not discouraged. Why? Because we understand their [sic] is no other peaceful option . . . to rein in an out-of-control federal government."[19]

*   *   *

"A LIVE WEAPON IN OUR HANDS"

Stubblefield's success in Arkansas and Manzella's decisive negative vote in Montana are just two episodes in a larger alarming story. Over the last two decades, a hushed effort to hold a convention under the Constitution's amendment provision—the nation's first ever—has inched through statehouses. And employing a dubious legal theory advanced by leading politicians, some now argue they only need to enlist a small handful of additional states to trigger the convening.

A convention would be a watershed moment in American history. Just like James Madison, Alexander Hamilton, and Benjamin Franklin in Philadelphia over two centuries ago, delegates would exercise almost unfettered authority to draft amendments that would change the contours of our fundamental law and civic life. Every contentious political and social issue could be on the table, creating or retiring constitutional rights and freedoms and restructuring basic elements of modern government. Unlike political skirmishes in Congress or presidential elections, constitutional amendments cut to the core of public life, silencing debate and quashing opposition. And as with all legal text, whoever holds the drafting pen exercises incredible power. The debates and proposed reforms of these new "framers" could shape American life for centuries.

The enormity of such an occasion is not lost on contemporary convention proponents. While many across the political spectrum have ignored their efforts, advocates have made their goals quite plain. As convention supporter Senator Rick Santorum remarked, "We're planning on putting resources, people in place to get us to where the safety's off and we have a live weapon in our hands."[20]

The claim is both disturbing and peculiar. What is it about this august constitutional mechanism, one envisioned as a means for national reckoning and reformation, that allows one to claim it as a new "weapon"? How can one say with such certainty that the "live weapon" will be theirs? And—perhaps most important—does the weapon pose any real danger? Might it have been decommissioned and discarded long ago?

Hard-right activists have seized upon the seemingly arcane constitutional convention mechanism for two reasons. First, some argue that state legislatures—not the voters—would select convention delegates. Second, some also argue that at a convention each state would get one vote, making the convention radically more malapportioned than the Congress or the Electoral College (California's 39.5 million citizens would have the same representation and vote as Wyoming's 579,000).[21] Neither of these two claims is a settled matter of law, and each has been the subject of intense debate among constitutional scholars for generations. Yet convention proponents embrace the uncertainty and praise its potential. Even if their extreme policies are rebuffed in Congress and at the polls, it is possible that activists might be able to use the amendment mechanism to foist their agenda on an unwitting majority.

In closed-door meetings with state legislators across the country, proponents explain these supposed realities with great excitement. Republicans have controlled a majority of state legislatures at multiple points during the last decades. These electoral fortunes, if continued, could make it possible for a faction to end-run a constitutional convening, pushing through radical proposals with no bipartisan support. "The number of states with Republican legislatures (governors have no role in the process) already approaches the necessary two-thirds," one leading convention proponent wrote in the far-right publication the *Epoch Times*. "Surely a convention dominated by conservative state legislatures can draft amendments popular enough to be ratified by [three-quarters of the] states."[22]

That final bit of mathematics—the three-quarters threshold for ratification—poses an uphill battle for changing the Constitution. But history makes clear that even *proposing* constitutional amendments can be a potent legal and political force. Once amendments are pending before the states for ratification, they can sit for decades until they receive sufficient support, upsetting state-level politics in the process. And even if they are never ratified, proposed amendments can have a profound effect on the development of legal doctrine and party agendas. One need only look to the Equal Rights Amendment, which was proposed in 1972 yet languished before the states for decades awaiting ratification, for a telling example. While the states sat on the proposal, the courts and political branches took the matter up themselves, expanding the Constitution's guarantee of equal protection to further encompass sex. While the proposed amendment did not have an immediate legal effect, it had a profound impact on political and legal debate.

Far from focusing on the three-quarters bar, many proponents likely are thinking only about a lower one: the majority of states (twenty-six) possibly required to propose amendments in a convention. And convention proponents have fashioned a wish list of radical amendment proposals that might clear such a lower threshold: new state authority to veto federal laws, onerous federal spending limitations that would eviscerate most national policy and imperil national defense, and a complete restructuring of the country's lawmaking and regulatory powers. Other topics, even more radical ones, are likely in the wings. With the math possibly on their side, many activists and their deep-pocketed funders are betting that it is preferable to lead the charge than catch up from behind.

Despite convention proponents' claims of legal certainty, the most important questions about how a convening held under Article V would be called and how it would function are unsettled. The Framers left no rules. In this uncertainty lies great danger and, possibly, great power. Those who act first—achieving the requisite number of state applications to call a convention or convincing Congress or the courts that the threshold has been met using dubious counting methods—gain the advantage of creating the rules for the process. With a decades-long head start and little opposition, proponents have thrust ahead into this vast constitutional void, creating robust advocacy networks and marshaling commentators to craft legal theories favorable to their interests, oftentimes out of near thin air. Capitalizing on an era defined by win-at-all-costs partisan rancor, factious elements have trained their eyes on the ultimate prize: the Constitution itself.

IMPORTANT EVENTS

1776: Declaration of Independence
1781: Articles of Confederation
1787: Constitutional Convention meets in Philadelphia
1788: Constitution is ratified
1789: Constitution becomes operative (Washington inaugurated as first president; first session of Congress held)

CONSTITUTIONAL AMENDMENTS DISCUSSED AT LENGTH HEREIN

See full text in Appendix.

- One through Ten (Bill of Rights): proposed, 1789; ratified, 1791.
- Eleven (state immunity from suit): proposed, 1794; ratified, 1795.
- Twelve (presidential election procedures): proposed, 1803; ratified, 1804.
- Thirteen through Fifteen (abolish slavery, define citizenship, establish equal protection and due process guarantees, establish voting protections, among other topics): proposed between 1865 and 1869; ratified between 1865 and 1870.
- Sixteen (income tax): proposed, 1909; ratified, 1913.
- Seventeen (direct election of senators): proposed, 1912; ratified, 1913.
- Eighteen (Prohibition): proposed, 1917; ratified, 1919.
- Nineteen (women's suffrage): proposed, 1919; ratified, 1920.
- Twenty-Six (eighteen-year-old vote): proposed, 1971; ratified, 1971.
- Twenty-Seven (congressional pay): proposed, 1789; ratified, 1992.

THE
CONSTITUTION
IN
JEOPARDY

INTRODUCTION

T HIS BOOK IS ABOUT ARTICLE V, the Constitution's amendment process. It examines the history and meaning of the mechanism, analyzes contemporary efforts to distort its procedure for factional gain, and proposes a path forward for reform. The book is thus, at its core, about legal machinery—constitutional bolts, nuts, and gears—and the impact of that machinery on modern life.

But it is also about an aspirational ideal and the need to rekindle that ideal. Article V enshrines one of the Founding generation's most profound beliefs: that in a constitutional democracy, the People are empowered to return to first principles in a regular and controlled way to reform their government.

As the earliest Americans formed state constitutions during the Revolutionary War, many believed that constitutional amendment would be the cornerstone in a new American conception of democratic self-government. They heralded procedures for formal constitutional change as a means of "bloodless revolution" that would allow their communities to avoid the horrors of war and the tumult that defined the nation's birth. It would be constitutional amendment, these early Americans believed, that would allow their experiment to endure.

When the Framers set out to draft the new national constitution a decade later, they built upon these early ideals, fashioning a completely new theory of constitutionalism and national union. The Framers put aside the Articles of Confederation, the nation's first governing charter, and its ill-fated notion that the national government merely mediated loose relations between disparate states. The government would be cast in a new image, securing its authority not from the "Delegates of the States," as did the failed Articles, but rather directly from "We the People" who would "ordain and establish" the Constitution.[1]

In few places was such a reframing of constitutional authority more profound than in the debates regarding constitutional change. The Framers shared those early American beliefs that constitutional amendment could provide the primary means for the People to ensure that the new nation would thrive. Article V was a middle way between the havoc of constant change and the dangers of stagnancy and ossification. As George Washington remarked before the document was ratified, the new Constitution was "not free from imperfections."[2] But the "People (for it is with them to Judge) can, as they will have the advantage of experience on their Side, decide with as much propriety on the alteration[s] and amendment[s] which are necessary," he wrote. "I do not think we are more inspired, have more wisdom, or possess more virtue, than those who will come after us."[3]

Throughout history, Americans have tried to take up Washington's charge, calling upon Article V as a mechanism for political and social reform. Constitutional amendments have proved necessary to outlaw slavery and pursue racial and gender equality. So too have reformers outside the political establishment, like those in the women's suffrage and Progressive Era movements, seized on Article V as a means for redress when those in power remained obstinate. In the critical moments when change was necessary, our forebears have often looked to the amendment process for renewal. And many of these amendments have paved the way for the celebrated (and sometimes detested) advances in American freedom and equality. The right to marry, to speak freely, to worship according to one's conscience, to be free from racial discrimination, and to have bodily autonomy all find genesis in the amendments and contemporary meaning in their judicial elaboration.

This is perhaps why American public debate about the Constitution is often focused squarely on the document's additions rather than its initial grand articles. As one recent poll found, only 51 percent of Americans could name the federal government's three branches (legislative, judicial, and executive). But four out of five could name at least one of the First Amendment's five freedoms (speech, religion, press, assembly, and petition).[4] Most of the acclaimed rights advances of the last century find their legal roots in the Fourteenth Amendment. Raise the Second Amendment at Thanksgiving dinner—should you be so bold—and someone is bound to have a strong opinion. So too are other amendments keystones in modern life, including the Fourth (regulating police search and seizure power), the Seventeenth (direct election of senators), the Nineteenth (women's vote), or the Twenty-Sixth (eighteen-year-old vote). The amendments, and the Washingtonian ideal of national reformation they represent, have continued to captivate the American constitutional imagination.

An Unsettled Article V

Yet over the last two centuries, Article V—the machinery of formal constitutional change—has often been seen as an afterthought. A dilemma has arisen with the passage of time as lived experience has failed to attain the aspirations of the Founding.

Ours is the world's oldest functioning written national constitution, yet it is also one of the least changed. Although more than eleven thousand amendments have been proposed in Congress, only thirty-three have been sent to the states for approval and twenty-seven ultimately ratified. And a convention has never been held under Article V, despite the submission of at least 445 applications by state legislatures since 1789.[5] While we celebrate those twenty-seven great moments of constitutional reformation, formal constitutional change has been the exception rather than a middle-way norm.

How can one explain this divergence between Founding ideals and historical practice? The common response is that the procedure is just too hard. Article V establishes an arduous path, requiring a supermajority of either state legislatures or both houses of Congress to propose amendments and an even larger supermajority of either state legislatures or state conventions to ratify. Many policy makers and scholars today argue that this is Article V's fatal flaw—its standards are too high to have any modern power. Indeed, the mechanism is so burdensome that some have come to consider it as almost dead and certainly not worth much attention. Article V might be printed in the Constitution, the thinking goes, but it is not usable in practice.

These onerous supermajority requirements no doubt contribute in large part to the paucity of amendments. They make the road to reform hard and long. But they do not make amendment impossible. History teaches that at times—and often to the surprise of many—Article V has been both workable and exceptionally powerful, taking quick hold in the political climate.

The majority of the twenty-seven amendments were ratified during a few short moments of amendment fervor: the Bill of Rights just following ratification (ten between 1789 and 1791); the amendments of the "Second Founding," which outlawed slavery and guaranteed equal citizenship for African Americans following the Civil War (three between 1865 and 1870); the Progressive Era amendments, which brought much-needed reform to Washington (four between 1913 and 1920); and the mid-twentieth-century reform period (four between 1961 and 1971). Yet outside these moments of rapid constitutional movement, amendments have been exceptionally rare: only six over the intervening 204 years.

This history offers a different conclusion regarding the nature of Article V. Rather than dead or useless, the mechanism might merely be sleeping—a giant waiting to be awakened. As James Madison wrote in *Federalist* No. 49, the amendment mechanism is a "constitutional road to the decision of the people . . . marked out and kept open for certain great and extraordinary occasions."

Article V remains a peculiar, unsettled element of the American constitutional structure. The provision is of foundational importance but is often ignored in public debates about constitutional change. So too does much of its procedure remain opaque. As Madison remarked before the 1787 Convention had even adjourned, Article V's convention route was flawed due to insufficient "constitutional regulations" dictating how it should work.[6] And as the following chapters detail, the provision has always suffered from inherent tensions, the result of a compromise between competing theories of constitutional change and popular autonomy. Where Washington and his colleagues envisioned constitutional amendment as an established, certain means to ensure the Constitution's vitality, over two centuries of lived experience have left more questions than settled answers.

TWIN JEOPARDIES

Despite these structural uncertainties, the Founding generation's noble aim to provide a means for peaceful, popular constitutional change remains. This book is an attempt to revive these aspirations and Washington's middle way, to spark public discussion of both the dangers and possibilities of formal constitutional amendment and a reevaluation of the legal mechanism that provides for such change.

For generations, scholars, policy leaders, and reformers have wrestled with Article V, attempting to add structure to its ill-formed procedures and fashion political environments that might guide public debate toward the high ideals of constitutional reform. Many academic articles have been written, draft revisions proposed, and bills introduced. These efforts have yielded few positive results. But recent events have rekindled the need for such debate and reform.

The Constitution sits in a precarious moment, confronted by twin jeopardies. The first jeopardy is a new effort, spearheaded and funded by far-right activists, to awaken Article V's convention mechanism and capitalize on its uncertain procedure almost entirely for factional gain. This is a particularly troubling danger, one rife with unanswered legal questions and animated by the divisive hyperpartisan sentiments of our era. This threat must be engaged with a cool head, its profound legal errors discounted, and its path blocked.

But in quashing the contemporary convention threat, Americans must address the Constitution's second profound jeopardy: the danger of stagnancy and ossification.

The limited record of constitutional amendment—just twenty-seven ratified in over two centuries—has caused many across successive generations to accept that Article V is useless. Even before ratification, many argued that the amendment mechanism would never work. Leading scholars and jurists in the nineteenth century echoed the same sentiment. So too do many policy and opinion leaders today believe that the amendment mechanism is fundamentally broken. The country will not, and indeed *cannot*, ever amend the Constitution again, they argue.

Over the last half century, this belief has become so dominant in political and popular thought that some have come to embrace an even more troubling claim. Formal constitutional amendment is irrelevant, these commentators argue. Article V *should not* have any real power in modern life. The Constitution has survived without formal change and will continue to do so, they believe.

The nadir of Article V in mainstream thinking has inspired a system of crafting constitutional meaning—what could be called a "constitutional politics"—rife with problems and bad incentives. It has emboldened a form of reasoning that places constitutional power only in the hands of lawyers, judges, and academics. The People, for all practical purposes, are nowhere to be found.

Such a constitutional politics is at odds with the vast experience of American constitutionalism. Over the course of the nation's first two centuries, citizens have continued to elaborate on those early Americans' belief that bloodless revolution could provide renewed vigor to their political communities. In developing their own constitutions, citizens of the states and American territories have made popular constitutional change a central mechanism of the political and legal order, allowing citizens to directly constitute and reform their government at relatively regular intervals.

The time has come to continue this work. We must rebuild Washington's middle way, fashioning a new form of constitutional politics that empowers the People to reclaim their authority to make constitutional meaning.

*   *   *

A Note About Sources

When embarking on a study of the Constitution, one must engage the process and deliberations of its drafters to attempt to understand what the legal text means and how it operates. Throughout this book, and especially in Chapters 2 and 4, we consider in some detail the relevant debates of the first Constitutional Convention.

The primary sources documenting what occurred in Philadelphia in the summer of 1787 are incomplete.[7] We take as our starting point, as do most others, James Madison's Notes, published in Max Farrand's 1911 edited volume, *The Records of the Federal Convention*.[8] This documentary record, when combined with the Convention Journal's procedural notations, remains the most detailed source from the Convention and is generally accepted as the leading account.

But Madison's Notes are still notes. They are not a transcript, taken down as if by a court reporter or a clerk recording legislative minutes. This is a crucial distinction of which the reader should be aware. When we quote a particular delegate's comments from the Convention, we are quoting not a verbatim recitation but rather Madison's recollection of those remarks. It is quite possible that Madison remembered comments incorrectly, substituted what he thought he heard, or maybe even wrote down what he wanted to hear.

In her extensive study of Madison's Notes, constitutional historian Mary Sarah Bilder details how the Notes are likely incomplete and were altered by Madison long after the Convention adjourned. Madison did not write the Notes for the public, Bilder argues, but rather as a personal record for himself and likely Thomas Jefferson, who was serving a diplomatic mission in Paris while the Convention met. The Notes were never intended to be an objective account; they were more akin to a detailed diary entry than a newspaper article.[9] James Hutson, a historian with the Library of Congress Manuscript Division, likewise has argued that the Notes are underinclusive, covering only one-tenth of what was likely said at the Convention.[10]

What are we to make of this? We cannot know for sure. But as others have done before us, we take the Notes as they stand—with a healthy pinch of salt and a serious engagement with the scholarly literature added in for good measure.

So too have we tried to make the Notes accessible to a modern reader, substituting (in brackets) synonyms for words whose meaning has changed in the intervening centuries. For example, when Alexander Hamilton remarked that "an easy mode should be established for supplying defects," he did not mean that a route should be provided to create *more* constitutional problems. He meant the opposite. In context, the term *supply* is an archaic form, meaning "to make up for the lack or absence of something by providing a substitute" or "to make good a defect."[11] We have thus substituted the modern synonym *repair*. We also note such alterations in the relevant endnotes.

Part I

FOUNDATIONS

1

BLOODLESS REVOLUTION

The Radical Idea of
Peaceful Constitutional Change

"I hold that a little rebellion now and then is a good thing, and as necessary in the political world as storms in the physical. . . . It is a medicine necessary for the sound health of government."

—Thomas Jefferson to James Madison (January 30, 1787)[1]

WHEN THE *Dartmouth* entered Boston Harbor and docked at Griffin's Wharf in November 1773 carrying the East India Company's first direct shipment of tea to America, the colonists demanded the ship return to England. Ensnared in a bureaucratic morass and foreseeing financial ruin, the captain refused. Soon two more ships carrying Company tea docked, only to be greeted by the same angry demand from the colonists. After nineteen days of impasse, a group of Bostonians boarded the three ships under the cloak of darkness. They lifted the imported tea to the decks—some ninety-three thousand pounds in 342 chests, worth about $1.7 million today—and dumped it into the harbor.[2] Although they likely did not foresee it then, those who participated in what would come to be known as "the Boston Tea Party" changed the course of history and had a profound impact on the formation of the United States Constitution.

Earlier that year, few in London had been thinking about constitutional theory when Parliament considered the Tea Act. The debate was

Destruction of the tea at Boston Harbor (Lithograph, 1846)

about money. The East India Company, which administered the British Indian territory and its lucrative tea trade, had amassed substantial debts and was close to default. With eighteen million pounds of tea in London storehouses, it needed a new market, and quickly. The Company's directors soon set their eyes on a promising prospect: the American colonies.[3]

Exporting tea from England to the colonies was a risky proposition in 1773. Three years earlier, the Townshend Acts had imposed a much-hated tax on tea imported to America. The colonists were fierce in their opposition and turned to the black market. Soon smuggled tea accounted for an estimated 77 percent of the colonial tea trade.[4] To break into the market while still paying the import tax, the East India Company needed a concession. Lord North, the British prime minister, devised a solution. The government would allow the Company to ship tea directly to the Americas, cutting out merchant middlemen and the export taxes charged in London to make the American market economically viable.

The Tea Act passed both houses of Parliament with no discussion of its impact on the American colonists. The London press showed a similar lack of concern. The few newspapers that mentioned the vote failed to note a basic element of the law: that the American colonies were the focus of the new arrangement. As Ben Labaree, a historian of the colonial era, remarked, "Perhaps no bill of such momentous consequence has ever received less attention."[5]

Response in the colonies was swift. Even though the price of Company tea likely would have been comparable to the smuggled drink already available, many colonists refused on principle to buy it.[6] Under the British constitutional regime, they argued, Parliament had no right to levy direct taxes like the Townshend tea tax on the colonies unless the colonists had elected representation in London. The price was no matter. A tax was a tax.

The Boston Tea Party sparked a movement up and down the Eastern Seaboard. Three years prior, the colonies had little sense of unified political identity. But the British response to colonial protests inspired a common cause. Parliament passed a series of ever more draconian measures to quell the unrest. Soon, the British revoked the Massachusetts Charter and dissolved the colony's representative assembly. When the colonists objected to this new affront, the British responded with deadly force. At Concord in 1775, three minutemen fell—the "shot heard around the world."

As John Adams wrote in his diary the day following the Boston Tea Party, "This Destruction of the Tea, is so bold, so daring, so firm, intrepid & inflexible, and it must have so important Consequences and so lasting, that I cannot but consider it as an Epocha in History."[7]

FUNDAMENTAL LAW, THE NEW KING

What was it about the tea tax that made Bostonians so angry? Unlike modern mischaracterizations, the tea partiers were neither small-government firebrands nor free-market crusaders out to fight any new tax with a vengeance. The colonists' objections were more nuanced. As Edmund Burke reflected in the House of Commons two years later, the American critiques of British rule were learned ones. Their intense study of law had fostered a keen sensitivity to constitutional structure and rights.[8] The Boston Tea Party was not a manifestation of brute political anger but rather a disagreement regarding the legal principle the tea tax conveyed.

The American Revolution erupted largely over disagreements about who had authority to change the constitutional order.[9] Informed by Lockean notions of representative government, the colonists believed that the unwritten British constitution contained an array of inviolable limitations on government authority. The English Bill of Rights of 1689 guaranteed all Englishmen one such right: to pay only those taxes approved by Parliament (rather than by royal fiat). Since the colonies were unrepresented in Westminster, the colonists argued, Parliament could not infringe their retained constitutional right, no matter the reason.

London countered, claiming the colonies enjoyed "virtual representation" in Parliament, meaning non-colonist politicians could effectively represent colonial interests in the same way that landholding men did for others in England. The Americans dismissed this argument outright as "fallacious sophistry, in opposition to common sense."[10] Representation meant representation by one's peers. Without Americans in Parliament, there could simply be no legal tax in the colonies. The famed revolutionary rallying cry "no taxation without representation" was not merely a statement of fiscal policy. It was a much bolder claim: that England's constitution was fundamental law. All other law—including acts of Parliament—had to conform to it.

The British struggled to understand this view. To most in England and beyond, the constitution had no distinct power. The term was merely descriptive, referring to "that assemblage of laws, customs and institutions which form the general system."[11] As the influential English legal scholar William Blackstone put it at the time, there was no distinction between "the constitution or frame of government" and the "system of laws."[12] This prevailing understanding of the British constitution at least partially explains ministers' lack of concern regarding the Tea Act and why it received so little attention in the London press. It was challenging for the British even to conceive of an unconstitutional parliamentary act. The constitution *was* Parliament, the sum of all law passed by that legislative body. If Parliament passed a new law, it was, by definition, constitutional.[13]

This disagreement regarding the nature of constitutions is of central importance to the Founding, to the development of the American system of self-government, and to the question of how constitutions can be changed. The colonists espoused radical views regarding constitutionalism, believing that fundamental law could define and limit government power.

When Thomas Jefferson penned the Declaration of Independence, he summarized this new way of thinking. The purpose of government and law, Jefferson explained, is to establish a society in which the unalienable rights of life, liberty, and the pursuit of happiness are made real and manifest. Such a government is made by the People and bound by the People's delegation of power. And when the government oversteps the bounds of its authority, the People have a right to recourse. He continued: "To secure these rights, Governments are instituted among Men, deriving their just powers from the consent of the governed; That whenever any Form of Government becomes destructive of these ends, it is the Right of the People to alter or to abolish it, and to institute new Government, laying its foundation on such principles and organizing its powers in such form, as to them shall seem most likely to effect their Safety and Happiness."[14]

More than a revolutionary manifesto, the Declaration was a short, brilliant treatise on the nature of government, law, and society. It encapsulated and solidified the three main elements of the nascent American vision of democracy and constitutional theory: first, the People as the source of authority; second, the power of written law to limit the government; and third, the retained authority of the People to alter their form of government. In the new United States, fundamental law would reign supreme, with all other law and government action conforming to it.[15] This new view would take quick hold.

Almost immediately after approving the Declaration in July 1776, the Continental Congress adjourned, and its members rushed back home from Philadelphia to re-form the thirteen colonial governments into new, independent states. When the United States declared independence, the colonies' governing charters had become void. Having repudiated the power of the Crown, the colonies lacked a legitimate government and had reverted to what most Americans would have understood to be the basic social compact—the fundamental laws of humankind. What precisely this compact included, however, was open to debate.

Well versed in the writings of Thomas Hobbes and John Locke, two leading political theorists of the age, the newly independent Americans understood the dangerous implications of this disarray. Hobbes and Locke wrote that without government, humans existed in the state of nature—what today we might call anarchy.[16] Both Hobbes and Locke intended their conception of the state of nature to be hypothetical. They were political theorists; their purpose was to consider why humans leave the state of nature to form political communities and submit themselves to government authority.

But their theories now had a pressing real-world significance. On July 4, the colonists had effectively chosen to *reenter* the state of nature by throwing off the yoke of the king. And when they did so, much evaporated into the summer air. Gone were the institutions that adjudicated the English common law and the structure they provided society and commerce, gone were the wide array of civil rights retained under the British constitution, and gone were all property rights under royal grants. Independence had created a dangerous void: no government, no legitimate law, and, many feared, no order.[17]

Under the prevailing Lockean understanding of popular sovereignty, the "United States of America" and its states could not yet fill this void. Without new constitutions, the states did not even exist, let alone have a right to govern. And a union of states could not be formed, as a legal matter, until the states were constituted.

Acting on advice from the Second Continental Congress in 1775, New Hampshire's provincial congress began the process of state f ormation, adopting a provisional constitution in January 1776. After independence was declared in July, the other states followed suit.

Independence advocates in Connecticut and Rhode Island acted first, arguing that their charters, approved in 1662 and 1663, respectively, remained valid. Because the documents allowed elected assemblies to appoint the colonial governor rather than requiring royal appointment as other colonies did, proponents reasoned that their uniquely independent charters could function in the newly independent states without alteration.[18]

But this first foray into constitution making in the months following the Declaration drew critics. For some, the bedrock principle of popular sovereignty couldn't be reasoned away so easily with legalistic quibbling over the colonial charters' terms. A constitution was a contract between the government and the governed, one with unique terms. The contract was not time bound, possibly lasting forever, and its provisions remained binding on each successive generation without their explicit assent. This legal form did not permit the substitution of one party (the king) for another (a newly independent government). If there was to be a new government, objectors argued, a constitution must be drafted anew.

Several Rhode Island towns adopted this theory, instructing their representatives to ignore the old colonial charter until a new constitution could be drafted. The settlers who had originally accepted Rhode Island's royal charter in 1662 did so recognizing the king's authority, these towns' representatives argued, meaning that when the king was deposed by the Declaration, the governmental power reverted to the People. Without a reconstituted government, the legislature had no legal right to rule.[19]

The arguments fell on deaf ears. Connecticut and Rhode Island would keep their charters-turned-constitutions until 1818 and 1842, respectively. But in these early disagreements, one can see themes that remain pressing even today in the ongoing debates regarding American constitutionalism: What is a constitution, what makes it legitimate, and how should it work?

The Americans of the Founding generation were in the vanguard, experimenting with new and complex ideas about government, politics, and law. Independence had prompted an array of new questions no society had yet to consider. How should a free and democratic community grounded on a theory of the rule of fundamental law be structured? Should written constitutions be allowed to change, and if so, how? And perhaps most perplexing, if one says the People are the source of all political authority, how does a political community make that popular sovereignty a reality rather than just a high ideal? Must, for example, a constitution be put to a vote in which all can cast a ballot (including women and racial minorities)? Well-trodden paths and clear answers were elusive. What before had been confined to the rarefied air of political theory and academic treatises now had become the stuff of town meetings, popular debate, and political wrangling. Americans had begun to experience the beauty and struggle of making democracy work.

While each state's new constitution embraced a different approach to self-government, one striking commonality united the documents.[20] In this opening democratic moment, the states all endorsed some version of the rule of fundamental law. Gone was the British notion that a constitution was merely the sum of all law, changing with each new legislative act. The uniquely American idea of higher law demanded more. It required a popular grant of authority embodied in the text of a constitution. And it mandated strict adherence to that grant, requiring that the workings of government be judged against the text, structure, and animating purpose of that constitution.

As the revolutionary writer Thomas Paine observed in 1791, this new American theory of constitutionalism demanded an entirely new political vantage and culture. Americans treated constitutions like "political bible[s]," he remarked, ones that were well-thumbed and treated with a certain reverence. "Nothing was more common when any debate arose on the principle of a bill, or on the extent of any species of authority, than for the members to take the printed Constitution out of their pocket and read the chapter with which such matter in debate was connected."[21] How far the country had come from the ill-fated Tea Act debates in Westminster less than two decades prior. In the United States, constitutions were written and referenced, and legislation was judged against them. Fundamental law was the new king.

BLOODLESS REVOLUTION

American insistence on the supremacy of written constitutions raised predictable problems. If the documents were to be the ultimate binding law, what were the People to do if they wanted to change them? How could a sovereign people reassert their right to alter their government if the document was set in stone?

One answer was clear from recent American experience: revolution. Political theorists like John Locke argued that constitutions must be unamendable. Ratification was a solemn act of the People etched in time. Any change to a constitution would upset this original grant of popular legitimacy, rendering the government void. If a new generation desired to change the constitutional status quo, these theorists reasoned, they must overthrow the previous regime—using force if necessary. Only then could reformers reconstitute the government under new terms—a new constitution.[22]

The Rhode Island and Connecticut critics who refused to accept their new state governments as properly constituted because the old royal charters remained framed their dissent in this revolution-laden language. To them, constitutional change could only occur in a linear, two-step process—revolution then reconstitution. The state legislatures' attempt to form new governments by amending the old colonial charters ignored this stepwise logic. The Declaration was the revolutionary act, vanquishing the former government's authority. The People then needed to complete the second step: forming the new government. The *old* regime could not give legitimacy to the new one; that got the sequence backward.

As an anonymous writer stated in the *Providence Gazette* in November 1776, if the legislature did not correct course and draft a new constitution, "we should have no remedy left us, but downright rebellion."[23] With the prospect that citizens might start fighting each other to resolve constitutional questions, it seemed as though the American democratic experiment was tilting toward a new, troubling kind of violent politics.

Here one can see the predictable conflict between high political theory and the practical, lived experience of both the Founding generation and our own. Acknowledging revolution as the only method for constitutional change might make sense in the halls of academia. The approach presents a clear theory of popular sovereignty and draws a bright line between legitimate and illegitimate governments. It simplifies hard questions—Who are the People and what is a legitimate government?—by embracing the base human instinct for brutality. The People are those who are willing to put their life on the line for the cause, and the legitimate government is the one left standing. Violence is what settles the matter: either the current regime repels the uprising, or the revolutionaries prevail with popular support against the despot. Blood has the final word.

As early Americans soon realized, such theoretical, barbaric purity was impractical. A functioning democracy required workable, nonviolent methods for constitutional change. Otherwise, citizens would kill the newborn experiment.

A method for amending constitutions was needed, the townspeople of Lexington, Massachusetts, declared in 1778, to "be a happy means, under providence, of preventing popular commotions, mobs, bloodshed and civil war." The town delegates of Essex County agreed. They urged the Massachusetts constitutional convention to make a provision allowing the people "to rectify the errors that will creep in through lapse of time, or alteration of situation." While the stability of a written constitution was desirable, they wrote, unamendable constitutions were known to fail and lead to violence. A formal amendment mechanism was the only peaceful method to mediate stability and change. The Roxbury town delegates also agreed. An amendment method was essential, they argued, so that "the people might recur to first principles in a Regular Way, without hazarding a Revolution in the Government."[24]

For the people of Lexington, Essex County, and Roxbury (now a neighborhood of Boston), revolution was not a far-off, heady topic. Its carnage

laid all around them. Over one hundred men, forty-nine of them local militiamen, had died at the Battles of Lexington and Concord just three years
before. The siege of Boston had left another four hundred of their own dead
and could have destroyed their city.[25] These new Americans knew the costs
of revolution. With war raging, their insistence on an amendment provision
expressed an ambitious hope—that, in America, revolution would be made
with law rather than with blood.

This early hankering for state constitutional amendment provisions
demonstrated a noble, even remarkable turn in American public life.
Assembled in town meetings amid war-torn wreckage, common citizens
thought intently about how to forge their fledgling democratic community
to reflect a new image of human nature. They believed that maybe, just
maybe, the new American democracies could cast off the human instinct
for violence and adopt the higher, more measured insistence on law and
debate as the appropriate means to address civic conflict. For them, constitutional amendment was about more than mundane, wonkish repairs. It
was needed to peacefully preserve the democratic community.

That the burgeoning American theory of constitutionalism should (or
even could) accommodate such peaceful constitutional amendment was a
controversial proposition. Early thinking regarding popular sovereignty
and fundamental law was still enmeshed in the realities of violent revolution. When Thomas Jefferson boldly claimed in the Declaration that the
Americans were exercising the "Right of the People to alter or to abolish
[the British regime], and to institute new Government," he was justifying
violent insurrection. The colonists had tried to use nonviolent, political
routes to seek change within the British constitutional framework, but
their efforts failed. The First Continental Congress relayed a petition to
the king in 1774, "filled with sentiments of duty to [his] Majesty," requesting the repeal of objectionable laws. The king never replied. Another petition
was sent the following year amid a series of additional pleas lodged with
British authorities, again to no avail.[26] Dissatisfied with these rebuffs,
Americans turned to war. When citizens set out to draft new state constitutional amendment provisions, General George Washington had been
leading colonial troops in campaigns for over two years to claim the right
of the people to alter or abolish their government. And more conflict was
likely imminent. The Declaration's vision of popular sovereignty was
hardly a peaceful one.

In this early moment, crafting a legal mechanism for bloodless revolution was a daunting task. With a new regime secured by violence, American statesmen and constitutional drafters needed to translate nascent ideas of popular sovereignty and regime change to the new, peaceful context of constitutional amendment. That translation posed knotty problems.

THE PEOPLE PARADOX

As the states began crafting their founding documents, they wrestled with the question of who exactly retained the right to change the government and how that change could occur. Echoing the Declaration's invocation of the "right of the people," all thirteen original states settled on some recognition of popular authority. The Virginia Bill of Rights declared that "a majority of the community" had the right to reform, alter, or abolish the government. Pennsylvania granted the authority to "the community" and "the people . . . by common consent." The others avoided specificity, invoking merely the power of "the people."[27]

But how could the People undertake peaceful regime change? How would it work, practically speaking? As the French political philosopher Joseph de Maistre remarked, the People are "a sovereign who cannot exercise sovereignty."[28] Unless they take up arms for revolution, the People cannot rule alone. They must work through legal institutions to make change. Put another way, the People are one example of Hobbes's "sleeping sovereign." Although omnipotent, their power remains delegated to the government until they decide to act. They must awake from their slumber to reign once more.[29]

Determining how exactly the People make constitutional law—how they wake up—remains an endeavor rife with paradox. Scholarly consideration of the issue has yielded more puzzling questions than sure answers.[30] For those of the Founding generation, however, the matter required practical solutions. The American project would have meant little without a workable way to make the People's authority real.[31]

To allow the People to amend a constitution using law and not violence, drafters had to undertake two challenging tasks. First, they had to figure out what precisely was (or who were) "the People." What was the critical moment that marked the transition from the individual opinions of many *persons* to the binding belief of *the People*? And who should be counted in the People's community—all citizens, only landowners, only men, only those of a certain race?

Second, once they had defined "the People," drafters had to determine how an amendment procedure could give the popular will binding authority. Could one measure the opinion of the People—discern what is sometimes called their univocality—with enough certainty to give it the power of law?[32] And how did the People express that opinion? Did they act individually, through individual votes? Or could they act through representatives in a legislature or convention?

The first task, defining the People, presented the more complicated question. To demarcate the People, one must both define the community's members and determine how that community speaks with an authoritative voice. During the Founding Era, the first prong of this analysis was stunted. Women, people of color, and those who did not own property were usually, but not always, denied the vote and thus refused functional representation in the People's community. Yet these groups were bound by laws the government instituted in the People's name. The long arc of the American constitutional experience has been defined by attempts to enliven and empower a broader interpretation of the People. But at the Founding, the People—as a practical, political matter—remained a small community.

Defining how that community spoke, however, posed other challenges. At the outset, one could argue that the People can only act in unison. Since "the People" refers to the entire body politic (a collective singular), all must be of the same mind. But unanimity is unworkable in practice. Few issues in life—perhaps none—enjoy universal agreement. And the fundamental matters enshrined in a constitution (like rights guarantees) tend to be both controversial and nuanced. Self-government requires compromise and second-best solutions.

Another possibility is that the People speak when *most* agree. This makes the most sense in theory, but the approach raises its own problems in practice. If the People are merely a simple majority (50 percent plus one), the threshold for constitutional amendment is no higher than that of normal electoral politics. But the Americans aimed to set constitutions apart from the general tumble of politics. Allowing the same simple majority that could elect a state's governor to also effectuate constitutional change could blur the line between fundamental and ordinary law.

If both the unanimity and simple majority approaches seem to miss the mark, then an in-between solution remains. The People must be some kind of *qualified* majority—insulated from normal political processes but not impossible to achieve. Ultimately most states, as well as the federal Constitution, would implement this approach in a variety of forms. Some states would adopt a supermajority logic, requiring high thresholds (some two-thirds, others three-quarters) to adopt constitutional amendments. Others would empower a simple majority (50 percent plus one) to approve constitutional amendments if the process was set apart from normal electoral politics by way of a convention, special referendum, or procedures that otherwise protected against hasty action. Many would mix and match. For all, the process of demarcating the People was defined by a guiding principle: slow, careful deliberation.

HARNESSING THE PEOPLE'S POWER: LEGISLATURES, CONVENTIONS, AND THE BALLOT

With some resolution to the first question, drafters still needed to consider the second: How and where do the People speak? In most political communities, even small ones, gathering all citizens together is not practical. Where and how then does public debate become the binding opinion of the People?

The Declaration offered two answers: legislatures and conventions. The document spoke of "the people's right" to revolution but acted through the Continental Congress, which the Declaration called "the Representatives of the United States of America, in Congress Assembled." The common Anglo-American understanding of representative government supported this approach. When the legislature passed laws, the thinking went, it was as if the People had gathered and acted in the first instance. Legislatures worked both for and through their constitutive communities. In this frame, the People as an identifiable, numerous whole existed only at the ballot box. Afterward, they acted through their representatives in a legislature.[33]

In addition to elected legislatures, conventions were also an established method for harnessing the People's power in the British tradition. Meeting as a unique representative assembly, conventions acted with authority independent of the legislature to address specific, extraordinary issues. Although not legislatures, conventions functioned like them. Their members were often chosen in special elections or sometimes appointed by other elected representatives to undertake a specific task, most often drafting constitutional provisions or settling constitutional problems. Unlike legislatures, however, conventions were not standing bodies. Formed only as needed, the body dissolved when its task was completed.

This unique form of popular lawmaking—a quasi-legislative body acting with exceptional authority yet formed on demand—was a relatively new creation when the Americans began drafting their constitutional frameworks. Prior to the mid-seventeenth century, the term *convention* was most often used as a pejorative, signifying an illegitimate meeting that lacked legal authority. But the English Convention Parliaments of 1660 and 1689 established new precedent for the method, granting the meetings a legitimacy that would prove influential to American constitutional framers.

The Convention Parliaments met to address constitutional questions regarding royal succession despite not being properly convened by royal mandate.[34] Even without Parliament's normal legislative authority, these conventions proclaimed themselves a true parliament.[35] As John Milton observed in 1689, the convention was a legitimate body because it was convened under the authority of the people, "not as heretofore, by the summons of a king, but by the voice of libertie."[36] And because the convention acted with popular authority, another observer noted, it wielded a unique set of powers: "Being the Representative of the whole Kingdom gathered together in an extraordinary case and manner . . . [it] seemeth to be something greater, and of greater power, than a Parliament. . . . If this Convention can do anything, cannot it make laws truly Fundamental, and which shall have the same Firmitude and continuance as the Government it sets up?"[37]

The Convention Parliaments had a rapid and lasting impact in the Americas. Conventions were soon used in the late seventeenth and early eighteenth centuries to settle political and constitutional disputes, most notably in Massachusetts, New York, and Maryland. They were also used to constitute new revolutionary governments.[38] In 1719, when the citizens of South Carolina desired to wrest power from their ruling landed proprietors and reconstitute the government as a royal colony, the people could not rely on the legislature to do their bidding. Because the proprietors had not given the rebel legislature authority to govern, the assembly appealed to a higher power: "We cannot Act as an assembly," the legislators declared, "but as a Convention, delegated by the People, to prevent the utter Ruin of this Government."[39]

In the months following independence, all thirteen new states would use a legislature or convention to draft their constitutions.[40] And in ten of the thirteen, these assemblies also ratified their draft constitutions, giving them binding power. No popular vote was taken.[41]

Using representative assemblies—legislatures and conventions—to harness the People's power made sense during the revolutionary period. States needed a quick, legitimate method to establish new governments. With peacetime on the horizon and the creation of constitutional amendment procedures a growing topic of debate, however, some statesmen and citizens began to consider whether there might be better ways for the People to make constitutional change. Maybe the constitutional amendment process should be more democratic, involving not just political elites but also the common citizen.

The artisan and mechanics guilds of New York City expressed this concern in the summer of 1776. The New York provincial congress had drafted and ratified the state's new constitution, but the guilds' members felt that their interests were not represented in the state legislature. Their claim was simple: If the Revolution had been fought on behalf of the People, how could average citizens like mechanics, farmers, and artists not be included in the process of crafting and ratifying the state's fundamental law? The constitutional power belonged to the "inhabitants at large," they argued. It was a "right which *God* has given them, in common with all men, to judge whether it be consistent with their interest to accept or reject a Constitution framed for that State of which they are members."[42] Only the People, through their personal consent, could approve and amend a constitutional regime. Conventions or legislatures were just an elitist end run around the popular will.

Massachusetts tried to give the People the direct power these advocates desired. The commonwealth ratified its constitution by a popular vote and gave the voters a key role in the amendment process. The new constitution required the legislature to poll the citizens gathered in town meetings at regular intervals to determine whether a convention should be called. And as they had in Massachusetts's first constitutional convention, delegates to such an amendments convention would be elected in a special election.[43]

While admirable, Massachusetts was a democratic outlier. Plebiscites (direct popular votes on constitutional questions) and the popular election of constitutional convention delegates would not become widespread until after the Civil War.[44] But even though direct, electoral forms of popular constitutional power were uncommon, there might have been other ways to harness the popular will. As Larry Kramer, the former dean of Stanford Law School, argues in his book *The People Themselves*, elections were not the sole method for popular constitutional governance at the Founding.[45] A nuanced culture of unwritten political mores allowed the People to exert binding power outside legal and institutional channels.

This culture was typified by the Revolution, which instilled in the Founding generation a sense of pride, both in the popular nature of the Founding and in the core belief that the project of republican democracy belonged to the entire community, not just a ruling clique. The People had spoken their government into existence, and so too would they continue to speak—providing ongoing meaning and form to the constitutions through which their governments had been formed. The People, according to Kramer, provided such ongoing meaning through both legal and nonlegal yet binding acts.[46]

Kramer argues that this history of popular constitutional authority (what he calls "popular constitutionalism") should change the way we understand the nature of American law and its processes.[47] So strong was the notion that the People retained the ultimate authority and responsibility to make constitutional meaning that constitutional drafters saw no need to reference it in the text. Whether through institutional processes, legitimate forms of violent protest, or otherwise, the People could and did speak in authoritative ways. The fact that the new constitutions were written did not change this foundational truth. The constitutional amendment processes, focused as they were on adding, deleting, or altering text, were not intended to limit the constitution-making power of the People. Rather, the Founding generation conceived of the amendment power as merely one small focus of the People's authority, an outgrowth and manifestation of the Revolution's embrace of popular sovereignty.[48]

The popular constitutionalism thesis offers a compelling case that early conceptions of the People's power prized direct authority. Like the view put forward by the New York artisans and mechanics in 1776, matters of constitutional concern were not the sole domain of the political elite. The People could harness their own power and act directly rather than relying solely on intermediary institutions like legislatures, conventions, and the courts.

Yet the early development of constitutional amendment procedures in the 1770s and 1780s would take a different approach. Most drafters would adopt the view that the People's power could be harnessed in the realm of constitutional amendment *only* through legislatures, conventions, and—sometimes—through the vote. But as a general rule, the People would rarely have an active role. In endorsing this turn away from direct popular authority, our constitutional framers made perhaps one of the most consequential decisions in the history of the American democratic experiment.

THE PEOPLE, IN CONGRESS OR CONVENTION ASSEMBLED

The New York artisans and mechanics' demands for more direct popular power, like those raised by many others, proved too radical for their time. The proposition that representative assemblies were appropriate conduits to harness the popular will was well settled in the British legal tradition and readily adopted by the Americans; whether these assemblies were prone to control by a social or economic faction, the clear concern of many even at the Founding, was no matter. When those in the political establishment did take issue with the assemblies—a rare occurrence—their concerns were often procedural. In Virginia, for example, Thomas Jefferson was the only dissenting voice among the leading planters to challenge the authority of conventions to draft constitutional provisions. He argued that a convention could not reconstitute the government without first holding a new round of elections.[49] This concern, however, was one of method. Few challenged whether the bodies themselves were a legitimate forum for democratic decision-making.

When faced with the choice of how to harness the People's power, these early constitutional drafters throughout the various states opted for approaches that insulated the constitutional amendment process from direct popular will. While the People perhaps retained the ultimate constitutional authority, as Kramer's historical account proposes (there was, after all, always the possibility of rebellion), drafters would vest the *institutional* power of constitutional change in the mainstream political process. But whether the legislature or convention would become dominant was a significant open question.

From the 1770s until the mid-nineteenth century, most states vested the bulk of the constitutional amendment power in representative assemblies. Following this early lead in the states, conventions and legislatures would also take center stage in the federal Constitution's amendment provision ratified in 1789. Yet the concerns raised by early eighteenth-century detractors continue today. To understand the contemporary role of constitutional amendment in public life, one must engage these critiques, examining the pitfalls of our amendment procedure and considering how its reliance on representative assemblies to harness the People's power might lead to problematic outcomes.

The first major question is whether allowing legislative assemblies to speak for the People in the constitutional amendment process has the potential to disrupt the nature of constitutions. As the Connecticut and Rhode Island dissenters so forcefully articulated, the Revolution endorsed the ideal that a constitution must reign *above* the normal workings of government. If the People could amend the constitution only through the electoral process, how was an American Constitution any different from ordinary law?

Using conventions with popularly elected delegates to draft and propose amendments was one way to avoid the problem.[50] When the People choose convention delegates directly through a special election, rather than relying on legislative appointment, the amendment process is insulated from legislative control. Massachusetts held such an election to pick delegates to draft its first constitution. Pennsylvania did the same, holding a poll in July 1776. Underscoring the popular nature of the task, Pennsylvania's provincial legislature expanded the franchise, allowing all adult militiamen to vote, regardless of landowning status.[51] But such popularly elected conventions would prove quite rare, and the federal Constitution's amendment provision drafted a decade later would not require a popular vote. How else then could the danger of legislative overreach be avoided?

Another way to resolve the problem was to insulate constitutional amendment from the rough waters of everyday politics through the calming effects of parliamentary procedure. Many states chose to vest the amendment power with the legislature but required additional supermajority safeguards to slow consideration of amendments and provide opportunities for popular input. Maryland, for example, empowered the legislature to propose draft amendments to the constitution by a two-thirds vote in both houses. These amendments, however, would only take effect after the next election and approval by a second, two-thirds vote in both new houses. This allowed the voters to have some say, at least from a distance.[52]

The federal constitutional amendment provision would follow suit, giving Congress an outsized role in one element of the process yet including supermajority requirements to set amendment apart from normal legislation. Later chapters consider whether such procedural safeguards are cold comfort for the democratically (with a small *d*) minded citizen. For the moment, however, it is important to consider how (and whether) the early rise of this procedural-protection logic can be squared with the radical notion of bloodless revolution.

Amendment provisions were intended to allow the People to peacefully rebel against the governing regime—to reclaim their right as the ultimate sovereign to form their government anew. Relying on legislative bodies to undertake the work of constitutional change causes an innate tension. How can the People change a governing regime if they must work *through* the very regime they aim to reform? This conundrum lies at the heart of the American constitutional system and its procedure for formal amendment. And it has wreaked havoc in our politics and distorted our law by placing inordinate pressure on the courts to arbitrate new constitutional meaning when the amendment mechanism does not, or cannot, be a useful means for constitutional change.

A second concern with empowering elected assemblies to speak for the People on constitutional questions perhaps rings louder today than it did in the 1770s and 1780s. Placing the amendment power in the hands of elected leaders assumes that political institutions—elections, legislatures, executive officials—can adequately represent the citizenry. But this has not been the case for most of our history. The vote was severely restricted at the Founding and for much of the proceeding two centuries. Does this mean that "the People" was meant not to include women, people of color, and those who did not own land?

Some invoke a version of this argument today to call into question the federal Constitution's legitimacy. They claim that the limited definition of the democratic community at the Founding and the document's failure to put asunder the sin of slavery necessarily sully any power the document might have in contemporary life. It is useful to consider these critiques in the context of crafting an amendment mechanism that claims to empower "the People." The colonists dismissed outright the British claim that, although the colonies could not elect representatives to Parliament, their interests were sufficiently represented to be bound by Parliament's taxation authority. One could, in the 1780s, have raised the same concerns many raise today about an unrepresentative political process as a potent argument challenging the authority of new state constitutions and the federal Constitution to speak for those who could not vote. After all, the constitutions were (and are) binding on all.

The political problems of today similarly call into question the ability of representative assemblies to truly represent the interests of the People. Take gerrymandering for example. State legislatures play a key role in the process of amending the federal Constitution. Yet state-level partisan gerrymandering has rendered many statehouses immune to the majority's will. In states like Wisconsin, one political party can win key statewide at-large elections (where there are no districts) by wide margins yet fail to gain control of either house in the state legislature due to radically skewed maps.[53] The modern era is one in which some embrace radical countermajoritarian political tendencies, and due to institutional failures, these tendencies often win the day. If representative assemblies suffer from these democratic shortcomings, how can they claim to speak in the name of the entire community? And in the context of constitutional amendment, how can gerrymandered state legislatures, acting on simple majority votes along partisan lines, act with popular legitimacy on the most important questions in our civic life?

These concerns regarding legislative control and undemocratic representation, hardwired into our federal constitutional amendment mechanism, form the foundation of this book. Americans today are heirs to amendment procedures embedded with inconsistencies, troubles, and landmines that impede the ability of our institutions to effectively harness the People's power. These difficulties are not merely the stuff of theory or historical analysis. As contemporary efforts to call a constitutional convention richly illustrate, these issues continue to have a profound impact on modern political life.

*   *   *

By 1780, FEWER THAN HALF of the states had adopted constitutional amendment procedures.[54] Yet the debates regarding the practical realities of constitutionalism, amendment, and the People's role in the institutions of self-governance had solidified generally accepted early American understandings of fundamental law. The principle that constitutions could be altered through a fixed method was well established; bloodless revolution was the norm. The idea that such change could occur in representative bodies, at a distance from the direct will of the People, was also an accepted proposition.

When the federal Constitutional Convention gathered in Philadelphia in 1787 to craft America's national governing text, these beliefs were the foundation upon which the rest of the constitutional architecture was built. A government constituted by "We the People" was not a new approach; it was one adopted by the states, given a certain meaning in practice, and bound up in the political and legal context of the previous decade. The federal Constitution's amendment procedure, contained in Article V, would set out a method to harness the People's power that was equally a product of its time. To understand Article V and assess its relevance to life today, one must understand the work of the Convention. How did the Framers construct the People's ultimate power to change their fundamental law?

2

COMPROMISE AND TENSION

The Creation of Article V

"The [constitution] now to be formed will certainly be defective. . . . Amendments therefore will be necessary, and it will be better to provide for them, in an easy, regular and Constitutional way than to trust to chance and violence."

—George Mason at the Constitutional Convention (June 11, 1787)[1]

IN NOVEMBER 1786, George Washington received an alarming letter from his former military aide and close friend David Humphreys. Newspapers had been reporting growing economic turmoil and civil unrest in Massachusetts for months. Violent scuffles between citizens and the authorities were becoming more frequent. But now, as Humphreys impressed upon the retired general, things were taking a turn for the worse. Massachusetts was on the verge of anarchy.

The problem was economic. Easy access to credit after the war had fueled a growing trade deficit with Europe. As Americans began purchasing more foreign goods, the amount of silver and gold in circulation in the United States fell dramatically—by as much as 80 percent since independence. Without a fluid money supply, the economy stalled. And with the added blow of lost access to the British Empire's markets, a crippling depression took hold.

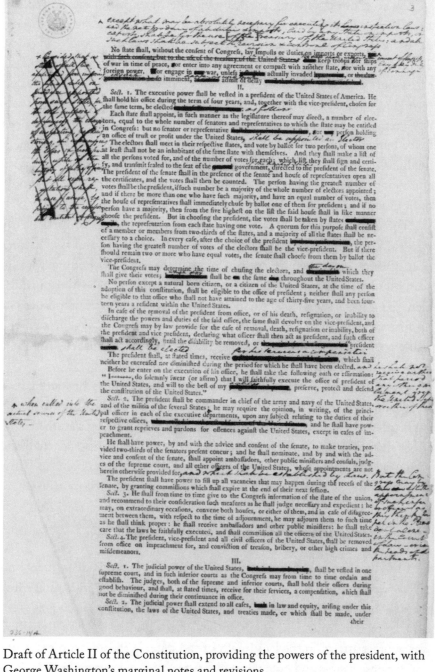

Draft of Article II of the Constitution, providing the powers of the president, with George Washington's marginal notes and revisions.

As access to hard currency dried up, the states faced a new problem. Both the state and national governments were carrying substantial foreign debts from the war, loans that could only be paid in silver and gold coins. To meet debt payments during the coin shortage, the Massachusetts General Court passed a series of draconian property tax hikes. Tax rates on farmland soon rose to multiple times those under the British. But to satisfy creditors, Massachusetts and other states had made the taxes even more burdensome by requiring the payment of the new property taxes in gold and silver, rather than in crops. Without enough currency and with commodity prices falling, farmers could not pay their tax bills. Their only options were to sell their land or default.

Foreclosures began quickly. In some Massachusetts counties, nearly two-thirds of farmers had their land seized by the state and sold at auction. Others sat in debtors' prison or fled the law, absconding west in search of better prospects. But even these forced land sales were insufficient to meet the state's loan payments. The sheer number of properties put up for tax sale, combined with the currency shortage, had saturated the market and depressed prices. While property values crashed, tax rates crept higher still. The situation was at a breaking point.

Much like the events that precipitated the Tea Party in Boston Harbor thirteen years before, the discontent in Massachusetts had begun with peaceful petitions for redress. Cash-strapped farmers urged the legislature to issue paper money to inflate the currency. But coastal merchants and creditors, who would have been hurt by inflation, quashed any hopes of reform. Their pleas unanswered, disgruntled farmers turned to more drastic measures.[2]

THE CONSTITUTION'S VIOLENT PRELUDE

Led by the charismatic farmer Daniel Shays, thousands of farmers and townspeople armed with muskets and swords converged in military formation on five Massachusetts county courthouses, blocking judges from hearing foreclosure cases. For Massachusetts's leaders, Shays's Rebellion was a direct attack on the legitimacy of the state. If the government could not dispense justice and hold wrongdoers to account, how could it claim to have the authority to rule?[3]

But Humphreys conveyed to Washington a more disturbing analysis: the Shaysites foreshadowed deeper problems for the young republic. "As to your question, my dear General, respecting the cause and origin of those commotions," he wrote, "I believe there are a few real grievances and also some wicked agents, or emissaries, who have been busy in magnifying the positive evils and fomenting causeless jealousies and disturbances. . . . It rather appears to me that there is a licentious spirit prevailing among many of the people, a leveling principle; a desire of change."[4]

Humphreys did not detail who precisely he thought these "wicked agents" were; perhaps the British? But he made it clear to Washington that the rebellion was about more than just debt. It was a movement for "leveling"—for populist mob rule and maybe even economic redistribution. As the weeks went on, more troubling reports made their way south to Washington at Mount Vernon. The general's former artillery commander Henry Knox echoed Humphrey's assessment, reporting that the protesters wanted to seize the property of the rich and give it to the poor.[5] Virginia congressman Henry Lee wrote that the farmers wanted "the division of property and re-union with Great Britain."[6]

By January 1787, the situation in Massachusetts had deteriorated further. Three well-organized bands of rioters, each under the command of a seasoned Revolutionary War officer, had attempted to take the federal arsenal at Springfield, the main armory for all of New England. In its stores were 7,000 new muskets with bayonets, 1,300 barrels of gun powder, and over 200 tons of shot and shells. As historian Leonard Richards argues, had the Shaysites succeeded they would have been better armed than the state militia. And the rioters' aims soon became well known. According to an alleged interview with Shays published in the *Massachusetts Centinel* shortly after the raid, the rioters had intended to march straight to the state capitol to "burn it and lay the town of Boston in ashes." Their aim, Shays declared, was to "overthrow the present constitution."[7]

Four years retired from public life, Washington had returned happily to farming on the shores of the Potomac. Yet the news from New England unsettled him. He was "mortified beyond expression" by the rebellion, he wrote one acquaintance. To another, Washington decried the protesters exhibiting "a melancholy proof of what our transatlantic foe has predicted . . . that mankind left to themselves are unfit for their own government."[8] If Massachusetts could fall to revolutionary bandits, then the other states could too. And with the others would go the union for which he had so valiantly fought. A political sickness was taking hold, and the current system could not control it. "No morn ever dawned more favorable than ours did," Washington wrote to the Virginia statesman James Madison just ten years following independence, "and no day was ever more clouded than the present!"[9]

Madison had been encouraging Washington to join the Virginia delegation attending a convention in Philadelphia, tasked with drafting amendments to the Articles of Confederation, the troubled national governing charter. Washington had initially turned down the invitation, but Shays's Rebellion changed his mind. The Shaysites had proved that the union was too tenuous, the national government too weak. "Without some alteration in our political creed," he wrote Madison, "the superstructure we have been seven years raising at the expense of much blood and treasure must fall. We are fast verging to anarchy and confusion!"[10] He would attend the Constitutional Convention.

THE ROAD TO PHILADELPHIA

The Constitutional Convention held in the summer of 1787 was the culmination of years of debate regarding the nature of the United States and the union between them. Following independence, citizens began to consider a challenging question: How was a union of coequal sovereign states to be constituted? How should a national government fit to address the pressing needs of the day be formed?

As discussed in Chapter 1, the initial American foray into constitution making focused on establishing state governments. The decision to overthrow the British regime and begin anew had thrust the colonial communities into a form of legal chaos. New, legitimate governments were needed to ensure the orderly functioning of society. Such were the demands of revolution. In this flowering of constitutional exploration, local communities in the states embarked on experiments in self-government, thinking intently and debating in public spaces the meaning of fundamental law and the role of popular will in changing that fundamental law. While this constitutional innovation was occurring in the states, the open question of national union loomed. If the United States were to remain united, something more than just a loose affiliation of friendship was required; a stronger, central structure needed to be developed.

Almost immediately after the Declaration was adopted, debate regarding the nature of the national union and the thorny problem of delineating the extent of the states' independence and sovereignty ensued. While these early national constitutional debates were crucially important for the development of American public life, their tenor differed from those in the states. The debates occurred primarily among the political elite, confined to the halls of power. Unlike the robust public debates in town meetings, newspapers, and in the streets regarding popular sovereignty and state constitutional norms, the national conversation was muted. Little public discussion of the nature of the new union, its structure, or its position in a political community constituted by fundamental written law occurred. As the noted colonial historian Gordon Wood has remarked, the early debate regarding a national constitutional union was "very limited and intellectually insignificant."[11]

The Articles of Confederation, ratified in 1781, set out America's first resolution of the question of national union. The Articles established a weak central government empowered to manage, in the Articles' terms, a "firm league of friendship" between the states. Under the Articles, the states retained most governing power. The national government, vested in the Confederation Congress, would only carry out foreign policy, provide for the national defense, and undertake minor duties.

By the time Shays marched on the Springfield arsenal in January 1787, it was clear that the Articles' restriction of the Confederation Congress's power had weakened not just the national government but also the union itself. Because Congress could not regulate interstate or foreign commerce, states had imposed discriminatory tariffs on each other, worsening the growing economic depression. When European states banned certain American exports, Congress could not retaliate with importation limitations of its own. Congress's inability to tax was also a key failing. In October 1786, Congress had attempted to borrow $500,000—roughly $14 million today—to finance an expansion of the national army to quell Shays's Rebellion. But domestic and foreign lenders, weary of the states' habit of not paying their voluntary share of the national government's budget, refused to extend a loan.[12]

With the economy in shambles, states descending into rebellion and lawlessness, and Congress unable to muster an army, American leaders began to question whether the national project was doomed to failure. "It is not possible that a government can last long under these circumstances," James Madison remarked.[13] Soon, many began debating whether the nation should be split into new, smaller confederacies, an idea that Madison reported "after long confinement to individual speculations & private circles, [was] beginning to show itself in the Newspapers."[14]

Calls to amend the Articles were almost immediate. But the path to change was steep. The Articles declared themselves to be perpetual and provided that no alterations could be made without the consent of *all* the states. Every attempt at amending the Articles between 1781 and 1787 failed, many blocked 12–1 by one state or another voting no. As frustration mounted, the unanimity requirement took center stage as the Articles' chief pitfall. Charles Pinckney, a congressional delegate from South Carolina and future delegate to the Constitutional Convention, remarked that "the depressed situation of the union is undoubtedly owing" to the Articles' "absurd" unanimity requirement for amendment.[15]

Following a failed attempt to draft a new constitution at a convention in Annapolis, the Confederation Congress succumbed to mounting pressure and issued a call for the states to send delegates to Philadelphia. The convention would be, according to Congress's call, "for the *sole and express purpose* of revising the Articles of Confederation and reporting to Congress and the several legislatures such alterations and provisions therein as shall . . . render the federal Constitution adequate to the exigencies of Government and the preservation of the Union."[16]

Washington, like many, doubted the "legality of this Convention."[17] But with the troubling events of the last decade growing to a fevered pitch in Massachusetts, bold action was required. Animated by fear, and likely anger, Washington reentered the public square, traveling to Philadelphia as a delegate to the Constitutional Convention. In short order, this hero of the Revolution, who had led the Republic to victory just a decade before, was elected the Convention's president.

From his perch presiding over the intense debates regarding how the nation's new constitutional system should be structured, Washington no doubt had a keen understanding of why he was there—why they all were there. As the events of the previous ten months had underscored, democracies were fragile, precarious things. Rebellion and revolution would always be at the door. But Washington fervently believed that the cynicism of "our transatlantic foe" was wrong, that mankind *was* fit for its own governance. Such governance was predicated on the peaceful ability to change the constitutional order. Without a mechanism to mediate stability and change, the American experiment would fail. Either the people would revolt, the country would splinter, or both.

A new constitution was needed, Washington was certain. But how the new instrument could provide for such essential mediation, how it could craft a workable release valve, remained an open question. Delegates gathered at the Constitutional Convention would need to craft the first workable amendment mechanism for a national constitution.

THE AMENDMENT QUESTION

The Constitutional Convention was called to order on May 14, 1787, in the Assembly Room of the Pennsylvania State House. The conditions were, by all accounts, unpleasant. The summer was unusually hot and humid, and a plague of biting flies had descended on the city. To avoid the swarms, delegates spent their days inside the convention hall with the windows shut, sweating in the heat with little reprieve. Yet the work of statecraft pressed forward.

Substantive debate began on May 29 with the introduction of the Virginia Plan, a draft federal constitution that would shape the Convention's debates and the final document. While much of the plan was the intellectual work of the young James Madison, it was presented to the delegates by Edmund Randolph, the respected Virginia governor. Among the plan's fifteen proposals was the explicit provision for an amendment mechanism: "[Resolved] that provision ought to be made for the amendment of the Articles of Union whensoever it shall seem necessary, and that the assent of the National Legislature ought not to be required thereto."[18]

The draft sparked consequential debate. While the development of amendment mechanisms in state constitutions over the previous decade had made the concept more acceptable, several states still lacked such provisions. So too had no national constitution in the world ever included a formal amendment mechanism short of unanimity.[19] For some delegates, it was unclear why the federal constitution needed such a procedure at all, especially when some states did not see a need for one.

Charles Pinckney of South Carolina, a twenty-nine-year-old plantation owner and lawyer, opened the debate along these lines, remarking that he "doubted the propriety or necessity of it."[20] Elbridge Gerry, a Massachusetts businessman and signer of the Declaration, however, quickly took the floor expressing what would become the prevailing view. The idea was reasonable and prudent, Gerry argued. "The novelty and difficulty of the experiment requires periodical revision," he remarked. An amendment mechanism would provide "intermediate stability to the government."[21]

Because delegates were divided on the question, the proposal was tabled. Within weeks, however, convention debate had reached some consensus, and soon delegates voted unanimously to include an amendment provision.[22] Even Pinckney would include an amendment procedure in his proposed constitution later submitted to the Convention.[23] But determining the appropriate role of the states or the Congress in the amendment process remained a controversial question, one that the delegates set aside.

Following this second round of debate, the Virginia Plan was sent to the Committee on Detail, which was tasked with gathering the various proposals and producing a revised draft for further debate. On August 6, the committee reported a draft of the amendment procedure to the convention floor: "On the application of the Legislatures of two thirds of the States in the Union, for an amendment of this Constitution, the Legislature of the United States shall call a Convention for that purpose."[24] The committee's text introduced two notable innovations that would shape debate and the ultimate adopted text of the Article V amendment power.

First, the committee forwent Randolph's complete exclusion of Congress from the amendment process, providing that "the Legislature . . . shall call a Convention" upon a sufficient application by the states. While Congress had some role under this revision, it appeared merely ministerial, procedural rather than substantive. There was no discretion or independent authority (as would be indicated by more permissive language, such as "may call").

Second, the committee's version provided that proposed amendments to the Constitution would be drafted by a convention. As discussed in Chapter 1, Americans had come to embrace the notion that a convention could function as a legitimate forum for harnessing "the People's" power. It is not surprising, then, that those assembled in Philadelphia would consider a convention a reasonable amendment method. The delegates were, after all, sitting in a convention called by the Confederation Congress to amend the Articles of Confederation.

Indeed, the notion that conventions were an appropriate means to conduct constitutional business was so strong that several delegates assumed amendment would be possible by convention even before the committee's proposal was brought to the floor. Elbridge Gerry remarked on July 2, just days after debate began, that although "the world at large expect[s] something from us[,] . . . defects may be amended by a future convention."[25] Gunning Bedford Jr., a lawyer from Delaware, echoed similar sentiments: "The condition of the U[nited] States requires that something should be immediately done. . . . [There is] no reason why defects might not be [remedied] by meetings 10, 15, or 20 years hence."[26]

However, while some delegates and the Committee on Detail supported vesting the amendment power in a convention alone, it was by no means a settled proposition. Other ways to harness the People's power on constitutional matters were also considered legitimate, including through legislatures. Delegates who supported a strong national government, many of whom were called "federalists," fervently disagreed with Randolph and the committee's design. To them, shunning congressional authority over amendment represented a troubling backstep toward the errors of the Articles and the political chaos they wrought. The proposal could not stand.

The Hamilton-Mason Compromise

Chief among these dissenting federalist voices was Alexander Hamilton, the then thirty-year-old lawyer from New York. The unrest and economic crises of the previous decade were the result of a weak national government, Hamilton argued. A new constitution was needed to rectify the errors in the Articles of Confederation. Excluding the national legislature from the amendment question would only prolong the backward ways of the Articles, allowing obstinate states acting to protect their own interests to inhibit important national policies. There was "no greater evil in subjecting the people of the U.S. to the major voice than the people of a particular State," Hamilton remarked.[27] Rather, there was a positive good in allowing Congress to propose amendments, which would still need to be ratified by the people of the states.

For Hamilton, the purpose of constitutional amendment was to provide a mechanism to *strengthen* the national union and its federal government.

It was only natural then that the federal government should lead the way. "The State Legislatures will not apply for alterations but with a view to increase their own powers," he continued. Where the states would succumb to petty infighting, "the National Legislature will be the first to perceive and will be most sensible to the necessity of amendments."[28] If the sum of the states were to be greater than its parts, Hamilton argued, then the body representing the sum—Congress—should dictate the path of change.

Many found Hamilton's views anathema to the new American experiment. And perhaps no delegate was more opposed to the Hamiltonian view than George Mason, the sixty-two-year-old plantation owner and principal drafter of Virginia's 1776 constitution. Mason forcefully advocated for a state-focused amendment process. A leading anti-federalist, he believed the union should be a bond that reserved the bulk of the governing authority for the states. Giving Congress a substantive role in the amendment process would undermine the very purposes of the Constitution, Mason argued.

The purpose of amendment, in Mason's estimation, was to allow the People to *check* the federal government, to ensure that the states' retained powers were not encroached by a wanton and reckless Congress. "It would be improper to require the consent of the National Legislature," he argued, "because they may abuse their power, and refuse their consent on that very account."[29] Only a provision that placed the amendment authority solely with the people of the states, thus insulating the Constitution from congressional control, would ensure that the document's freedoms and guarantees prevailed.

Despite Mason's forceful claims, Hamilton's rebuke of the Committee of Detail's convention-route proposal was convincing. Soon Roger Sherman of Connecticut moved to add "or the Legislature may propose amendments to the several States for their approbation."[30] Following Sherman's motion to provide for legislative control, James Madison proposed a draft that removed the convention route altogether, centering the entire amendment proposal process in the federal regime. The state delegations voted nine to one, with one state divided, to support Madison's proposal.* It would seem Mason and the anti-federalists had lost the day.[31]

---

* The delegates voted as a state delegation, not individually. This means a near-unanimous vote does not necessarily show near unanimity of opinion. It is likely that some anti-federalists, including Mason, did not support the motion. They likely lost the vote in their respective state caucuses.

While the Hamilton-Mason dispute informed most of the Convention's debate on the amendment question, a deeper tension was also festering below the surface. Amid consideration of the Sherman and Madison proposals, the South Carolinian planter and slaveowner John Rutledge took the floor to express his concerns with Madison's draft. He "could never agree to give a power by which the articles relating to slaves might be altered by States not interested in that property," he stated.[32]

Rutledge was concerned that the amendment power would be used by nonslaveholding states to remove the fugitive slave clause, which required the return of slaves escaped from slaveholding states, and the provision ensuring the continued importation of slaves to the southern states, both hard-won additions to the draft constitution on the part of southern states. The historical record provides little detail about the debate over Rutledge's objection and his proposal to make the Constitution's slavery provisions unamendable. Madison's Notes—the leading historical source of the Convention's debates—do not record any discussion of the matter, only that language shielding the slaveholding clauses from amendment until 1808 was added to "obviate this objection."[33] But one can speculate.

As James Iredell explained at the North Carolina Ratifying Convention, "a compromise . . . took place in regard to the importation of slaves."[34] Likewise Mason reported that the "southernmost states . . . struck up a bargain" that would protect their slaveholding interests.[35] The Convention's quick acceptance of Rutledge's proposed alteration to the amendment power was part and parcel of this odious bargain. It ensured that the tenuous balance between slaveholding and nonslaveholding interests would remain intact for the coming decades.

On September 12—five days before the Convention adjourned—the Committee of Style and Arrangement brought what was now called Article V to the floor:

> The Congress, whenever two thirds of both Houses shall deem necessary, or on the application of two thirds of the Legislatures of the several States shall propose amendments to this Constitution, which shall be valid to all intents and purposes as part thereof, when the same shall have been ratified by three fourths at least of the Legislatures of the several States, or by Conventions in three fourths thereof, as one or the other mode of ratification may be proposed by the Congress: Provided

that no amendment which may be made prior to the year 1808 shall in any manner affect [the Constitution's provisions regarding slavery].[36]

Roger Sherman of Connecticut, while pleased that the Convention had supported placing the power to propose amendments in the federal government, expressed concern that the article as drafted did not do enough to protect small states.

"Three fourths of the States might be brought to do things fatal to particular States," he argued, such as "abolishing them altogether or depriving them of their equality in the Senate."[37] To address this concern, he proposed an alteration to the draft: "no State shall be affected in its internal police, or deprived of its equality in the Senate."[38] His proposal was voted down, three to eight.[39] But upon the "circulating murmurs of the small States," a revised version that made states' representation in the Senate immune from future amendment passed without opposition or debate.[40]

With the objections of the slaveholding and small states addressed, the amendment question seemed to be settled. But George Mason, still frustrated with the convention's adoption of Hamilton's proposal to vest amendment proposition authority in the federal government alone, took the floor in one last-ditch effort to challenge the federalist position. "The plan of amending the Constitution [was] exceptionable & dangerous," he argued, because "the proposing of amendments is in both the modes to depend, in the first immediately, and in the second, ultimately, on Congress." Such a design would prove disastrous, Mason argued, because "no amendments of the proper kind would ever be obtained by the people, if the Government should become oppressive, [as] verily . . . would be the case."[41]

To appease Mason, Gouverneur Morris and Elbridge Gerry moved to amend the Committee's draft to add an alternative route for amendment proposal—a convention, which would be called upon application of two-thirds of the states.[42] The addition remains mysterious even to this day. Madison's Notes report no debate regarding the alteration save Madison's own comments on the proposition. Madison saw no problem with a convention but believed that "difficulties might arise as to the form [and] the quorum, which in Constitutional regulations ought be as much as possible avoided."[43] While an insightful critique (the modern problems of which are discussed at length in Part 3), Madison's fellow delegates still did not see a need to alter the proposal. Without further debate, the addition of a convention method passed unanimously. The next day, the Convention adjourned, and the Constitution was sent to the states for ratification.

ARTICLE V'S UNRESOLVED TENSIONS AND HAMILTON'S UPPER HAND

The final amendment provision ratified by the states is one of the great compromises of the Constitutional Convention. Article V erects a two-route amendment method, one that allows amendments to be proposed both bottom-up by the people of the states and top-down by Congress. This middle way did not give ultimate sanction to either Hamilton's or Mason's absolutist views about the federal-state separation of powers and the nature of constitutional amendment. Rather, Article V allows both conflicting views to coexist. It endorses an institutionalist theory of amendment—members of Congress, acting with special expertise on matters of state, crafting amendments and sending them to the states for ratification. But it also endorses a more radical resistance theory of amendment—the People of the states independently altering the terms of the federal regime without the federal government's consent or involvement.[44]

After the Convention adjourned, Hamilton and his fellow federalists championed the two-route compromise during the ratification debates as evidence of the Constitution's reasonable, cautioned approach.[45] Even though the document engineered a stronger central government, they argued, it was worthy of ratification because the amendment provision mandated a balancing of interests. As James Madison wrote in *The Federalist*, the constitution was "neither wholly *national* nor wholly *federal*."[46] Rather, Article V "equally enables the general and the State governments to originate the amendment of errors, as they may be pointed out by the experience on one side, or on the other."[47]

But as Mason and the anti-federalists argued during the ratification debates, the supposed security of Article V's two-track method was a mirage. The convention method—the very compromise for which Mason had fought and won—was hopelessly complicated, they believed. The thresholds for proposal and ratification were too high to render the provision useful in reining in the federal government's power. As the Virginian anti-federalist Patrick Henry argued, the amendment routes were practically "shut" because "two-thirds of the Congress, or of the state legislatures, are necessary even to propose amendments. If one-third of these be unworthy men, they may prevent the application for amendments." So too was the three-fourths ratification requirement an unreasonable bar—one that "suppose[s] that [the states] will possess genius, intelligence, and integrity, approaching to the miraculous."[48] Because amendment would be too hard, the anti-federalists argued, the Constitution posed an inherent and unacceptable risk—that of an enlarged and emboldened federal regime, the expanse of which could not be curtailed by the states. Far from the constitutional cornerstone that Hamilton and the federalists portrayed it to be, Article V was one of the document's cardinal sins. As Mason famously remarked, he "would sooner chop off his right hand than put it to the Constitution as it now stands."[49]

Even though the anti-federalists opposed ratifying the Constitution, the provisions for which they fought, including the two-track compromise of Article V, remained enshrined in the final document. As was evident even during the ratification debates, the Constitution's acceptance of the divergent federalist and anti-federalist theories of governance and constitutional change created inherent tensions in the document. There is perhaps no provision where these tensions are more fraught than in Article V, envisioned as a mechanism both to embolden the federal regime and also to restrict it.

Discerning what to make of Article V has been a perplexing question in American constitutional law and public life. Its compromise provisions were opaque and controversial even before ratification and have remained contradictory in the time following. So how should one think about Article V today?

One possible response is that the Hamilton-Mason compromise was a middle-course concession in name only. Hamilton always had the upper hand—and he probably knew it. The anti-federalist critiques were essentially right. Article V's thresholds are indeed challenging, the pathways too onerous to make amendment a routine method for change. And even when change is politically feasible, the congressional route has always prevailed due to its relative procedural ease. Where Mason desired the specter of state-led restructuring of government to be a check on federal power, Hamilton aimed to set a dominant federal government in stone. And with an amendment provision too challenging to be useful in practice, many believe Hamilton prevailed.

This assessment of Article V represents the generally accepted narrative. Hamilton and his fellow federalists successfully built a tall wall around their federal edifice, one that has held back anti-federalist assaults for over two hundred years. No amendments radically curtailing federal power have prevailed since ratification.[50] Rather, in the annals of American legal history and in the popular psyche, amendment is portrayed in a markedly Hamiltonian frame. Constitutional amendments have advanced freedom, equality, and prosperity by strengthening federal power. They have reformed the federal government to allow it to address new challenges, providing for a federal income tax, for example.[51] And amendments have made the federal Constitution the dominant repository for civil rights, and the federal courts the forum for vindicating those rights. The post-Reconstruction amendments of the 1860s, for example, provided the constitutional text animating most of the major civil rights advances of the last century, from *Brown v. Board of Education* (1954, racial segregation in schooling) to *Roe v. Wade* (1973, abortion) and *Obergefell v. Hodges* (2015, same-sex marriage).[52] This is the common Article V account often told by law professors, historians, and legal commentators. Constitutional amendment is part and parcel of an ongoing march toward a more powerful federal government, ensuring a brighter future—a manifestation of the preamble's lofty goals of establishing "a more perfect Union."

But there is an alternative, equally legitimate story to be told. Just as Article V endorses the Hamiltonian theory of top-down, union-strengthening constitutional change, so too does the Article endorse Mason's bottom-up, union-limiting theory. As the coming chapters detail, a long-running effort to engage Mason's convention mechanism has gained traction in recent decades. While the road to success is long and arduous—the anti-federalists were right in their critique—potential pathways to victory remain. Latent cracks in Hamilton's federalist rampart have long existed, and as this book lays out, now the long-developing fissures are becoming more apparent.

*   *   *

IMPERFECTION AND OTHER CONSTITUTIONAL COMPLEXITIES

While traveling through the United States some five decades after the Founding, the French philosopher Alexis de Tocqueville reflected upon the nature of the United States' experiment in popular self-governance.

Alexis de Tocqueville (Lithograph, 1901)

In his widely acclaimed two-volume study *Democracy in America*, he had this to say about American constitutionalism:

> An American constitution is not supposed to be immutable as in France, nor is it susceptible of modification by the ordinary powers of society as in England. It constitutes a detached whole, which, as it represents the determination of the whole people, is no less binding on the legislator than on the private citizen, but which may be altered by

the will of the people in predetermined cases, according to established rules. In America the constitution may therefore vary, but as long as it exists it is the origin of all authority, and the sole vehicle of the predominating force.[53]

Through the trials and tribulations of democratic adolescence, our forebears had made good on their revolutionary cry. In the United States, fundamental law was the new king; constitutions were binding on all, even those in power. And so it seemed bloody revolution would be no more. The People could change their founding documents "according to established rules" when necessary.

The importance of the amendment procedure was clear from the beginning. As George Washington remarked after the Convention concluded, the new Constitution was "not free from imperfections, but . . . as a constitutional door is opened for future amendments and alterations, I think it would be wise in the People to accept what is being offered to them."[54] For Washington, the ingenuity of the new American experiment in constitutional self-government was not the document alone—its finely wrought separation of powers or federal structure. Its genius was the wise recognition that the young republic was a work in progress.

The People, according to Washington, would best discern the path of that progress. The "People (for it is with them to Judge) can, as they will have the advantage of experience on their Side, decide with as much propriety on the alteration[s] and amendment[s] which are necessary," Washington wrote. "I do not think we are more inspired, have more wisdom, or possess more virtue, than those who will come after us."[55]

Washington's support for the Constitution, predicated in large part on the document's amendment provisions, remains perhaps one of the most important, fortuitous occurrences in American history. Washington, previously unwilling to engage in the work of the Convention, had written in haste to Madison and Humphreys just ten months before expressing his dismay at the unrest rocking Massachusetts. If it were not for Shays's violent uprising, and Washington's fear that the viability of the American project was in question, he likely would not have attended.

It is impossible to know whether the Convention that many—including Washington—suggested may have been illegal would have proceeded if the nation's future first president had not presided at the helm or publicly endorsed its handiwork. As the legal historian Michael Klarman notes, "nothing about the process that produced the Constitution was inevitable," and Washington's "absence would have deprived [the Convention] of his extraordinary legitimizing influence."[56] Perhaps the Convention would have ended with no draft, a second convention would have been held, as the anti-federalists desired, or the Constitution would not have been ratified at all.

Yet under the storm clouds of rebellion and Washington's careful gaze, the Convention crafted a new regime, one that would enshrine the radical American notion of bloodless revolution into fundamental law. Providing for amendment "in an easy, regular and Constitutional way" would, as Mason argued at the Convention, ameliorate the need "to trust to chance and violence."[57] Rebellion would no longer be necessary.

PART II

CONSTITUTIONAL AMENDMENT: DISMISSED AND MISUNDERSTOOD

3

THE ARCHAICS

Some Trouble with Conventional Wisdom

I F THE IDEA of a twenty-first-century constitutional convention seems unthinkable, consider how equally unlikely these three possibilities struck those growing up in the mid-twentieth century: the assassination of a president, the impeachment of a president, and the decisive role of the Electoral College in selecting a president who did not win the popular vote. These scenarios were almost impossible to imagine because they had not occurred in recent memory. And the constitutional provisions concerning these improbable crises were likewise not on most citizens' radar, often seen as fun fodder for trivia night or history buffs but of no real modern consequence.

With the stunning assassination of President Kennedy in November 1963, the first of these unlikely possibilities occurred. In the following years—at the height of our advanced constitutional democracy—we have endured three impeachments, one attempted impeachment, and two Electoral College obstructions of the popular vote (as well as a number of attempted assassinations). The implausible has repeatedly become reality.

Many today believe the calling of a constitutional convention is effectively impossible. Article V has no real role in our public life, they think. The application procedures are too difficult, our country too divided, and the state of our politics too acrimonious. And even if there were a time during which a convention call could possibly succeed, a once-in-two-centuries goldilocks moment when all the right political factors aligned, it

is surely not now. Congress cannot even pass its annual spending bills on time, a far simpler political task. (Congress last met the appropriation bill deadline in 1997.[1]) How could a movement ever secure sufficient momentum to gain support from thirty-four state legislatures—thousands of individual legislators—to successfully force a convention call? And even if a movement could somehow manage to *call* a convention, the amendments it proposed could never clear the even higher three-quarters bar for ratification. The prospect is so remote, so unlikely, that it is not worth much focus.

This common view of Article V can be persuasive. Informed by one understanding of history and political probability, it seems both reasonable and intuitively correct. The common view can feel so plainly obvious that many do not give it much thought. The history of the use and attempted use of Article V, however, suggests that a successful convention call, or meaningful constitutional change resulting from a potential call, are at least as plausible today as those three unfathomable possibilities were in the last half century. And as monumental as those unforeseen events have been in our recent history, a constitutional convention could go well beyond the issue of a particular president's tenure. By its very nature, a constitutional convention could—and most surely would—set in motion attempts to fundamentally alter our system of government, pursuing regime change by peaceful and legal means.

The country may well be on the verge of a new chapter in constitutional history, one animated by the awakening of a long-dormant provision—Article V. Far-right activists have seized on Article V's provision for a constitutional convention as a new route to advance their political agenda. Their road to success is steep, to be sure. But they have already gained significant ground with little scrutiny or opposition.

This effort should not come as a total surprise, nor should the possibility of claims of a successful application effort and convention call catch citizens off guard. These efforts can be tracked and their consequences foreseen. Yet those who would likely find the results most disturbing—including progressives, liberals, many moderates, and perhaps even some conservatives—tend to discount the threat. Because Article V has been so infrequently used, and the convention route *never* successfully deployed, they consider the provision to be toothless, a quirky vestige of a time long ago.

*   *   *

The Archaics

Americans have generally trusted that the nation's constitutional order rests on firm footing. Two centuries of remarkable stability have fostered a fervent faith in the Constitution, one predicated on its sure—some even say divinely inspired—structuring of political life. Most Americans believe that the Constitution's main provisions are settled and strong. They trust its guardrails and take solace in its ability to calm and check the base instincts of power. The Constitution is known, dependable, and, many believe, essentially unchanging.

This culture of constitutional trust, what some have called our "civil religion," can be a productive and even noble thing.[2] The trust inspires a sense of shared citizenship and purpose, sets firm expectations of institutions and elected leaders, and ultimately ensures a robust yet steady form of democratic self-government. But this trust can sometimes breed complacency. Citizens can grow comfortable with the Constitution. A bit too comfortable.

One troubling way this comfort has taken hold in public life is through a phenomenon one might call "the archaics."[3] Many Americans, often informed by prevailing opinion in the political and legal establishment, consider some parts of the Constitution to be archaic—dusty, quaint, and irrelevant. They relegate these old constitutional provisions to the storage closet, to a lesser status that over time removes them from the public consciousness. The archaics are never struck from the Constitution. But conventional wisdom assumes them to be dead and inoperative.

Take the Third Amendment's prohibition that "no Soldier shall, in time of peace be quartered in any house, without the consent of the Owner, nor in time of war, but in a manner to be prescribed by law." Beyond a parody Twitter account posting jokes and memes about the amendment, the provision is rarely discussed.[4] While exceptionally important to the Founding generation, and a textual "penumbra" used by the Supreme Court in the landmark 1965 case *Griswold v. Connecticut* to find a constitutional right to privacy, the provision now seems old, strange, and largely unimportant.[5] The same could be said of the Seventh Amendment's requirement that a civil case allege injury greater than $20 (not pegged to inflation) to be tried by a jury, Article I's prohibition against Bills of Attainder (legislative acts finding a person guilty of a crime without a trial),[6] Article I's prohibition of noble titles,[7] the republican guarantee clause,[8] or Congress's authority to regulate piracy in American waters by granting letters of marque and reprisal. All are often seen as odd remnants of a time gone by.

Yet sometimes these archaics can awake from their slumber, seemingly plucked from their dusty constitutional storeroom to change history.[9] Consider one archaic that took hold deep in the heart of the legal and political establishment. In the 2008 landmark decision *District of*

Columbia v. Heller, the Supreme Court held five to four that the Second Amendment protected a personal right to own a firearm in the home.[10] Before *Heller,* however, the generally accepted consensus was that the Second Amendment contained no real power at all, let alone a robust personal right. It merely regulated Congress's power over state militias, which had become less and less important since the Revolution.[11]

So dominant was this prevailing conception that one constitutional scholar wrote in a respected 1969 treatise that "this amendment is not overly important."[12] The first edition of Harvard Law Professor Laurence Tribe's leading constitutional law casebook, published in 1978 and spanning over one thousand pages, mentioned the Second Amendment exactly once—in a footnote.[13] The same was true of the second edition, published in 1988.[14] "To put it mildly, the Second Amendment is not at the forefront of constitutional discussion," Professor Sanford Levinson wrote in a 1989 *Yale Law Journal* article.[15] Another professor, writing in 1987, was even more direct: "The second amendment is not taken seriously by most scholars."[16]

But again the unforeseen happened. While the mainstream establishment had relegated the archaic amendment to the trash can, an alternative narrative was taking shape in other corners. Conservative and otherwise contrarian thinkers began reconsidering the amendment's text (which, after all, remained in the Constitution) and the history of its drafting. Indeed, as one of us observed in a 1975 senior honors thesis at the University of Wisconsin, entitled "The Armed Amendment: The Bases and Prospects for the Modern Significance of the Second Amendment to the United States Constitution," there was a "striking discrepancy between the low legal status of this provision and its potent symbolic role in the gun control controversy."[17] Noting the contemporary state of the scholarly and political debate, that same author commented:

> The Second Amendment has been dismissed frequently or even ridiculed as a largely insignificant and certainly not important right. Often these "barbs" come from the pens of those who have devoted their careers to the study and sanctification of the Bill of Rights; which is just as surely the home of the Second as of the First and Fifth Amendments. . . . In effect, the Second Amendment has been granted, by many legal scholars and especially those in favor of gun control, the unenviable

status of perhaps the most ridiculed and disdained provision in the U.S. Constitution.[18]

This discrepancy between elite scholarly opinion and activist fervor provided, the author reasoned, "perhaps the perfect case study" to examine "the process by which an alleged 'archaic' law becomes interpreted and revitalized through the political and legal processes to reemerge as a significant statement on individual rights and social policy." The ferment apparent among gun activists and conservative scholars made clear that an alternative interpretation was not only possible but could be correct. "The Constitution (that is, what the courts have said the Constitution means) may give way to the pressures of important or highly controversial political or social issues. . . . Now is the time to determine the possible ways in which the Second Amendment may be interpreted and by whom."[19] During the last quarter of the twentieth century, similar arguments were made in law reviews and academic symposia. Soon, judges began noticing and agreeing.[20]

By the third edition of Professor Tribe's casebook, published in 2000, the Second Amendment received its due treatment: ten full pages of dense analysis of the history, text, academic scholarship, and judicial interpretation of the provision. The text even noted that it was an open question whether the Amendment contained a personal right.[21] Eight years later, in *Heller*, the Supreme Court radically upended over a century of jurisprudence. Two years following, in *McDonald v. City of Chicago*, the Court applied the new doctrine to the states, invalidating large swathes of gun regulations across the country.[22] The supposedly dead Second Amendment had become very much alive, seemingly overnight.

One cannot overly fault those who have embraced these dismissive attitudes toward the archaics. That the constitutional provisions were dead (or so disused as to be almost dead) was accurate as a backward-looking, descriptive matter. The conventional wisdom, informed by one interpretation of history and political probability, would have seemed reasonable and instinctively right. As more recent history illustrates, however, such conventional wisdom can be wrong. Ignoring or minimizing these archaics can fog one's thinking about the Constitution, law, and public life with potentially perilous effect. The tendency to consider some provisions as defunct and useless, and thus remove them from mainstream scholarly and political debate, fosters an apathy toward the array of possible futures the provisions might entail. And with such apathy comes unpreparedness.

For many, Article V is yet another example of the archaics, one bound up in a reasonable yet potentially misleading understanding of history and political probability. Because the provision has not been used often, and its convention route *never* used, many think it has no real power in the modern era. Like other archaics, however, the inclination to overlook Article V could lead one to underestimate its potential—with detrimental effect.

THE CONVENTIONAL WISDOM: AN ARCHAIC ARTICLE V

If the ability to amend is one of the Constitution's great cornerstone principles, the arc of history leaves one with an intriguing dilemma. Ours is the world's oldest functioning written national constitution. Yet it is also one of the least changed. The People have adopted only twenty-seven amendments, ten of which (the Bill of Rights) were proposed by the First Congress and ratified just years after the Constitution took effect in 1789. The most recent, concerning congressional pay, was ratified in 1992 but proposed in 1789.

It would seem that the vast social, political, and technological change of the last two centuries should have necessitated more frequent revision. Other important issues of the last three decades, such as campaign finance, climate change, and voting rights, seem ripe for constitutional reform. So how can one explain the relative absence of amendment?

The common answer is that Article V is too challenging to deploy. The two-step amendment method (proposal by Congress or convention, then ratification by state legislatures) and three-quarters ratification requirement erect a high threshold for change. Article V forces amendment proponents to build exceptionally mature, cross-group coalitions and well-funded, savvy advocacy efforts to secure the support of thousands of state legislators and (sometimes) hundreds of congresspeople across a diverse political terrain. Such advocacy is hard, expensive, and can take decades. Most movements cannot do it.

This view of Article V is dominant in the legal, political, and academic establishment. Formal constitutional amendment, a rich topic for scholarly writing and engagement as recently as 1980, is now seen by some as a stagnant backwater.[23] Constitutional scholars from across the ideological spectrum pronounce Article V as "too onerous to provide for sufficient adapt-ability,"[24] as a "formidable obstacle course,"[25] the "Constitution's most truly egregious feature,"[26] and cause for "both embarrassment and evasion."[27]

These assessments of Article V are fair and accurate under any reason-able criteria. There is no disputing that the provision erects a very high bar. Compared to constitutional amendment mechanisms in state constitutions and those of other advanced democracies abroad, the federal Constitution is an outlier. According to one study by comparative constitutional schol-ars, Article V makes our national constitution among "the most inflexible" in the world.[28] The amendment mechanism requires more individuals, in more legislative bodies, to agree at a higher rate. The path to change is particularly steep.

Yet many debate whether such inflexibility poses a problem. As many scholars and jurists have theorized, constitutional change does not only occur through Article V. There are *informal* methods to change the mean-ing of the Constitution through political and judicial action.

The common method, and the source of most public and academic debate, is the Supreme Court's ongoing interpretation of constitutional text, through which the Constitution's meaning is applied and adapted case by case.[29] Professors William Eskridge and John Ferejohn have argued that Congress can also informally change the Constitution through the creation of "super-statutes" such as the Civil Rights Act or the Clean Air Act, which frame government structure and regulate public values.[30] So too can the political branches, in union with popular support, craft what theorists have called "non–Article V" amendment.[31] In his multivolume study *We the People*, Professor Bruce Ackerman argues that the People have effectuated legitimate and settled constitutional change during great "constitutional moments" when intense public reckoning yields a certain, generally accepted conclusion.[32] The reforms of the New Deal, for exam-ple, fashioned a functional amendment to the Constitution, granting Congress an array of new powers to regulate the economy and public life.[33] In each of these ways—through the courts, Congress, or the political sys-tem at large—the Constitution does change with force and legitimacy, just not through the strictures of formal amendment. As Professor Ste-phen Griffin has put it, "By making it difficult to change the Constitution, the Framers forced a significant amount of constitutional change off the books."[34]

Most would agree that the Constitution does change outside the confines of Article V. And most argue that such informal change is necessary, an inherent element of any robust constitutional system. While discerning the means and magnitude of such informal change has been highly controversial, that it occurs—at least in some fashion—is indisputable from lived experience. The Constitution of today is different from the Constitution of two decades ago, and even more different from the Constitution of a century ago. Some of this informal change is slow and hard to gauge. But in other core areas, like foreign affairs, executive authority, and war powers, overt theories of non–Article V amendment have been particularly powerful and decisive.[35] Any serious analysis of our constitutional tradition must account for this change.

But in making sense of informal change, many scholars, politicians, and civil society leaders of all ideological stripes go a step further. In response to Article V's rough road to constitutional change, many make normative claims about formal amendment itself. Article V should be seen as "irrelevant," many claim.[36] The Constitution has survived without it and will continue to do so. The work of informal change has proved workable and good. Others who eschew theories of informal change nonetheless embrace another version of the "irrelevancy" thesis. That "Article V makes it almost impossible to amend the Constitution" is a good thing, these commentators argue, as it entrenches the Constitution's supposedly conservative ethos and enforces a theory of "intergenerational lawmaking."[37] Article V is irrelevant not because informal methods prove workable but because it makes the Constitution fundamentally unchangeable. In both iterations, modern commentators embrace a defunct formal amendment mechanism. That Article V is disused is not a problem to be fixed but a sign the mechanism can be ignored, or maybe even a feature to be praised.

The accepted wisdom that Article V can be (or ought to be) ignored is so widespread that mainstream political debate regarding constitutional amendment has come to a halt in recent years. Since the 1990s, no serious efforts have been undertaken in Congress to pursue constitutional reform by amendments. Rather, political debate regarding the Constitution in Congress and the mainstream political establishment has focused almost exclusively on the mechanics of Supreme Court nominations and court reform. These debates are timely and important, to be sure. The role of the Court's informal alteration of the Constitution's meaning is of exceptional significance. But these debates are often predicated on a core assumption—that the amendment mechanism is broken, and the Supreme Court is the dominant institutional method to change constitutional law and meaning.

Within the nation's law schools, informal methods are likewise often considered the only viable means to change the Constitution. Students study the great amendments from history—the First, Fourth, and Fourteenth—debating the nuances of the cases interpreting them, possible new futures for that interpretation, and the philosophical underpinnings of the jurisprudence. But few classroom minutes are spent discussing formal constitutional amendment as a present and future possibility, as a wellspring of opportunity to correct the many ills infecting our law and body politic or as a threat to long-held norms. Formal amendment is almost always discussed in the past tense.

This tendency in the academy to overlook formal amendment took one of your authors by surprise. When he became a visiting professor at one of the nation's leading law schools, several colleagues questioned why his course on the Senate and legislative process addressed Congress's consideration of proposed amendments. "It's not done that much," one colleague remarked. After proposing to teach a course on Article V, that same author was even more surprised to learn that it was among the first (if not *the* first) in the country devoted to the subject.[38]

Leaders in civil society, including prominent editorial boards and public intellectuals, have also embraced the conventional narrative. In a 2021 opinion piece, one *New York Times* columnist remarked it was unlikely "anyone alive today" would see a new amendment successfully ratified.[39] Another columnist noted in the pages of the same paper that there was "almost no chance" Article V could ever prove functional.[40] As part of its multiyear series "The Battle for the Constitution," the *Atlantic* published hundreds of pieces examining "the constitutional debates in American life." Authors have attempted to read the tea leaves of recent Supreme Court voting rights decisions, parsed the meaning of the "nondelegation doctrine" (a legal theory regarding legislative delegation to administrative agencies), and even examined the nuances of chief judge rotation policies on the nation's courts of appeals. Only two articles discussed the role of Article V in our constitutional structure.[41]

Under this prevailing view, the historical memory of Article V becomes more powerful than the provision itself. Among liberals and progressives, debate often assumes the impossibility of amendment yet attempts to rekindle a culture of constitutional change inspired by Article V. Many tell stories about how the People harnessed Article V to claim new rights, correct political and social wrongs, and make the country a better place. Amendment was the august constitutional tool used to bring about equality and justice, to advance the Preamble's goal "to form a more perfect union." But those times are past, the conventional story goes. Article V *was* the mechanism used to make ours a "good" Constitution. Now the country must find new political and constitutional pathways to further that effort.[42]

Many mainstream conservatives likewise see Article V as dead yet celebrate its history in a different light. Recognizing the disproportionate power with which they have been vested due to the Constitution's baked-in malapportionment, conservatives see the provision as giving the ultimate sanction to a logic of limited change and minoritarian rule. Where liberals and progressives remember Article V by way of its laudable products, mainstream conservatives now speak of the provision as hardwiring the supposed conservative ethos of the Founding. Article V's rough road is the ultimate protection and vindication of their political agenda, a provision to be often cited in full belief that it will likely never be invoked—a convenient talisman to quiet calls for change.[43]

SOME TROUBLE WITH THE CONVENTIONAL WISDOM

Because Article V is "unworkable," the argument goes, it is little more than useless text. It sits enshrined behind glass in the National Archives as a testament to the possibilities of yesteryear, an artifact of a bygone era when constitutional change with relatively direct popular sanction was possible. But now, Article V can be ignored and maybe even forgotten. It has no real power in the modern age.

This conventional wisdom is dangerous for two interrelated reasons. First, it discounts and ultimately forecloses the fundamental importance of formal amendment to a healthy, functioning constitutional democracy. It endangers, either willfully or by implication, the Founding generation's bold claim that a new theory of bloodless revolution should be the cornerstone of the American constitutional experiment, one that ensures the country's ongoing vitality. The United States has moved on from the Founding generation's youthful naivete, many believe. The Constitution has matured. This turn in popular thinking is subtle and has taken broad, bipartisan hold over multiple decades. And its implications, discussed in Part 4, pose grave problems for the future of the American democratic community.

But the conventional wisdom is also dangerous because it has bred widespread complacency. Most assume without question that the wisdom is *correct*, that Article V does indeed have no power in modern life. Such certainty permits relegating movements for formal constitutional change to the sidelines of political life. Anyone who takes Article V seriously can be ignored, most think. They will never achieve anything of note.

When one examines how Article V has functioned in practice over the last two centuries, however, a certain truth becomes clear: the formal amendment mechanism has never been dead. Like the other archaics, it merely sits in a silent slumber waiting to be awakened. And in the case of Article V's convention route, that awakening often occurs seemingly out of the blue, taking most by surprise and demanding rapid response.

*   *   *

THE CONVENTIONAL WISDOM OF YESTERYEAR

While troubling, contemporary thinking about Article V is hardly a new phenomenon. As the country approached the Constitution's centennial in 1887, an almost holy aura had developed around our founding document. With words like *reverence*, *sacredness*, and *shrine*, Americans praised the Framers' work as "an inspiration from God" and supremely perfect.[44] They spoke of the Constitution as the "Ark of the Covenant" and called Philadelphia's Independence Hall the "holiest spot of American earth." Visitors were pilgrims to the hallowed ground of the Constitution's birthplace. At centennial parades and celebrations from Philadelphia to Minnesota, Utah to Texas, and Tennessee to California, orators repeated again and again British prime minister William Gladstone's remark that the American Constitution was "the most wonderful work ever struck off at a given time by the brain and purpose of man." What greater vindication of the Revolution could there have been than a British head of government extolling the constitutional virtues of a former foe? The Constitution's first century had rendered it flawless, an object of reverence and worship. And like the Bible, many believed it should not, or could not, ever be changed.[45]

"The Shrine of the Constitution in the Library of Congress" (1924)

Constitutional scholars agreed. In his widely acclaimed 1885 study *Congressional Government,* the Princeton political scientist and future president Woodrow Wilson remarked, "It would seem that no impulse short of the impulse of self-preservation, no force less than the force of revolution, can nowadays be expected to move the cumbrous machinery of formal amendment erected by Article Five."[46] Such was the clear teaching of recent history. Herman Ames, in his meticulous 1897 study of constitutional amendment that won the American Historical Association's annual prize for best manuscript, wrote, "Nothing of strength has been added to the Constitution by amendment except in the case of the 'reconstruction amendments,' and these were carried only after a civil war." Reflecting the prevailing conventional wisdom of his day, Ames concluded that it was unlikely the Constitution would ever be amended again due to the "insurmountable constitutional obstacles."[47]

In the early years of the twentieth century, many in the country's political and legal elite had likewise accepted the common view of Article V. In an address at the American Bar Association's 1907 annual meeting, Judge Charles F. Amidon chastised those who clung to Article V in certain hope of its resurrection. "The Constitution cannot be amended," he boldly declared, citing the over two thousand failed attempts in the previous century. Except the anomalous Civil War amendments, none had passed despite rigorous debate, he argued. The record spoke for itself. Informal amendment methods, including judicial elaboration of the Constitution's meaning, Amidon continued, have "the entire approval of the nation, and must now be accepted as a part of our frame of government, of equal validity with the Constitution itself."[48] The speech was so notable that Justice William Potter of the Pennsylvania Supreme Court quoted it (almost) verbatim three years later in an address at the University of Pennsylvania on amending the Constitution.[49] "It cannot be denied that the process is so difficult that it discourages any attempt to bring about any change," Potter remarked.[50]

But outside the halls of power, the conventional wisdom had yet to gain such firm footing. From New York to California, bloody clashes between workers and the government strengthened the growing belief that the political and economic system of the Gilded Age needed reform. Far from a moment of idyllic stability, the Constitution's centennial was animated by a spirit of brooding unease. America was, as historian Jackson Lears put it, "dreaming of rebirth."[51]

While it would not reach culmination for nearly two decades, amendment fervor was taking hold even as those in Washington, Princeton, and beyond sang requiems for Article V. In the states, movements for political reform were successfully pursuing a broad program of state constitutional amendment.[52] And citizens across the country, responding to widespread corruption, a nation awash with economic and social woes, and a recalcitrant establishment bent on halting reform, soon set their sights on the federal Constitution's amendment mechanism as another means for redress.

Starting with Nebraska in 1895, two years before Ames published his study and six years before Wilson's final edition, state after state began passing applications to call a constitutional convention under Article V.[53] By 1912, thirty-one states had filed applications—one short of the number necessary to trigger a convention (there were forty-eight states in 1912, making thirty-two the application threshold, not the thirty-four required today). The rapid success of the convention movement was a shock to many. As the *Washington Post* journalist Henry West observed, "Very few persons realize how close the nation is to a constitutional convention. . . . It would take but a slight degree of missionary work among these legislatures to secure the two-thirds action."[54] Less than two decades following Nebraska's opening salvo, a convention—whether a threat or an opportunity—seemed imminent.

As a sense of both excitement and trepidation set in, debate consumed Washington and the country. Should a convention be called or not? How would such a meeting work? And perhaps most interesting, how had this looming convention call come to fruition so fast?

Senator Weldon Heyburn of Idaho argued that he hoped "we would never again meet to make a constitution. With all the conflicting interests of this day and this age, with the great corporations, with the great labor question, with the hundred issues, you never could get 90,000,000 people to agree upon a constitution." His fears that a convention could come to consider the deepest questions facing society were not an exaggeration. All could be on the table, as "when the constitutional convention meets it is the people, and it is the same people who made the original Constitution, and no limitation in the original constitution controls the people when they meet again."[55] Henry West agreed, arguing that a convention "would open Pandora's box" and that, if called, it would do grave harm to the country and the economy.[56]

Perhaps due to these fears, the final state application never materialized, and a convention call was averted. Yet the rapid surge of convention applications between 1895 and 1913 had a profound, sea-change effect on the country's political life. The applications demonstrated an insistence in the states that Article V was workable, that formal amendment was not only a real possibility but also a political necessity. While the requisite number of applications was never achieved, Washington could not ignore the People's clamor. Soon Congress would propose a series of reform amendments that ushered in a flourishing of constitutional change.

Convention applications played a decisive role in sparking the burst of formal amendment that followed. Between 1913 and 1920, the states ratified four congressionally proposed amendments that transformed American public life—the federal income tax, direct election of senators, Prohibition, and women's right to vote. Over just seven years, the People resurrected formal amendment, forcing Article V's machinery to operate with remarkable speed. And through Article V, the People fundamentally reformed aspects of the Constitution, equipping it for a new, modern century. Writing in the *Yale Law Journal* in 1915, Professor Joseph Long reflected on how quickly the conventional wisdom had changed: "When the ratification of the required three-fourths of the states can be obtained within twelve months," he wrote, "there is little room to complain."[57]

This rapid shift in popular opinion regarding Article V caught the legal and political establishment off guard. But for no one was it likely so jarring as for President Wilson. During his two terms in office—starting just twelve years after he published the fifteenth edition of *Congressional Government* in 1901—four amendments radically altering the constitutional status quo were ratified and a movement to hold a constitutional convention nearly prevailed. Over just eight years, Article V's "cumbrous machinery" had moved with great speed, ushering in a revolution in constitutional thought and a new flowering of civic engagement on questions of fundamental law.

Wilson never published a sixteenth edition of his magnum opus, a study that one contemporary commentator praised as "the best critical writing on the American constitution which has appeared since *The Federalist Papers*."[58] One is left to wonder whether he ever considered revising his bleak assessment of the amendment mechanism. But Wilson's initial certainty about the demise of formal amendment stands as a warning for concerned citizens today, a reminder that Article V has often been misunderstood and its risks underestimated.

4

A SLEEPING GIANT

The Enduring Importance of
Article V and the Convention Route

"A constitutional road to the decision of the people ought to be marked out and kept open, for certain great and extraordinary occasions."

— *Federalist* No. 49 (Attributed to James Madison, February 5, 1788)

F OR GENERATIONS, Americans have rehearsed eulogies for Article V. Many anti-federalists argued even before ratification that the provision would never be useful in practice. "Who is there to be found among us, who can seriously assert, that this Constitution, after ratification and being practiced upon, will be so easy of alteration?" a leading anti-federalist wrote in 1787.[1] John Marshall—who, as the fourth chief justice of the United States, relied in part on Article V to establish a theory of judicial review in *Marbury v. Madison* (1803)—is said to have remarked that the mechanism was "unwieldy."[2] So too with Woodrow Wilson, Herman Ames, and so many others at the turn of the last century, and with the conventional wisdom dominant today. Lamenting Article V's supposed inutility is perhaps one of the most consistent through lines in the American constitutional story.

But history makes clear that Article V is not useless. Twelve amendments were ratified in the last century alone, following decades of minimizing Article V in the late nineteenth and early twentieth centuries. So why has luments whereof shall have been encreased during such time; and no person holding any office under the United States, shall be a member of either house during his continuance in office.

Sect. 7. The enacting stile of the laws shall be, " Be it enacted by the senators and representatives in Congress assembled."

All bills for raising revenue shall originate in the house of representatives: but the senate may propose or concur with amendments as on other bills.

Every bill which shall have passed the house of representatives and the senate, shall, before it become a law, be presented to the president of the United States. If he approve he shall sign it, but if not he shall return it, with his objections to that house in which it shall have originated, who shall enter the objections at large on their journal, and proceed to reconsider it. If after such reconsideration two-thirds of that house shall agree to pass the bill, it shall be sent, together with the objections, to the other house, by which it shall likewise be reconsidered, and if approved by two-thirds of that house, it shall become a law. But in all such cases the votes of both houses shall be determined by yeas and nays, and the names of the persons voting for and against the bill shall be entered on the journal of each house respectively. If any bill shall not be returned by the President within ten days (Sundays excepted) after it shall have been presented to him, the same shall be a law, in like manner as if he had signed it, unless the Congress by their adjournment prevent its return, in which case it shall not be a law.

Every order, resolution, or vote to which the concurrence of the Senate and House of Representatives may be necessary (except on a question of adjournment) shall be presented to the President of the United States; and before the same shall take effect, shall be approved by him, or, being disapproved by him, shall be repassed by ~~two thirds~~ of the Senate and House of Representatives, according to the rules and limitations prescribed in the case of a bill.

Sect. 8. The Congress ~~may by joint ballot appoint a treasurer.~~ They shall have power

To lay and collect taxes, duties, imposts and excises; to pay the debts and provide for the common defence and general welfare of the United States: *but all duties, imposts and excises shall be uniform throughout the United States*

To borrow money on the credit of the United States.

To regulate commerce with foreign nations, among the several states, and with the Indian tribes.

To establish an uniform rule of naturalization, and uniform laws on the subject of bankruptcies throughout the United States.

To coin money, regulate the value thereof, and of foreign coin, and fix the standard of weights and measures.

To provide for the punishment of counterfeiting the securities and current coin of the United States.

To establish post offices and post roads.

To promote the progress of science and useful arts, by securing for limited times to authors and inventors the exclusive right to their respective writings and discoveries.

To constitute tribunals inferior to the supreme court.

To define and punish piracies and felonies committed on the high seas, and offences against the law of nations.

To declare war, grant letters of marque and reprisal, and make rules concerning captures on land and water.

To raise and support armies: but no appropriation of money to that use shall be for a longer term than two years.

To provide and maintain a navy.

To make rules for the government and regulation of the land and naval forces.

To provide for calling forth the militia to execute the laws of the union, suppress insurrections and repel invasions.

To provide for organizing, arming and disciplining the militia, and for governing such part of them as may be employed in the service of the United States, reserving to the States respectively, the appointment of the officers, and the authority of training the militia according to the discipline prescribed by Congress.

To exercise exclusive legislation in all cases whatsoever, over such district (not exceeding ten miles square) as may, by cession of particular States, and the acceptance of Congress, become the seat of the government of the United States, and to exercise like authority over all places purchased by the consent of the legislature of the state in which the same shall be, for the erection of forts, magazines, arsenals, dock-yards, and other needful buildings—And

To make all laws which shall be necessary and proper for carrying into execution the foregoing powers, and all other powers vested by this constitution in the government of the United States, or in any department or officer thereof.

Sect. 9. The migration or importation of such persons as ~~the several~~ *any of the* states now existing shall think proper to admit, shall not be prohibited by the Congress prior to the year one thousand eight hundred and eight, but a tax or duty may be imposed on such importation, not exceeding ten dollars for each person.

The privilege of the writ of habeas corpus shall not be suspended, unless when in cases of rebellion or invasion the public safety may require it.

No bill of attainder shall be passed, ~~nor any ex post facto law.~~ *nor any ex post facto law*

No capitation tax shall be laid, unless in proportion to the census herein before directed to be taken *~~nor any indirect taxes shall be laid unless in proportion to~~* *State over in another*

No tax or duty shall be laid on articles exported from any state. ✗ *or pay duties in another*

No money shall be drawn from the treasury, but in consequence of appropriations made by law.

No title of nobility shall be granted by the United States. And no person holding any office of *and no persons holding* profit or trust under them, shall, without the consent of the Congress, accept of any present, emolument, office, or title, of any kind whatever, from any king, prince, or foreign state. *of the United States shall expend the public money without the consent of Congress*

Sect. 10. No state shall coin money, nor emit bills of credit, nor make any thing but gold or silver coin a tender in payment of debts, nor pass any bill of attainder, nor ex post facto law, nor law altering or impairing the obligation of contracts; nor grant letters of marque and reprisal, nor enter into any treaty, alliance, or confederation, nor grant any title of nobility. *No*

Sect. 10. No state shall enter into any treaty, alliance or confederation, nor grant letters of marque and reprisal; coin money; emit bills of credit; make any thing but gold & silver coin a tender in payment of debts; pass any Bill of attainder, ex post facto Law, or Law impairing the obligation of contracts, or grant any title of nobility

the view of a moribund Article V taken such a recurring hold throughout history? What is it about the amendment mechanism that has caused so many individuals across successive generations and different political and social contexts to discount its power?

One obvious answer is procedural. Chief Justice Marshall was right. Article V's rules are some of the most "unwieldy" in the world. As discussed in Chapter 3, these rules make the path to amendment so steep that most political movements cannot achieve sufficient momentum. And over time, policy and opinion leaders have given up hope, favoring easier methods to pursue constitutional reform. This is the conventional wisdom expressed by Wilson in 1885, Ames in 1897, Judge Amidon in 1907, and Justice Potter in 1909, and echoed with striking similarity by many commentators throughout the last century and up to the present.

But there might be a deeper reason why so many have discounted Article V's power, one rooted in the nuances of the Hamilton-Mason compromise. The Constitutional Convention of 1787 crafted an amendment mechanism with two ideologically opposed routes for amendment proposal: Hamilton's union-enhancing, top-down congressional method and Mason's union-checking, bottom-up convention method. This compromise between the federalist and anti-federalist views introduced an inherent tension in Article V: constitutional amendment can be not only an institutionalist means to strengthen and embolden but also a revolutionary mechanism to subvert and destroy.

Many throughout history have discounted this second element of the compromise, ignoring Mason's revolutionary logic in favor of a markedly Hamiltonian conception of constitutional change. As Hamilton remarked at the Convention, constitutional amendment should be "an easy mode . . . for [repairing] defects which will probably appear in the new System."[3] Unlike Mason, who took an oppositional tack, Hamilton foresaw amendment as a way to update the document to modern times, fix the Framers' oversights, and change provisions that have proved flawed. And as Hamilton forcefully argued at the Convention, such reform should be sparked and driven by those in power. "The National Legislature will be the first to perceive and will be most sensible to the necessity of amendments," he believed.[4]

Article V in this framing entrusts the question of constitutional change to the normal process of federal politics. This Hamiltonian vision seems to anticipate that amendments will fall in a (relatively) evenly spaced manner throughout constitutional time. Every few years Congress would debate new changes to fix problems arising as the country matures, and sometimes the states would adopt them. Under this scenario, the Constitution endures through incremental change. Constitutional repair and maintenance would occur in a normal cadence, much like changing a light bulb or seasonally cleaning the gutters. Amendment proposals and political debate about formal constitutional change would be common and standard in public life, the Hamiltonian thinking goes.

Yet Congress has not proposed a single new amendment within the last half century. This absence of consistent, linear, and rhythmic constitutional amending has caused many to regard Article V as not worthy of much focus. But rather than being a sign of its demise, might Article V's sporadic success suggest the resilience of Mason's—not Hamilton's— amendment logic? Could it be a sign that Article V is more about constitutional revolution than constitutional repair?

The American experience is defined by brief moments when constitutional amendment proved both workable and decisively powerful. As discussed in the introduction, twenty-one of the twenty-seven amendments were ratified during a few, short periods: ten following ratification, three following the Civil War, four during the Progressive Era, and four during the mid-twentieth century. But outside these moments of rapid change, amendments have been quite rare—only six over the intervening 204 years.

How can one explain this phenomenon of intermittent amendment fervor, what Madison predicted in *Federalist* No. 49 would be the "great and extraordinary occasions" of constitutional amendment? The answer lies, in part, with the nuanced interplay between Hamilton and Mason's two dueling methods and rationales. History makes it clear that rather than being a seemingly defunct Hamiltonian mechanism for congressionally led repairs of defects, Article V and particularly its convention option exhibit a markedly Mason-like character: that of a sleeping giant waiting to be awakened to check the status quo.[5]

Most amendments have been the result of movements that used the political process and Article V's own mechanism to force Congress to act. In this way, Mason's conception of amending as a bottom-up revolutionary tool has found great power. And even though Mason's convention route has never fully prevailed, *attempts* to awaken Article V through convention applications have often played decisive roles in sparking amendment fervor. This is why amendment moments often arise so suddenly, taking those in power—like Wilson and, as discussed below, many others—by surprise.

To understand the full power of Article V, one must consider these moments of fervor. What was it about certain moments in time that caused the sleeping giant to wake?

THE UNSETTLED CONSTITUTION: CALLS FOR A SECOND CONVENTION AND THE BILL OF RIGHTS

The first moment of amendment fervor occurred before the Constitution was even ratified as the possibility of another convention loomed. Even before the Constitutional Convention adjourned in 1787, discontent with the new Constitution was widespread. The anti-federalist delegates, including Mason, had already expressed grave concern about the newly emboldened central government and the Constitution's lack of an express guarantee of essential personal liberties. Once the draft Constitution was put to the states for ratification, these critiques gained momentum. The ratification debates, occurring on the floors of ratifying conventions and in newspapers, pamphlets (including *The Federalist*), and town squares, soon made it clear that the question of adopting the new Constitution was far from settled. As the states considered ratification, the anti-federalist argument sparked intense debate. For many, it seemed that a second convention was necessary. The work of the first was flawed.

Writing under the pseudonym Publius in *The Federalist*, Madison, Hamilton, and John Jay attempted to alleviate citizens' fears. They extolled the virtues of the new Constitution, recounted with woe the troubles under the Articles, and attempted to dispute the anti-federalist argument point by point. Yet concern continued to grow.

The anti-federalist critique of the new Constitution was, as the scholar of the Founding Herbert Storing has argued, firmly rooted in a "conservative posture."[6] The anti-federalists were not naive; they agreed that the Articles of Confederation were flawed and that the current regime needed change. But their approach was cautious and slow.[7] "The framing [of] entirely new systems, is a work that requires vast attention; and it is much easier to guard an old one,"

one dissenter wrote.[8] The Constitution, drafted over just a few short months and immediately submitted for ratification, was conceived too quickly.

More troubling still was the drafting process itself. The Constitutional Convention was arguably illegal from the beginning. And even if it was legal, its final product was not. The Confederation Congress had called the Convention "for the sole and express purpose of revising the Articles of Confederation." That the Convention would draft a whole new constitution (hardly an act of "revising" the Articles) clearly overstepped its mandate. Adding even more complexity and subterfuge, the Convention had similarly claimed that the new Constitution would be deemed ratified upon acceptance by three-quarters of the states, not by the *unanimous* vote required to amend the Articles. This meant that under the Convention's theory, a state might be functionally bound by the new Constitution even if it did not consent, or it could be strong-armed into accepting the new status quo against its will.[9] Both propositions were anathema to the Articles' plain text and guiding spirit.

The fear was far from exaggerated. Rhode Island put the ratification question directly to the people in a popular vote. After the legislature printed a thousand copies of the document so voters could "have an opportunity for forming their sentiments" on it, citizens gathered in town meetings to cast their votes in a referendum.[10] The result was a resounding rejection of the new Constitution, by a vote of 2,708 to 237.[11] Even after the Constitution had taken effect upon ratification by nine states, Rhode Islanders remained obstinate. Multiple ratifying conventions in the state failed to approve the document. Others sparked angry, violent mobs. Only following Congress's threat of a trade embargo on the small state did the legislature ratify the Constitution in 1790, over a year after it had taken effect.[12] And even then, it was approved on a razor-thin margin of thirty-four in favor to thirty-two opposed. "The extreme Distress we were reduced to by being disconnected with the other States," the Rhode Island governor remarked, had finally caused the state to capitulate.[13]

This perceived radical, coercive ethos of the Convention's work and the new federalist program worried the anti-federalists. Even if the Articles needed reform, with the nation awash in unpaid debt obligations and unable to muster an army for national defense, the Convention was still a step too far. It had offended the very ideal of America: that here, fundamental law, not the whims of a few powerful men, had the final word.

In their view, the Convention and the new Constitution it drafted were nothing less than an attempt at a constitutional coup.[14]

This legal argument seems compelling to many even today and should inform one's thinking about the possibility of a constitutional convention being held under Article V in the coming years. But in the ratifying conventions, the argument that the 1787 Convention had overstepped its legal authority proved uncompelling. Responding to the oft-raised concern, James Wilson, a delegate to both the Constitutional Convention and Pennsylvania's state ratifying convention, remarked, "The truth is, that, in our governments, the supreme, absolute, and uncontrollable power *remains* in the people. As our constitutions are superior to our legislatures, so the people are superior to our constitutions. Indeed, the superiority, in this last instance, is much greater; for the people possess over our constitutions control in *act*, as well as right. The consequence is, that the people may change the constitutions whenever and however they please."[15]

The new Constitution sought the ultimate and most direct public sanction—ratification by the People. What higher form of lawmaking was there? The Articles' amendment procedures, and the legalistic quibbling over the Confederation Congress's convention call, were no inhibition. Rather, the work of the Convention and the ratifying debates had proved the insistence on bloodless revolution, Wilson argued. Americans were demonstrating to the world "a gentle, a peaceful, a voluntary, and a deliberate transition from one constitution of government to another."[16]

While their arguments about legality did not pose significant problems on the path to ratification, the anti-federalists' substantive critiques of the document inspired some doubts. The anti-federalists could not argue that the Confederation was worthy of being saved; it clearly was not. Without an alternative proposal, and in the face of the federalists' strong, proactive case, the anti-federalists were forced to raise only negative arguments and to induce fear and worry regarding the plan.[17] Prime among these concerns was the perceived aristocratic nature of the new federal government, the feared demise of state governments, and the abuses they thought would likely result.

The Constitution purposefully made Congress small, a feature Professor Akhil Amar has called its "skimming principle": it hoped to skim the cream (representatives) off the top of the milk (the people).[18] The anti-federalists found such an idea abhorrent and believed it would render the federal government an aristocratic institution. Only men of exceptional wealth or fame would seek high office and be able to mount successful campaigns, they argued. And once seated, these aristocratic legislators would hold a certain disdain for the ordinary citizen of average means and status.[19] "Let us never flatter ourselves that we shall always have good men to govern us," one anti-federalist remarked. "Constitutions are not so necessary to regulate the conduct of good rulers as to restrain that of bad ones."[20]

Likewise, the anti-federalists believed that the new Constitution would annihilate the powers of the states, and with them the personal liberties for which Americans had fought. The anti-federalists argued that the history of self-government had proved that geographic size was a determining factor for the longevity of democracy. The farther away the leaders are from the governed, the less public oversight and the higher the possibility for waste, graft, and despotism.[21]

These two elements of the new constitutional structure—the size of its legislature and its expanded power—justified the anti-federalists' most convincing critique, one that posed a real threat to final adoption of the Constitution. If a larger, more muscular democratic union was to be created, certain safeguards were necessary. Only a constitutional guarantee of enumerated rights, including criminal procedure rights, freedom of religion and conscience, and freedom of the press, could ensure that the enlarged government would not impede Americans' cherished freedoms.[22]

Seven of the new state constitutions had included a textual rights guarantee as a preface to forming the state governments. Thomas Jefferson's famed Declaration of Rights in the Virginia Constitution, for example, set a paradigm that many of the states emulated and that would ultimately serve as the guiding ethos for the federal Constitution's Bill of Rights. Many historians argue that the British paradigm of nontextual, unenumerated rights guarantees was strong in the new United States, and that these early attempts at textualizing rights were not seen as *fixing* them, as if text were stone. Alexander Hamilton, for example, noted in 1775 that "the sacred rights of mankind are not to be rummaged for, among old parchments, or musty records. They are written, as with a sunbeam, in the *whole* volume of human nature."[23] Nonetheless, these early attempts at providing an explicit textual limitation on the government's authority were widely supported and admired.[24] And in the context of the

Constitution's new experiment in federalism, which created a system of separate and perhaps dueling sovereigns, the desire for textual guardrails and guarantees seems even more reasonable. As Thomas Jefferson wrote Madison from Paris, "A bill of rights is what the people are entitled to against every government on earth, general or particular, & what no just government should refuse or rest on inference."[25]

CALLS FOR REFORM

Even before the ratification debates had begun, New York governor George Clinton had penned a public letter calling for a second convention. On July 26, 1788, the New York ratifying convention formally adopted the circular letter, calling on the states to withhold ratification until a second convention could resolve the problems. Several elements of the proposed Constitution were "so exceptionable," the New York circular declared, "that nothing but the fullest confidence of obtaining revision of them by a General Convention, and an invincible Reluctance to separating from our Sister States, could have prevailed upon a sufficient Number to ratify it, without stipulating for previous amendments."[26]

By September 1788, over forty newspapers throughout the country had printed the circular. In state after state, the argument that ratification should be contingent on amendment was raised. And at multiple critical junctures—in Massachusetts, Virginia, and New York, for example—the promise of future amendment providing a Bill of Rights was the critical element swaying the states in favor of ratification. New York and Virginia made the contingency of amendment quite explicit, immediately calling for a second convention under Article V's mechanism. North Carolina went a step further, refusing outright to ratify until a new convention was called, lest the federalists' promises of future amendment proposals through the congressional route be reneged.[27]

While New York and Virginia's two convention calls came nowhere near the nine required under Article V, the New York circular was exceptionally influential, possibly decisive, in changing the tide of the ratification debates. It demonstrated that states' acceptance of the new Constitution was contingent. A second convention had wide support throughout the country, and if Congress did not provide amendments, that pressure could and probably would lead to something greater.[28] Recognizing the new Constitution's

The Conventions of a Number of the States having, at the Time of their adopting the Constitution, expressed a Desire, in Order to prevent misconstruction or abuse of its Powers, that further declaratory and restrictive Clauses should be added : And as extending the Ground of public Confidence in the Government, will best insure the beneficent ends of its Institution—

RESOLVED, by the Senate and House of Representatives of the United States of America in Congress assembled, two thirds of both Houses concurring, That the following articles be proposed to the Legislatures of the several States, as amendments to the Constitution of the United States, all or any of which articles, when ratified by three fourths of the said Legislatures, to be valid to all intents and purposes, as part of the said Constitution—Viz.

Articles in addition to, and amendment of, the Constitution of the United States of America, proposed by Congress, and ratified by the Legislatures of the several States, pursuant to the fifth Article of the original Constitution.

ARTICLE the FIRST.

After the first enumeration, required by the first article of the Constitution, there shall be one Representative for every thirty thousand, until the number shall amount to one hundred ; to which number one Representative shall be added for every subsequent increase of forty thousand, until the Representatives shall amount to two hundred, to which number one Representative shall be added for every subsequent increase of sixty thousand persons.

ARTICLE the SECOND.

No law, varying the compensation for the services of the Senators and Representatives, shall take effect, until an election of Representatives shall have intervened.

ARTICLE the THIRD.

Congress shall make no law establishing articles of faith, or a mode of worship, or prohibiting the free exercise of religion, or abridging the freedom of speech, or of the press, or the right of the people peaceably to assemble, and to petition to the government for a redress of grievances.

ARTICLE the FOURTH.

A well regulated militia, being necessary to the security of a free State, the right of the people to keep and bear arms, shall not be infringed.

ARTICLE the FIFTH.

No soldier shall, in time of peace, be quartered in any house, without the consent of the owner, nor in time of war, but in a manner to be prescribed by law.

ARTICLE the SIXTH.

The right of the people to be secure in their persons, houses, papers, and effects, against unreasonable searches and seizures, shall not be violated, and no warrants shall issue, but upon probable cause, supported by oath or affirmation, and particularly describing the place to be searched, and the persons or things to be seized.

Enrolled congressional act proposing the first ten amendments to the Constitution precarity, James Madison championed a slate of reform amendments in the first Congress based on proposals from the ratification debates. "If we . . . refuse to let the subject come into view," Madison worried, "it may occasion suspicions" that could "inflame or prejudice the public mind." The only way to "extinguish opposition" to the new Constitution once and for all was through reform, he believed.[29]

The package of amendments was introduced in Congress in June 1789, twelve proposed amendments approved by September, and ten—what today we call the Bill of Rights—ratified by December 1791. The remaining two were not ratified in the initial moment. The first, concerning congressional pay, would be ratified in 1992, nearly 203 years after it was proposed.[30]

The Bill of Rights was the first attempt in world history to amend a written constitution.[31] And it was a resounding success. The machinery worked quickly and provided a body of constitutional text essential for the country's continued development. But the Bill of Rights also provided insight into a deeper truth about Article V and the amendment mechanism.

Article V was the critical lynchpin that reconciled the anti-federalists to the new Constitution. As a potential second constitutional convention loomed, the prospect of Article V constitutional amendment and the promise on the part of the federalists to provide for necessary changes following ratification became the final, necessary component of the Constitution's ratification and popular acceptance. As constitutional historian David Kyvig has argued, "Without immediate amendment, the Constitution faced the prospect of being stillborn." The ability to amend was the Constitution's "price and proof."[32] Article V provided the essential forum within which to mediate conflict and constitutional unrest with the status quo.

THE ELEVENTH AND TWELFTH AMENDMENTS: HAMILTONIAN REPAIRS

Following ratification of the Bill of Rights, there was little emphasis on Article V during the Constitution's first seven decades. Perhaps signifying the relative importance of the topic, Thomas Jefferson's *Manual of Parliamentary Practice for the Use of the Senate of the United States*, which compiled rules and procedures in over fifty categories and is considered a masterpiece of early legislative history, included no reference to the Senate's consideration of issues relating to Article V.[33] Even though over four hundred amendments were proposed in Congress between 1804 and 1860, only two were considered and adopted by the states—the Eleventh and Twelfth. Both typify a Hamiltonian approach to amendment, repairing defects in the Constitution.[34]

Consider the Eleventh. Article III, relating to the judiciary, was the least detailed and defined of all the Constitution's provisions following ratification. The article provided for the Supreme Court but left the formation of inferior courts and most of the courts' rules to the legislature. To create the federal judiciary, Congress passed the Judiciary Act of 1789 establishing inferior federal courts. Soon troubling questions of jurisdiction came to light. The Constitution provided that federal jurisdiction extended to all suits "between a State and Citizens of another state," but it did not stipulate whether citizens could sue a *state* without its permission. In English courts, the long-standing common-law doctrine of sovereign immunity exempted the king from suits without consent. Whether and how to import this doctrine to the United States remained an open question.

In the 1793 case *Chisholm v. Georgia*, the Supreme Court rejected the claim that states enjoyed sovereign immunity in federal courts, as did the king in England. This holding opened the states up to lawsuits against their will.[35] With many states still paying debts from the Revolutionary War, the Court's holding in *Chisholm* posed a serious financial threat. The Eleventh Amendment provided a narrow repair, overruling *Chisholm* and affirming that the English common-law doctrine of sovereign immunity would apply to the states.[36]

So too was the Twelfth Amendment a technical repair, one intended to fix an unresolved error in the method by which presidential electors cast their ballots. Despite its long-lasting and important consequences, the Twelfth Amendment was a tweak that sought to perfect the Constitution rather than the result of a groundswell of disagreement with constitutional arrangement.

The Electoral College has been subjected to some of the most intense and relentless attacks in the history of constitutional amendment. Between 1800 and 2020, more than eight hundred proposed amendments altering the Electoral College were introduced in Congress, more than on any other subject.[37] That pace yields a (conservative) average of almost four a year. Some scholars put the number even higher, perhaps north of nine hundred.[38] Yet despite the continuing calls for change, only one amendment altering the presidential selection regime has been ratified—the Twelfth, in 1804.

Following the 1800 election, Congress engaged in heated debate regarding Electoral College reform. Political strategizing had started to infect presidential campaigns, as state legislatures adopted different elector-selection systems to benefit the party dominant in the statehouse. The Twelfth Amendment soon arose as a compromise. Under the Constitution's original design, the vice president was the runner-up in the Electoral College's presidential balloting. Candidates all ran for president; there was no election for vice president. This procedure created an unforeseen problem, an error—what constitutional historian Akhil Amar has called the original Electoral College's misfire.[39] The Electoral College vote in 1796 had yielded a president and vice president of opposing parties. In 1796, John Adams of the Federalist Party was president, and Thomas Jefferson of the Democratic-Republican Party was vice president, a mismatch that proved problematic for both domestic and foreign policy. In 1800, the House of Representatives selected Jefferson and his running mate Aaron Burr in a contentious election, following a failed attempt by Democratic-Republicans to game the voting system to yield a president and vice president of the same party, causing a tie in the College between Burr and Jefferson. Had certain federalists successfully gamed the outcome, Burr might have become president rather than Jefferson. The Twelfth Amendment modified the voting rules, requiring electors to vote for both president and vice president together rather than only president.[40]

The reform did not pursue profound change aimed at resolving brewing national unrest (say, a loss of faith in the electoral system resulting in a real, palpable constitutional crisis). Nor was it a response to broad-based unease in society, intended to mediate between conflicting political or social interests to ensure national stability. In effect, it engineered a clerical resolution to a procedural problem.[41]

CIVIL WAR AND NATIONAL RECKONING

For the next 109 years, between 1804 and 1913, only three amendments were ratified: the Thirteenth, Fourteenth, and Fifteenth Amendments of Reconstruction following the Civil War. These amendments outlawed slavery, established equal rights of citizenship, and forbade the abridgement of the right to vote. Often aptly called the "Second Founding," these

"Under providence, Washington made and Lincoln saved our country" (1866)

amendments are of utmost importance in the American national story, attempting to ensure racial and political equality following the horrors of war and slavery.

Yet like the Bill of Rights, the Reconstruction Amendments' exceptional, foundational importance and singularity make it challenging to use them to derive conclusions about the nature of Article V. As Herman Ames observed in the late nineteenth century, the amendments were the result of the ultimate kind of great and extraordinary occasion—civil war. Woodrow Wilson had put it differently, intuiting from the Reconstruction Amendments that "no force less than the force of revolution, can nowadays be expected to move the cumbrous machinery of formal amendment erected by Article Five."[42]

Constitutional historian Bruce Ackerman has argued that the Reconstruction Amendments, while legitimate, should be considered as having occurred outside the frame of Article V, set apart by their singularity and the procedural irregularities of their ratification.[43] Prime among these irregularities in Ackerman's view is the federal government's active role in managing the governance of the southern states during Reconstruction, and Congress's refusal to seat representatives from those states. For example, the Fourteenth Amendment was proposed in 1866, when Congress had almost no representatives from the southern states; had the southern representatives been seated, it is likely the amendment would not have been proposed. Akhil Amar has challenged this view, arguing that, despite the procedural irregularities, the amendments were legitimate under a strict reading of Article V.[44]

Academic debate regarding the scope, meaning, and legitimacy of the Reconstruction Amendments aside, the fact remains that they pose difficulty for those today who wish to glean lessons from the past to attempt to understand how Article V functions today. While necessary to begin the process of correcting the evils of slavery and racism, these amendments were not the result of a grassroots movement working within the constitutional system seeking redress. The war had settled the political questions, not Article V.

Between 1830 and 1860, however, many statesmen including former president and then-congressman John Quincy Adams and President James Buchanan had tried and failed to resolve the slavery question through Article V.[45] As early as 1832, southern states had also seized upon Article V's convention mechanism as a means to address perceived federal overreach.[46] Later, fearing that a constitutional amendment might successfully ban slavery, South Carolina statesman and former vice president John C. Calhoun developed and promoted a constitutional theory that would protect the South even if the northern states were able to meet Article V's three-quarters threshold for ratification. The theory, called "concurrent majority," held that if a state rejected a proposed amendment, it would be a sufficient constitutional, sovereign act to allow the state to secede from the Union.[47] While no such need arose, Calhoun's theories regarding state sovereignty—namely, his doctrine of nullification, which held that states can nullify federal laws such that they have no force within the sovereign territory of the state—remain a potent force today in contemporary conservative constitutional amendment movements. For example, in 2019, a proposed amendment was introduced in Congress to codify a form of nullification, providing that the states should be empowered to override congressional acts and federal administrative rules.[48]

Desperate for redress as war loomed, the states turned to Article V and specifically its convention mechanism. Kentucky, New Jersey, Illinois, Indiana, and Ohio applied to Congress for an Article V convention to address the slavery question. Their requests were rebuffed. The Peace Conference of 1861, convened by Virginia outside the auspices of Article V and to which twenty-one states sent delegates, provided a set of amendments to Congress in hopes of allaying violence. Their proposed amendments would have maintained slavery yet constitutionalized certain geographic restrictions. The proposals were soundly defeated in the Senate and never taken up in the House. Ohio representative Erwin Corwin's last-ditch effort to resolve the tension through Article V, which would have introduced an unamendable provision allowing slavery where it existed, was also not enough to stem the rush to war. While Congress successfully approved the amendment—it is technically still pending before the states—the southern states had already ratified the Confederate Constitution.

After many attempts, turning to Article V had been futile.[49] While the original Constitutional Convention had struggled with the slavery question, striking compromises between states with different interests, the amendment mechanism had proved inadequate for the purpose prior to the bloodshed of war.

THE PROGRESSIVE AWAKENING

When the country celebrated the Constitution's centenary in 1887, the several states had made only ten applications for a constitutional convention since ratification. Two of these applications, Virginia's and New York's, were part of the immediate push for reform that hastened proposal and ratification of the Bill of Rights in the late eighteenth century. Three others, passed in 1832 and 1833 by South Carolina, Alabama, and Georgia, aimed to curtail federal regulatory power, primarily regarding tariffs.[50] The remaining five, passed in 1861, sought to avert the Civil War. Meanwhile, over 1,800 amendment proposals had been introduced in Congress during the Constitution's first century. But only fifteen were ratified.[51]

This meager amendment record helped inspire the awe-filled discourse anointing the Constitution as a holy text. In contrast, some believed fundamental constitutional change was required. Only through an overhaul of the amendment mechanism itself could change be secured, many believed. Wisconsin senator Robert La Follette shared the view, introducing an

"The Bosses of the Senate" (1889)

amendment in Congress to overhaul Article V itself, replacing the ratification procedure with a direct, democratic plebiscite.[52] Like so many others, the proposal failed.

A Nation in Crisis

Yet even in 1887, a movement for change was growing. Just a year before, over two hundred thousand Union Pacific and Missouri Pacific railmen had gone on strike demanding higher wages, stopping rail traffic in five midwestern and southern states. The government's swift, violent response had left ten workers dead, carnage and injustice that hastened the founding of the American Federation of Labor a few months later. In Milwaukee, the Wisconsin State Militia—acting on the governor's order to fire on them—had killed a child and six Polish rail workers striking for an eight-hour workday. After the Haymarket Riots in Chicago, in which a bomb exploded during an otherwise peaceful labor demonstration, seven anarchists were tried on dubious evidence and convicted of conspiracy. On November 10, 1887, four were hanged. Thirteen days later, in Thibodaux, Louisiana, the Knights of Labor conducted the first strike by a formal labor organization, bringing sugar cane plantations to a standstill. The state militia ultimately broke the strike, killing around sixty people.[53]

Soon, as clashes between state and citizen became more and more frequent, signs of an unraveling political and social fabric began to appear. Labor organization was merely one manifestation of a greater unease as the Gilded Age's period of unparalleled economic and demographic growth gave away to feelings of distrust, discontent, and an almost religious, moral fervor for reformation.

Corruption and injustice festered, but in no place was the rot more pronounced than within the government itself. Municipal governments, run by political machines, were saddled with patronage and bribery. The Congress was likewise enmeshed in a web of graft and dishonesty. Senators, appointed by the state legislatures rather than popularly elected, were especially vulnerable to the influence of industry. As one congressman remarked on the floor of the House in 1892, "Men have gained seats in the Senate of the United States whom the people of their State would never have chosen to go there, and who never would have gone there but [f]or the corrupt use of money to secure their election."[54] But the problem was not only corruption in the state legislatures. The issue distorted public policy. As William Jennings Bryan, an Illinois lawyer turned Nebraska congressman and great champion of the Progressive Era, argued on the House floor in 1894, "Great corporations . . . are able to compass the election for their tools and their agents through the instrumentality of Legislatures, as they could not if Senators were elected directly by the people."[55] In 1906, David Graham Phillips's series of influential articles in *Cosmopolitan Magazine* entitled "The Treason of the Senate" painted an ugly picture for all to see: a legislative body defined by wealth that abused the public trust. The Senate was, in Phillips's words, "The House of Dollars."[56]

Social and economic troubles also unsettled the status quo. Inhumane work conditions in urban factories, dangerous child labor, limited health care and quality education, and the effects of alcohol soon became the subjects of intense debate. Farmers, like the urban working poor, lived on the edge due to what many perceived as a rigged economic system that shifted profits from farmers to powerful intermediaries like the railroads. The gap between rich and poor was also widening—with the top 10 percent living in a degree of luxury never seen in American history, while the bottom 10, often recent immigrants, toiled in poverty. When Congress attempted to address growing income inequality in 1894 with a 2 percent tax on incomes over $4,000 (about $127,000 today), the Supreme Court struck down the tax as unconstitutional. Article I, Section 2, of the Constitution forbade direct taxation not apportioned by population.[57] Whether through industry's stranglehold on Congress or the Court's repeated rebuffs of reform, it seemed that with each successive year the government was less and less responsive to the needs of the common man.[58]

Most in the political, intellectual, legal, and business elite did not sense the constitutional tenor of changing political tides at the end of the nineteenth century. For those in the upper echelons, there was little question that the constitutional system would continue to work in their favor, as it always had. They *were* the system. Power in Washington, industry, the courts, and the banking and finance sector was remarkably centralized among a small upper crust. The labor unrest and general social unease growing throughout the country was not a sign of imminent political change, many thought, but of anarchist agitators swaying the immature and undisciplined spirits of a new class of uneducated and poor immigrants. Rather than a constitutional threat, the political climate was emblematic of a backward underclass, one that had to be suppressed with the civilizing power of the state.

The triumph of the traditionalist, pro-business Republican William McKinley over the "great commoner" Democrat William Jennings Bryan in the 1896 presidential election seemed to dispel any reason for worry. Bryan, the rousing Nebraska politician, billed his campaign as a crusade of the working class versus the rich. Lambasting the sins of the Gilded Age, he called for a massive overhaul of the American economy and government. His reformational platform was perhaps best encapsulated by the promise to cast American currency in both gold and silver, thus eliminating the dominance of the gold standard and inducing inflationary pressures that many believed would help bolster the economy following the Panic of 1893. Bryan's boisterous battle cry, "You shall not crucify mankind upon a cross of gold!" called the common man to arms. But for the bankers and business owners active in foreign trade, the elimination of the gold standard would have caused great harm. Bryan posed an existential threat.

In a stunning show of political force, McKinley's campaign manager Mark Hanna capitalized on this fear, engineering what was then the most ambitious and advanced campaign finance operation in American history. Hanna made the proposition clear: the business elite could either put substantial weight behind McKinley or be ruined by Bryan. The establishment could

either snuff out the populist calls for change in 1896 or live with the consequences of a radical Bryan administration. The call was heard, and McKinley
drew massive contributions. His alliance with the establishment proved decisive in the final poll, as Bryan's call for reform was resoundingly defeated.

An Awakening

For those who sought change, the ordinary political system clearly could
not provide it. The Senate was corrupt. The presidency could be bought by
moneyed interests. And political pressure was building.

In 1894, as Woodrow Wilson reiterated his sobering analysis of
Article V in the eleventh edition of *Congressional Government* and Ames
prepared his own eulogy for the amendment mechanism, 250,000 labor-
ers in Chicago and across the Midwest again halted national rail service.
A strike against the Pullman Company helped set in motion a movement
for political change that would transform American public life. Amid a
deep recession in the 1890s, Pullman had slashed wages while refusing to
adjust rents in the company-owned towns where employees lived. Strapped
for cash, workers demanded recognition of their union and lower rents.
Pullman refused. As the strike stopped the flow of interstate commerce,
the federal government intervened. Attorney General Richard Olney
urged President Cleveland to take bold action. The strikers could not be
allowed to win the day, he argued. They had to be subdued.

To the strikers, Olney represented the corrupt political establishment
bent on using the government to protect industry at the expense of the
common man. A former director and lawyer for a Chicago railroad, Olney
continued to receive a $10,000 retainer (about $330,000 today) while
attorney general on top of his $8,000 public salary (about $261,000
today)—an obvious conflict of interest. His swift response to the Pullman
Strike confirmed where his loyalties remained. To quell the strike, Olney
sought and received on behalf of the United States an injunction from a
federal judge in Chicago. Yet the American Railway Union, headed by
labor leader and future Socialist Party presidential candidate Eugene Debs,
pressed forward. Soon President Cleveland ordered the army to enforce the
injunction and stop strikers from obstructing trains. The resulting violence
left many dead. Yet even with the strike broken, Olney sought further
revenge. The growing labor unionist movement had to be destroyed.

Olney urged the federal court in Chicago to exact personal punishment against Railway Union leader Eugene Debs for his role in organizing the strike. The court agreed, holding Debs in contempt for violating the injunction and ordering him jailed for six months. In a sentence controversially upheld by the Supreme Court in 1895, Debs was imprisoned about fifty miles northwest of Chicago in Woodstock, the seat of rural McHenry County, Illinois.[59] As a reporter for the *St. Louis Post-Dispatch* wrote in response to Debs's imprisonment, "This little jail out here in this quiet country town is today famous the world over. Behind the bars and bolted doors is confined a man who not many months ago, by one stroke of his pen, paralyzed the railway traffic of this great continent."[60]

Far from a sentence of state-imposed reformation, Debs would later write, his time spent in this midwestern farm town sparked an awakening.[61] The injustice of his imprisonment, and the time spent reading and studying philosophy and law, had solidified his turn toward socialism and a newfound conviction that the constitutional order needed reform.[62]

While those in Washington and beyond celebrated the Constitution and its unchangeable perfection, Debs saw a different reality. From his jail cell window overlooking a rose garden across the way, Debs reflected on the state of the nation and of the law. The bloody repression of labor was a symptom of a deep disease, he thought. The government's willingness to use the entire arsenal of state violence—the courts, police, and military—against workers seeking a better life proved that there was an unholy alliance between the political class and industry, one that was subverting both democracy and the Constitution.[63]

Released six months later, this Indiana grocery-clerk-turned-revolutionary, as *Time* put it, "came from his cell with a gospel."[64] Later that day, emboldened by his captivity, Debs delivered a rousing speech to over one hundred thousand gathered outside the Federal Armory in Chicago that would galvanize the labor movement against the evils of the Gilded Age. The topic was liberty and constitutional change: "This 'Liberation Day' demonstration . . . means that American lovers of liberty are setting in operation forces to rescue their constitutional liberties from the grasp of monopoly and its mercenary hirelings. It means that the people are aroused in view of impending perils and that agitation, organization, and unification are to be the future battle cries of men who will not part with their birthrights and, like Patrick Henry, will have the courage to

exclaim: 'Give me liberty or give me death!'"[65] For Debs, the labor movement was more than a struggle between workers and management. As he
came to understand in the Woodstock jail, it was a battle for the soul of
the nation—one that would require both political and constitutional
reform.[66]

Yet only "within the limitations of the federal constitution," did Debs
believe true change could be achieved. Two years later, in an 1897 article
published in the *New York Journal* entitled "The Coming Republic," Debs
situated his political goal of forming an American socialist "cooperative
commonwealth" squarely in the language of formal amendment: "After
achieving success at the polls," he wrote, "the [state legislatures] will be
convened and a constitutional convention called."[67] Socialism would come to
America not through violence or a coup, he argued, but through Article V
and its convention mechanism. The Founding generation's old dream of
bloodless revolution was having a rebirth.

Amendment Fervor

Throughout the 1890s, Debs and many others disaffected with the state of
the nation began to fix their sights on a seemingly dormant conduit to
pursue radical change. The Progressive Movement, which would come to
ascendency at the turn of the century, aiming to reform government and
address the ills of industrialization and urbanization, was a manifestation
of deep, underlying problems. Faced with an obstinate Washington establishment bent on blocking change, the movement soon turned to other
methods for redress.

In 1893, Nebraska—the state that Bryan represented in Congress—
passed the first application for an Article V constitutional convention in over
thirty years to provide for the direct, popular election of senators.[68] The
Nebraska application would set off a constitutional firestorm unlike anything
the country had seen before. Texas followed suit in 1899.[69] In 1900, a Pennsylvania legislative committee encouraged coordination between the states to
utilize the Article V mechanism. The Congress—especially the corrupt
Senate—would not act on its own accord. The House had approved an
amendment providing for the direct election of senators five times between
1893 and 1899, only for the proposal to languish in the Senate.[70] Reformers
had to *force* the question, the Pennsylvania commission argued.

"Plutocracy," wearing a top hat, trains his parrot "State Legislature" to repeat a phrase after him, "We don't want an Income-Tax Amendment!," promising it "some nice crackers" in return for correctly learning to repeat the phrase. (1909)

In 1901, fourteen more states had passed applications, most of which implemented Pennsylvania's recommendation that the resolutions be placed in the mandatory language of Article V: that Congress "shall call a Convention." In 1902, Kentucky joined the effort.[71] In 1903, eight years after Debs's release and just seven after Ames's award-winning book proclaimed Article V's demise, Illinois became the twentieth state to pass an application for a constitutional convention.[72] By 1912, only one more state was needed to trigger the convening.[73]

Over two decades, the movement for constitutional amendment had reached a crescendo. While a successful convention call was averted, the movement sparked a moment of amendment fervor in Congress. Between 1913 and 1920, the states would ratify four amendments proposed by Congress. The Sixteenth Amendment provided for federal income tax, the Seventeenth required the direct election of senators, the Eighteenth prohibited the sale of alcohol, and the Nineteenth provided women the right to vote. Combined with pathbreaking legislation of the Progressive Era, including the increased regulation of industry, crackdowns on the centralization of economic power, and legislation prohibiting corporate contributions to campaigns, the constitutional change hastened by the Progressive Era radically transformed public life.

Historian Jill Lepore has gone so far as to argue that the progressive amendments were a third founding, a moment of constitutional "rewriting" (her term) on par with the Convention of 1789 and Reconstruction.[74] Whether or not one conceives of the Progressive Era's reforms in that high register, the amendment movement of the 1890s to the 1910s did manifest a moment of great constitutional fervor. Rather than implementing an establishment-driven agenda for constitutional repair, the Progressive reforms—like the Bill of Rights—provided much of the necessary constitutional redress demanded by the People. When faced with widespread social unease and a political system unable or unwilling to address the discontent, the People seized upon the machinery of formal amendment to force change. Article V, and its potential to authorize a constitutional convention, was the release valve that ensured the constitutional system's stability.

Making Sense of the Progressive Era Amendments Today

The Progressive Era's moment of popular amendment fervor, which awakened the machinery of Article V following a long slumber, provides an essential episode and historical record from which to glean insights into the meaning of Article V today. One must be careful not to carelessly attribute historical certainty to what one's own reading of the past might

Sketch for the April 1915 edition of the *Suffragist* newspaper: "The Spirit of '76: On to the Senate"

mean for the present. Yet even with such a cautious approach, one can draw a few important lessons that are useful today.

First, consider the pivotal role of convention applications in spurring Congress to begin a program of constitutional reform through Article V. Prior to the Progressive Era, Article V had sat functionally dormant for almost a century. The rapid movement of convention applications during the Progressive Era, and the popular movements that encouraged state leg-islators to pass applications, had a powerful, and possibly decisive, effect in awakening Article V. This ability of convention movements to prod Con-gress is an essential element of our contemporary amendment regime, one that is often overlooked, understudied, and underestimated.[75]

Historians debate whether the near-miss threat of a successful con-vention call was the direct cause of Congress's proposal of the Progressive Era amendments. This scholarly debate is often focused on the role of the convention movement in securing the proposal of the Seventeenth Amendment, which provided for direct senatorial election. Some argue the applications were but one factor in a widespread movement for change. Congress would likely have pursued a constitutional amendment agenda even without a credible convention threat. Many argue the political goals of the convention effort were focused on a narrow issue: reforming the Senate. This was a task the Senate would not undertake on its own, mak-ing an Article V convention necessary to force this idiosyncratic question.

As constitutional scholar Russell Caplan argues, by 1913 a significant number of senators represented states that had already adopted direct elec-tion through state law. The growth of convention applications, although important, was not uniquely pivotal in breaking the senatorial stalemate. Rather, the Seventeenth Amendment should be understood as a conflu-ence of multiple, equally important factors—a constitutional crescendo of sorts.[76] David Kyvig and other scholars disagree, arguing that the conven-tion applications played an essential role. As Kyvig notes, the number of state legislatures applying for a convention was only five fewer than those needed to ratify an amendment (Arizona and New Mexico were admitted to the Union earlier in the year).[77] Were not the applications themselves a sign of political and popular will for changing the constitutional status quo, one that would spark representatives to do as the public demanded?

The historical record is clear on several essential points. Consider again the meager record that caused Ames, Wilson, and so many others to write their eulogies for Article V in the 1890s. In the Constitution's first century, the states had made only ten applications for a constitutional con-vention: two following ratification, three in 1823 and 1824 regarding tariffs, and five in 1861 hoping to avert civil war. While the record of con-gressionally proposed amendments was abysmal—eighteen hundred proposed yet only fifteen ratified over a century—the convention route's record was far worse. Whereas those in Washington were at least *trying* to move the machinery of Article V's top-down congressional proposal route, it seemed as though the states had completely forgotten about the bottom-up convention route. This is perhaps why Ames devoted barely three pages to the convention route in his five-hundred-page opus.

Yet between 1893 and 1916, the states submitted a staggering 107 convention applications.[78] The wildfire growth undoubtedly took Congress by surprise. Never had the great unknown of an Article V constitutional convention been so imminent, the danger so real. Senator Weldon Heyburn's concern that Article V "does not contemplate that any constitutional convention shall assemble with a limitation on it to deal with a particular question" likely embodied the fear that many felt. "When the constitutional convention meets," Heyburn argued, "it is . . . the same people who made the original Constitution, and no limitation in the original constitution controls the people when they meet again."[79] The country was on a precipice.

Heyburn's claim was neither hyperbole nor alarmist. As discussed in Chapter 5, the overwhelming majority of legal scholars over many decades have argued that a convention's agenda indeed cannot be limited. And if one were to look to the single historical precedent—the 1787 Convention—for answers, one would find definitive proof that conventions can go far beyond their legal mandate without reproach or consequence.

But as a practical matter, congressmen in the early twentieth century did not even need to ponder Heyburn's points of high political theory nor consider historical precedent. They needed only to look at the political ferment in the states. While the political movement for a convention may have been animated by reform of the Senate, whether a potential convention would be limited to that topic alone was very much an open question. To a focused and cautious observer in Congress, the political debate's supposed limited emphasis on the Senate question might have just been noise. Either by design or happenstance, once the movement reached an ascendency, the political tides could change, and the ambit of a potential convention expand. The convention could, to use a phrase common in debate today, "run away."

This observation is of critical importance. Scholarly examination of the role of Article V's convention route in the late nineteenth and early twentieth centuries often focuses narrowly, too narrowly, on the direct election question and Congress's consideration of the Seventeenth Amendment. This approach ignores the broader importance and impact of a potential convention call in awakening the congressional route. During a period rife with political and social upheaval, would not the many uncertainties of a possible convention have sparked a moment of pause and concern in Washington, one that would spur Congress to action?

As the *Washington Post* journalist Henry West wrote in 1905, a convention would "in all probability, be in session for a year, during which time the business interests of the country would pass through a period of uncertainty that would be almost disastrous."[80] West's focus on economic interests is perhaps revealing. While Senate reform was animated by an attempt to rein in corporate influence in Congress, so too could a convention undertake more radical reforms that would hurt the business and political establishment emboldened and enriched during the Gilded Age. When considered in the context of the political, social, and economic landscape of the early twentieth century, there is little doubt that the prospect of a freewheeling, uncontrolled convention would have thrust constitutional amendment to top-line political importance in Congress. Had Congress not attempted to alleviate popular discontent by undertaking a series of constitutional reforms, the convention movement might have reached its ascendancy. And what would the People have done if they had been given the opportunity?

Eugene Debs had argued that an Article V convention was the appropriate mechanism for the People to seize the means of production and establish a communitarian commonwealth only sixteen years before. While some might have laughed at such a proposition in 1897, the claim posed a real possibility in 1913. What protections were there to prevent such an outcome, what guardrails to control popular passions? Perhaps, as many do today, congressmen might have looked to the high ratification threshold as the ultimate calming force: no radical proposals could possibly achieve that impossible three-quarters bar. Yet for those watching the rapid, unforeseen, and formerly unthinkable rise of amendment fervor in the states, such a procedural protection might have been cold comfort. The possibility that populist tendencies or the nefarious influence of corporate and special interests already rife in Congress might overcome the small group of convention delegates was a risky gamble. A successful convention call could become the American Rubicon. If the nation were to cross the two-thirds threshold, it could usher in a whole new political order.

The Progressive Era amendments thus provide an essential lesson: fear of a convention, and the constitutional reforms that fear can inspire, are core elements of how Article V works in practice. The potent possibility of a successful convention call—one more state!—played a significant, perhaps decisive, role in waking up Article V and revitalizing formal amendment in the public square. Even though the movement failed in the technical sense, it was remarkably successful in sparking an era of profound constitutional change. For decades, many in Washington had assumed formal amendment posed insurmountable obstacles and was thus not worthy of serious political attention. But the surge of state applications was an incontrovertible sign that Article V's dam was breaking, prodding Congress to provide constitutional redress lest the ultimate danger of an unchecked convention be realized. While the Framers perhaps did not foresee this kind of interplay between convention applications and the Hamiltonian top-down congressional route, the Progressive amendments make clear that Congress also can act as the release valve that George Mason anticipated a convention would provide.

The other primary lesson is the coequal nature of the two amendment proposal routes. Article V's seismic success during the Progressive Era has engendered an inaccurate yet widespread view today that Congress holds the "primary" or "only functioning" amendment proposal route. While many believe that both of Article V's two routes are dead, an even *greater* number apply the same kind of thinking to the role of conventions. Despite the rapid success of convention applications and the near-miss of a successful call in the early twentieth century, many view Progressive Era convention zeal as yet another sign that the convention route was stillborn. The reality that a convention call did not prevail even when the political stars had seemingly aligned and there was massive popular engagement on constitutional questions teaches a certain lesson: we will likely never have a convention, and the convention process therefore can be ignored.

But an observer need go no further than the Progressive Era to see Article V's possibilities and the convention route's true, perhaps counterintuitive power. As a legal and historical matter, the convention route maintains a powerful position within our constitutional structure, one that should be taken seriously and watched carefully.

THE MODERN ERA: BACKLASH, REPAIRS, AND SILENCE

Prohibition and Its Aftermath

The frenetic movement of Article V during the Progressive Era left the country with something akin to a constitutional hangover. Prohibition—the third of the four Progressive Era amendments, ratified in 1919—sparked intense debate regarding the purpose of the Constitution and the appropriate nature of its provisions. Fundamental law was no place for moralizing legislation, many argued. Liquor regulation lacked a certain constitutional gravitas. Why not leave it to the normal political process? And even if the Constitution were an appropriate venue for settling hotly contested social questions, the policy implications of the liquor limitation had proved too grave. Prohibition's emboldening of organized crime and the rise of dangerous drinking habits in unregulated speakeasies had made the problem of liquor in America even worse. As Pauline Sabine, the founder of the Women's Organization for National Prohibition Reform, remarked, "Nothing since the days of the campaign for woman's suffrage equals the campaign which women are now conducting for repeal of the Eighteenth Amendment. It is a crusade and it can only be explained by the fact that women throughout the country feel that their children and their homes are endangered by the evil of prohibition."[81] For Sabine and many others, the rapid use of Article V to settle complex questions had proved misguided: too quick, too blunt, and too difficult to change course.[82]

Adding complexity to the backlash against the Progressive Era's missteps was the growing unease that Article V was fundamentally undemocratic, a misgiving sparked by the trouble of Prohibition and its ratification. The states adopted the Eighteenth Amendment's alcohol limitations by legislative ratification in 1919. But this ratification had not necessarily coincided with broad popular support for the reform in the states. To many, the amendment was not the work of the People but rather a small, nonrepresentative group of special interests and power brokers who had a stranglehold on the often malapportioned and gerrymandered state legislatures.[83]

In few places was this mismatch between popular will and legislative action clearer than in Ohio. Both houses of the Ohio legislature had overwhelmingly ratified Prohibition in January 1919 (by a vote of twenty to twelve in the state senate and eighty-five to twenty-nine in the assembly). Yet in a statewide referendum held in November of the same year,

51.9 percent of the voters expressed disapproval of ratification.[84] Despite this clear manifestation of popular will at the polls, the referendum was of no significance. Article V does not provide for ratification by popular vote, only ratification in representative assemblies: either the legislature or special state ratifying conventions. Following a judicial challenge to Ohio's ratification, this constitutional truth was reiterated by the Supreme Court in its 1920 decision *Hawke v. Smith*, which held that the referendum had no force of law.[85] The legislative action stood.

Even with a bad taste in the nation's mouth following Prohibition's ratification, the ensuing process of repealing Prohibition through the Twenty-First Amendment left many equally frustrated. Indicative of the backlash against Article V and the growing unease with its undemocratic tendencies, Congress provided that the Twenty-First Amendment should be ratified not in state legislatures, as had been the norm before, but through state ratifying conventions—a distinct form of convention contemplated in Article V. With the Ohio debacle top of mind, many in Congress believed that the state legislatures were not the appropriate venue for channeling the popular will, as they could too easily be swayed by vocal yet nonrepresentative interest groups. The Twenty-First Amendment's repeal of Prohibition was ratified in state conventions in just 288 days in 1933. These conventions, unique in our national history, operated differently in each state. But each generally had popularly elected delegates who were either bound by a statewide referendum on repeal or whose position on the question was clear on the ballot, making delegate election a proxy for a statewide referendum on the question.[86]

The Modern Era

Despite the successful repeal of Prohibition, the Progressive Era continued to cast a long shadow over Article V in the popular and political psyche. The history of constitutional amendment in the following century was defined not by groundswell popular movements for constitutional change but rather by relatively small constitutional repair efforts. These repairs have often been initiated by Congress to address a particular new problem and to generally expand rights in line with broader federal governmental policies: the Twentieth Amendment (1932), changing the date on which presidential terms begin; the Twenty-Second (1951), establishing a two-term limit for the presidency; the Twenty-Third (1961), granting the voters of the otherwise disenfranchised District of Columbia electoral votes; the Twenty-Fifth (1964), establishing procedures for presidential succession (and removal) in case of incapacity or vacancy; the Twenty-Sixth (1971), setting the national voting age at eighteen, which although inspired by the war in Vietnam was more focused on rectifying confusing discrepancies between federal and state law regarding voter qualifications;[87] and the Twenty-Seventh (1992), altering regulations of congressional pay. Few of these amendments were inspired by groundswells of bottom-up, popular discontent; rather, they were primarily the result of congressionally led efforts to update and repair, to enliven the Constitution for the modern age.

A snapshot view of formal constitutional amendment since 1919 presents in stark relief the now-dominant centrality of the top-down Hamiltonian view of Article V. Like the historical record upon which Wilson and Ames reflected in their own time, the last century appears to those looking back at it today not as a period of robust amendment but rather as one marked by relatively small-bore efforts at constitutional repair and maintenance. The centrality of this approach in the modern era is best encapsulated by the work of Senator Birch Bayh, a Democrat who served three terms in the Senate representing deep-red Indiana from 1963 to 1981. Bayh holds the estimable position of being the only non–Founding generation American to have authored multiple constitutional provisions—the Twenty-Fifth (presidential succession and disability) and the Twenty-Sixth (eighteen-year-old vote).

When Tennessee senator Estes Kefauver, then the chairman of the Senate Judiciary Subcommittee on Constitutional Amendments, died of a heart attack in August 1963, the Senate slated the subcommittee for dissolution. Running the subcommittee was too expensive. But Bayh, then a freshman senator seated just months before, offered to fund the subcommittee from his own office's budget if he could be named chairman.[88] He would go on to hold the post for almost two decades. Under Bayh's watchful eye, the subcommittee ushered in a flourishing of imaginative debate about possible futures of the Constitution. Among Bayh's proposals was the Equal Rights Amendment, which aimed to constitutionalize gender equality; the abolition of the Electoral College; and providing statehood for the District of Columbia.[89] Yet beside the two more minor efforts at constitutional repair—presidential succession and voting age—most (or some would say all) of these proposals failed. The proposal for D.C. statehood received only sixteen ratifying votes.

Bayh's efforts were the high-water mark of formal constitutional amendment in the modern era. Since ratification of the Twenty-Sixth Amendment—the work of Bayh's hand—in 1971, the states have ratified no new amendments written by modern authors. Following his tenure, the Subcommittee on Constitutional Amendments was dissolved and its subject-matter mandate assigned to a new Subcommittee on the Constitution (on which one of your coauthors served as chair or ranking member for over a decade). This small technical change in committee structure alone demonstrates the shift in opinion over the last five decades regarding formal amendment. The prevailing approach toward constitutional amendment in Congress has become one of staid restraint and formalism.

For example, a 1999 Century Foundation publication, authored and endorsed by a panel of leading legal scholars and practitioners, set out to codify if, when, and how Congress should propose amendments.[90] The report expressed alarm at the "sudden rash of proposed amendments [in Congress] that have moved further in the process than ever before." These new efforts at constitutional reform were a sign that the "system of self-restraint may be breaking down" and that further efforts should only be considered if they met eight strict "guidelines" that demarcated appropriate amendments from inappropriate ones.[91]

Perhaps indicative of a resurgence of a "system of self-restraint," or out of fear of what one legal scholar called "amendmentitis," Congress has not successfully proposed any new amendments since 1971.[92] And proposed amendments do not get far in Congress's parliamentary process, either. Despite thousands introduced, Congress has only held votes on around twenty proposed amendments since 1999.[93] All were voted down. Two amendments did get close to successful proposal. The first, a ban on flag burning, was deeply disconcerting as a constitutional and civil liberties issue. As one of your authors remarked following the proposal's defeat in the Senate, the amendment would have "cut back the Bill of Rights for the first time."[94] The second, a balanced budget amendment, posed equally troubling concerns for the functioning of the federal government and was narrowly defeated in the Senate.[95]

Indeed this "system of self-restraint" is now so engrained that many see no real problem in letting the Constitution calcify. While the document might not exude the holy aura those in the 1870s sensed, many believe the Constitution in the twenty-first century still should remain untouched. Other ways to fix the small problems—through the courts, presidential executive action, or legislation—remain viable. The Constitution might have missed a few years of maintenance, but there is little to worry about. As many looking back at recent history probably think, Article V encodes only the Hamiltonian, top-down repair-focused view of amendment. That work can be delayed while there are larger concerns to address.

Rather than possibility and potential, constitutional amendment has become synonymous with danger, wonkiness, and political posturing. In Congress today, legislators often submit proposed constitutional amendments more for retweets and cable news hits than out of a bona fide, Bayh-esque desire for needed constitutional reform. Amendment proposal has become a useful form of grandstanding. Politicians can claim to address an issue in the highest, most grave manner with almost complete certainty that the proposal is destined for the political graveyard. Repealing the income tax.[96] Capping the number of Supreme Court justices.[97] Overturning Obamacare.[98] Giving state legislatures power to repeal federal laws.[99] Denying the District of Columbia electoral votes (undoubtedly due to D.C. voters' history of supporting Democratic nominees).[100] Banning global currency.[101] The list of bizarre proposals goes on. The charade has become so routine that one might reasonably think that today Article V has taken on a new purpose: as a convenient venue for political theater.

* * *

THE EVENTS OF THE LAST ten to twelve years have unearthed great tensions within this nation—tensions that transcend one president, election, or political moment. For liberals and progressives, the lack of action on deep moral questions like racism and the threat of climate change is a cause for anger. But others are also frustrated with structural legal issues— the malapportionment of the Senate and the Electoral College, the problematic politicization of the Supreme Court—roadblocks that seem to impede necessary change. On the other side of the political spectrum, many on the right believe Congress is corrupt and too wanton in its spending. Those on the far right worry the country's demographic changes and liberalizing social mores pose an existential threat to their understanding of America, a dangerous shift that requires more drastic efforts to stem the flow.

This frustration is about more than just electoral politics. Those of many political stripes see the *system* as broken, unable or unwilling to respond to calls for reform. The widespread protest and civil unrest of the last few years—not to mention the failed insurrection at the Capitol on January 6, 2021—underscore the brooding discontent. In these social and political ills, one can hear echoes of the amendment fervor of previous generations. As a keen reading of history demonstrates, when the political system lacks solutions, or the system itself is the problem, citizens look elsewhere.

Over the last few decades, many disaffected with the status quo have turned to Article V, aiming to use constitutional amendment to fundamentally transform American public life. The country may well be happening upon another "great and extraordinary occasion," one that could take years or even decades to come to complete fruition. But the time is now to understand the growth and aims of the contemporary amendment fervor.

Part III

A WARNING

5

WHAT TRUMP AND THE TEA PARTY COULDN'T DO

The Modern Conservative Push and the Mirage of a Limited Constitutional Convention

"We're planning on putting resources, people in place to get us to where the safety's off and we have a live weapon in our hands."

—Sen. Rick Santorum (December 2021)[1]

IN SEPTEMBER 2016, over one hundred state legislators from all fifty states gathered in Williamsburg, Virginia, for a constitutional war game. The enemy: the federal government. The warriors: a who's who of the hard-right establishment. The battlefield: Article V.

George Washington—really an actor in period costume appearing on horseback via video—began the meeting. "I am presently concentrating my forces where I have no doubt that we are on the verge of a great and important victory," he declared.[2]

In the same video, Michael Farris, a founder of the Convention of States Project, which sponsored the simulation, and a lawyer who later spearheaded legal attempts to delay certification of the 2020 election, was no less dramatic.[3] "It's been said that heroes are not born," Farris remarked. "They arise out of the opportunity provided by the course of history. . . . Today statesmen must join together and . . . build a network of new American heroes."[4]

The simulated convention was really just a meeting in a large conference room at the Williamsburg Lodge Hotel. But the talk of the day
among the delegates and those joining via livestream from home was the
supposed historical significance of the gathering. Mark Meckler, founder
of the Tea Party Patriots and briefly CEO of the far-right social media
company Parler, told those watching the proceedings at "thousands of
watch parties" across the nation to remember the occasion, as history certainly would. "You ought to write this moment down in your journal," he
urged. "When historians study [constitutional change in the twenty-first
century] . . . they will look to this event. They will want to know who was
here, what amendments were made and passed."[5]

The comments might seem to be exaggerations, but these were serious
people laser-focused on a legitimate goal. The three-day simulated constitutional convention did indeed have a truly historic aim: to plan how a real
convention would work.

The delegates war-gamed the whole scenario. Referring to themselves as "commissioners," a term of art with little relevant legal or
historical significance crafted by conservative convention proponents in
the last decade, delegates planned how to engineer a convention to meet
their radical political goals.[6] They wrote parliamentary rules, established
committees and subcommittees, and drafted and debated proposed
amendments.

Even to a casual observer, the debate would have been impressive.
Delegates, the vast majority of whom were conservative Republicans
aligned with the Tea Party movement, approached the affair seriously and
engaged in good faith debate. Working committees parsed amendment
text, weighed the legal meaning of certain terms and phrases, and hashed
out draft proposals. When proposals were brought to the floor, objections
were raised and compromises reached. For example, regarding a proposal
to allow a vote of thirty of the fifty states to nullify federal law (John C.
Calhoun's dream, as discussed in Chapter 4), one delegate questioned its
propriety and said he was inclined to encourage his delegation to vote no.
Supporters of the proposal responded respectfully and countered. The
entire affair was akin to a collegial legislative session.

Meeting in state delegations to deliberate among themselves, delegates ended the meeting by rendering their state's single vote on each
proposal. And in so doing, the dramatic reading of the roll call caused

those present to celebrate the element of the convention process most essential to their plan to radically transform American fundamental law: its malapportionment. As was the case in the 1787 Constitutional Convention, the states meeting in convention each cast one single vote. The discrepancies today are stark: Wyoming (population: 577,000) had the same say as California (population: 39.5 million), Alaska (population: 733,000) the same vote as New York (population: 20.2 million).

This malapportionment, which gives enormous power to small states in both the proposal of amendments and their ratification, is one of the aspects of Article V that makes a convention so promising for conservative activists. Article V has no direct democratic mechanism. "The supreme law of the land is the Constitution. The supreme power of the land is to be able to lawfully change the constitution by yourself. Only state legislatures have that power," Farris claimed.[7]

And it is relatively easy to influence state legislatures, as the majority are currently controlled by conservative Republicans, Farris argued. Whether the People desire the proponents' plan for hard-right constitutional regime change is of no consideration, convention activists argue. "If you put enough pressure on state legislatures, you can get stuff done. You don't need a majority of America, because a majority doesn't participate. . . . In state legislative matters, less than 1 percent of the people ever participate. With 1 percent of the American public, that's three million people, I guarantee you we can get this done. This will pass."[8]

"A Dry Run"

The results of the mock convention—a hard-right constitutional wish list—invigorated those present. Proposed amendments that would radically transform modern government were adopted: restricting Congress's lawmaking authority to a tiny fraction of its current extent (removing its ability to pass most modern legislation); restricting federal agencies' rulemaking authority (neutering the government's ability to effectively implement law); repealing the income tax (a death knell for national defense and most federal programs); requiring onerous supermajorities akin to the filibuster to raise other taxes (ostensibly tariffs and other non-income taxes); placing term limits on Congress; and a provision allowing a vote of thirty state legislatures to nullify federal laws and regulations—which Farris proclaimed was "gonna give us a new weapon to stop congressional and con-stitutional decisions, but also statutory- and regulatory-level decisions and have the states—not all of them, but a good majority—have the ability to override federal overreach."[9]

"This gives us a hint of what would come at the official convention later on," Farris reflected. "We're giving hope that the federal government really can be curtailed."[10] Mark Meckler agreed. "This is the real deal," Meckler remarked on the last day of the proceedings. "This is kind of the precursor to the real Super Bowl. It's sort of a dress rehearsal."[11]

The dress-rehearsal convention had crafted a competitive advantage, allowing conservative activists to study how a convention would work under real-life conditions before anyone else, helping them prepare an end-run once a real convention is called. They studied the key procedural pressure points and the potential pitfalls to avoid. They hashed out advantageous parliamentary rules—essential to controlling any legal body—and were able to establish precedents. "When you're doing some-thing of this magnitude," Meckler remarked, "it's really important that you do a dry run. And we've learned a lot. There are so many things you couldn't possibly anticipate until you've hit the floor, put the rules in place. And when we move forward into the real convention, this experience will form the actual convention."[12]

And as many commentators remarked throughout the three-day meeting, many of the state legislators participating in the mock conven-tion likely would be the delegates at the real thing. An interwoven network was forming, one with deep wells of experience on this notori-ously esoteric and confusing yet powerful topic. Paraphrasing Proverbs 15:22, former Texas state representative Rick Green remarked, the prac-tice convention "truly is wisdom in a multitude of counselors."[13]

Writing in the *National Review* in 2016, Jenna Ellis—who, along with Rudy Giuliani and Sidney Powell, hawked 2020 election conspiracy theories and spearheaded Donald Trump's legal efforts to overturn that election—sang the praises of the delegates' handiwork.[14] The mock convention was "one of the most significant events in the history of our constitutional republic," she declared in an article coauthored with Farris. "The future of our country doesn't rest solely on the results in November. There is a much bigger and better solution in the U.S. Constitution itself—in Article V."[15]

MODERN ARCHAICS

Most mainstream coverage ignored the supposed significance of the mock convention, casting it not as a historic moment but rather as strange, maybe even humorous. The *Huffington Post* called it "a week of Founding Fathers cosplay" (meaning "costume play") and remarked that delegates "partied like it was 1787."[16] The *Guardian* noted that the simulation was "complete with period costumes and wigs."[17] Another account saw the delegates' procedural obsessions, "fussily parsing *Robert's Rules of Order*," and their fastidious "iron[ing] out [of] drafting disputes" not as a cause for worry but rather as a sign of its peculiarity.[18] The "most amusing conceit of the enterprise," the writers argued, "was the shared belief among this group of Article V enthusiasts that *they* would actually get to run such a convening." The event "had all the authenticity of a fantasy football league."[19]

The bulk of the commentary regarding the simulation outside conservative and far-right media channels served a healthy dose of the archaics, the troubling phenomenon of commentators ignoring constitutional provisions, pegging them as old and maybe even dead. Anyone who takes Article V seriously—very seriously, as was the case in Williamsburg—must be a bit off, the thinking goes. Attempts to resurrect the provision must be mostly make-believe, the stuff of fringe conservative fever dreams. Just like the arguments of gun rights activists in the late twentieth century that the Second Amendment contained a personal right, these attempts by Article V convention proponents pose no trouble. Beyond a newspaper article here or there, they can be ignored, and maybe even are cause for a chuckle or two.

But the Williamsburg gathering was not a cosplay Civil War reenactment or costumed rendition of the musical *1776*. The delegates wore business attire and discussed contemporary topics. Nor was it a fantasy, like a Boys State or Model United Nations conference for high schoolers. These were real politicians discussing real topics.[20]

Neither was it an "amusing conceit" that the delegates believed "*they* would actually get to run such a convening" (emphasis in original). If a convention were called, who is to say whether these attendees would run the affair? Some argue the votes of only twenty-six states would be necessary to elect a convention president and establish parliamentary rules. And many of the delegates at Williamsburg held roles essential to their states' involvement in a potential convention, including membership on state leg-islative judiciary committees. In the future, many likely could be delegates at a real convention. Would not those present at the 2016 gathering, those with the deepest body of practical experience on the matter, rise to the top of conservative states' consideration for leadership? If the mock conven-tion was any gauge of intentions, it seems clear that a hard-line factionalist approach would try to ensure that procedural control of the convention rested in the hands of well-studied and shrewd true believers.

Dismissive mainstream accounts can cause one to ignore or downplay a danger hiding in plain sight. Far from a joke, the Williamsburg gather-ing provided a rare public glimpse at the scale and sophistication of a very real effort: a coolheaded long-term strategy to make seismic alterations to our constitutional regime through legitimate, legal means. And like previ-ous slow-burn plays, the effort could prove supremely consequential.

Over the last two decades, conservative activists have engineered arguably the most systematic and effective effort to awaken Article V's convention mechanism in American history. The effort has flourished under the radar with little public attention or opposition, reported in leg-islative minutes and discussed extensively in conservative circles but often ignored by the mainstream press and even by careful observers. And con-vention proponents are much closer to success than many think.

THE LONG PATH TO A MODERN CONVENTION

That the country has yet again broached the question of holding a conven-tion under Article V should not come as a surprise. The conservative convention movement has suffered multiple setbacks and two near-miss losses, getting close to the threshold in 1967 and 1987 and then faltering. But after each setback, a vision for radical constitutional change through the convention route has come back more impassioned than before. Study-ing this long path of the conservative convention movement provides insight into what current activists desire and how they might achieve their goal.

Dirksen and the First Campaign

The idea for a modern constitutional convention was first born as a backlash against the liberalizing decisions of the Supreme Court in the 1950s and

DAILY NEWS

TEMBER 12, 1963—Twenty-four Pages (Two Sections)   Price Ten Cents

Justice Horace W. Wilkie (seated center), one of the state's newest supreme court judges, discussed the role of the lawyer and judge at the September meeting of the Rock County Bar association in Janesville Wednesday night. Other honored guests included (from left, seated) Leon Feingold, association president, Justice Myron L. Gordon, and (standing) Justice E. Harold Hallows, Judge Sverre Roang, Edgerton, J u d g e John Boyle, Janesville, and Senator Peter Carr, Janesville. (Daily News photo by Bill Heath)

Wilkie Is Opposed To 'Court of Union'

County Lawyers Hear Justice Reject Proposals convinced our founding fathers that we needed a federal system that recognized the national interest and led to the adoption of our treasured constitutional form of government,

Wisconsin Supreme Court Justice Horace Wilkie opposes "Court of Union" at Rock County, Wisconsin Bar Association (*Beloit Daily News*, 1963)

1960s. Under the gavel of Chief Justice Earl Warren, the Court had issued sweeping opinions advancing civil rights and expanding suffrage. In *Brown v. Board of Education* (1954), the Warren Court unanimously held that racial segregation in schooling was unconstitutional.[21] In *Gideon v. Wainwright* (1963), the Court held that criminal defendants were entitled to the assistance of counsel, even if they could not afford a lawyer.[22] Both decisions were controversial and charted a new course in constitutional jurisprudence.

But few decisions irked those in most statehouses and in Washington more than the Court's apportionment rulings. In two companion cases, *Baker v. Carr* (1962) and *Reynolds v. Sims* (1964), the Court held that the Constitution required legislative districts of equal size, that one man meant one vote.[23] These two cases nullified the long-standing districting practices in many states that had often overrepresented rural areas in the state legislature.[24]

When reflecting on his time on the Court, Warren remarked that *Baker* was "the most important case of [his] tenure."[25] Rather than *Brown, Gideon*, or any of the other pathbreaking civil rights decisions, it was the Warren Court's decision to forgo the Court's previous hesitancy to wade into the "political thicket" that Warren believed would render the political system responsive to the growing needs of modern life.[26] It was a decision that one biographer remarked "would forever change the nature of politics in the United States."[27]

With Illinois senator Everett Dirksen leading the charge, conservatives soon worked to call a constitutional convention to overturn the decisions.[28] The proposed reforms varied. Some focused purely on the apportionment issue. Others, including those advanced by the Council of State Governments, hoped a convention would propose an amendment creating a "court of the union," allowing the states to overturn Supreme Court decisions.[29]

By 1967, thirty-two states had made applications for a convention, two shy of the threshold. The *Chicago Tribune* called it a "revolt."[30] In March 1967, the *New York Times* reported "a campaign for a constitutional convention . . . is nearing success," but it had occurred mainly under the radar.[31] "Most official Washington [was] caught by surprise because the state legislative actions [in attempting to summon a convention for this purpose] have been taken with little fanfare," the *Times* went on to report.[32]

Conservative convention fervor had taken hold with remarkable speed and success. Soon, representatives in Washington began quibbling over the legal technicalities of applications. Senator Robert F. Kennedy argued that disparities in application text meant they could not be aggregated.[33] Twenty-six applications were invalid, two other senators claimed, and could not be counted.[34] Dirksen and convention proponents disagreed, noting Congress's limited ministerial role in counting. Senator William Proxmire of Wisconsin questioned Dirksen relentlessly on the Senate floor about the likely possibility that "a convention if called can go in any direction."[35] The three-quarters bar was no guard, Proxmire warned: "Frankly if the Congress should call a constitutional convention, I would expect a number of extreme amendments to be offered and adopted."[36] Fearing looming disaster, Senator Sam Ervin of North Carolina introduced a bill to "provide procedures for calling constitutional conventions," the first comprehensive act of Congress purporting to establish a legal framework for a convention.[37]

As the danger drew nearer and nearer, Washington danced the predictable convention waltz, rearguing debates as old as the Constitution itself: a convention could run away (no, it would not), Congress should be mindful of technical problems with applications (no, it should not), Congress could pass rules guiding a convention (no, it could not), states could rescind applications (no, they could not). In early 1969, Iowa passed the thirty-third application—one short of a call. Hearings were held, expert panels convened, and all braced for constitutional crisis.

But the blow never came. Later that year, Wisconsin voted down an application. No other state took up the issue.[38]

Historians have debated why the movement fizzled. Many point to Senator Dirksen's unexpected death in September 1969. Others note the oddly technical nature of the issues; unlike the question of direct senatorial election during the Progressive Era, the apportionment decisions never sparked a groundswell public movement for constitutional redress. The apportionment decisions mostly engaged the focus of state-level politicians, as they directly addressed the composition of state legislatures. And since some have argued that Republicans ended up benefiting politically from reapportionment, winning in many newly drawn suburban districts, the conservative movement to overturn the decisions waned.[39]

Others point to three state rescissions that pulled the country back from the convention brink in the last days of 1969, each of which, at least partially, expressed fear of a runaway convention. Then-recent sea changes in civil rights law, and the prospect that a convention would take on the issue of civil rights itself, surely were top of mind. The Civil Rights Acts of 1964 and 1968 had cast a new, tenuous balance of national power in Washington, as cross-party coalitions worked to route segregationists. Dirksen himself, a conservative Republican, had proved essential in securing the interparty truce needed to advance the civil rights bills. A convention, which Dirksen insisted could always set its own agenda, could certainly enter into the civil rights debates, upsetting the statutory rights framework many had fought to establish.

States were likely also worried about the Council of State Governments' proposal to create a "court of the union" to overturn Supreme Court decisions. While the apportionment decisions were seen by many legislators as troubling judicial overreach, the list of major civil rights cases decided while states considered convention applications includes some of the most consequential decisions of the twentieth century: *Heart of Atlanta Motel* (1964), finding it was within Congress's constitutional authority to outlaw discrimination in privately owned accommodations; *McClung* (1964), finding that Congress had authority to regulate discrimination in restaurants; *Harper* (1966), holding poll taxes unconstitutional; and *Loving* (1967), nullifying state laws banning interracial marriage. As the Wisconsin chief justice Horace Wilkie remarked prior to Wisconsin's decision to forgo a convention, "Those who would now tear up the document and provide a whole new system for running the country would return us to the faltering and disjointed form of government that existed prior to the adoption of our Constitution."[40] In North Carolina, one legislator worried about how a nationally televised convention would attract troubling personalities and "some degree of violence."[41]

Some contemporary observers posited another theory: that Dirksen hoped his movement would fail. As noted in one 1969 *Wall Street Journal* article, "Most Dirksen-watchers agree he doesn't really want a constitutional convention. The idea rather is to terrorize liberal senators with the thought of a runaway convention that would start tinkering with the Bill of Rights. To avoid such a calamity, the reasoning goes, Congress itself would propose to the states for ratification a constitutional amendment."[42] Whatever the case, Dirksen and the apportionment debates planted an intriguing seed in the minds of conservative reformers. Article V's convention mechanism had surprising purchase in statehouses across the nation. That thirty-three states would submit applications in just the seven short years following *Baker* was a sign that Article V was a viable path to constitutional change, one to which resources should be dedicated.

The Reagan Years and the Stealth Campaign

A second convention effort took hold just a decade later in 1978, following a state constitutional amendment push in California. In a surprising upset, nearly two-thirds of California voters approved Proposition 13, a state constitutional amendment that radically cut property taxes. Long the dream of libertarian economists and conservative activists, Prop 13 aimed to limit state government by starving it. The year after the proposition passed, California property tax revenues fell dramatically. Cuts to public programs and mass layoffs of public employees ensued.[43] What conservatives were unable to do through the legislature was accomplished with spectacular results through constitutional amendment. Others took notice.

Prop 13 injected constitutional amendment fervor into the conservative mainstream. After stunning success in California, a wave of copycat anti-tax amendment proposals arose in other states, and some of these were adopted. Activists soon set their eyes on translating state-level tax restraints to the federal Constitution. The obvious path was Article V's convention mechanism.

Conservative activists took a page from the apportionment convention movement's playbook from just a decade before, when the possibility of a successful call had taken Washington by surprise. Keeping a low profile would allow the movement to work to gather convention applications with haste and little opposition. Stealth was the strategy. As one commentator reflected, "The movement's sponsors nurtured their obscurity to keep opposition down. . . . They also encouraged impressions that their project was outlandish and their resolutions about as meaningful as endorsements of apple pie."[44]

The quiet antipublicity plan achieved remarkable success. Five years after the Prop 13 vote in California, thirty-two states had passed applications for a constitutional convention to consider adding a balanced budget provision to the Constitution. Just two more states were needed. But the movement, like that of the Dirksen era one decade earlier and the Progressive Era six decades earlier, suddenly sputtered—unable to reach the threshold.

Opposition to a convention had developed among a broad swath of interest groups. Anti-tax advocates themselves worried about the convention route. Howard Jarvis, the Los Angeles businessman who wrote Prop 13, was one of the most outspoken critics. A convention would allow "weirdos" to write a "screwball" version of California's anti-tax amendment into the Constitution, he worried.[45] Delegates would lose the nuance of the matter, failing to deliver a fine-tuned proposal like California had adopted. A convention was just too risky.

When California governor Jerry Brown, a Democrat, announced support for a budget-focused convention, fear yet again gripped Washington and the political establishment. As they had ten years before, many worried that a convention could—and would—tinker with foundational elements of the constitutional structure like the Bill of Rights. President Carter cautioned that a convention "would be completely uncontrollable" and thus "extremely dangerous."[46] The White House soon organized a task force to counter the convention drive in the statehouses. But was it too late?

The surge in national focus affected how state legislators considered the topic. Before, the movement's "nurtured . . . obscurity" had allowed applications to breeze through state legislatures. But now the nation was watching. "It was one thing when you could just pass the thing and send it off to Washington with nobody looking," one Ohio state senator remarked. "But now the newspapers are watching, you've got to have hearings. Everybody's more careful when this comes up in a legislature now."[47] The covert campaign had been thrust into daylight.

Convention proponents grew frustrated at the new public attention on their aims. "It would have been better to let a sleeping dog lie" and continue quietly working until the two-thirds threshold had been achieved, William Bonner, the treasurer of the conservative advocacy organization National Taxpayers Union, remarked. "There was no point in heating things up."[48]

Despite enthusiastic support from then-president Ronald Reagan, the convention movement struggled in statehouses. And with the passage of the Graham-Rudman Act and other Reagan low-tax policies, the need for a balanced budget amendment seemed much less pressing. Soon statehouses changed hands and the two last states necessary to cross the threshold never materialized. Attempts to resurrect a balanced budget amendment proposal through the congressional route likewise failed in the Senate by three votes in a 1995 showdown.

The Modern Movement: Surprising Success, a Hard-Right Tilt, and Dangerous Aims

But the dream did not die. As Republicans began a targeted push to exert more control over state legislatures in the early 2000s, the prospect of a constitutional convention resurfaced in political backwaters. Then the election of President Obama propelled the goal into the mainstream once again.

In the fourteen years between 1994 and 2008, not a single application for a constitutional convention was lodged with Congress.[49] But following the election of President Obama in 2008, a movement to resurrect Article V's convention mechanism surged. Between 2009 and 2021, at least twenty-three states made forty-seven new applications under Article V calling for a constitutional convention.[50]

Over just a few years, the effort became deeply enmeshed in the political efforts of the right and the burgeoning far right, supported by leading conservative luminaries, backed by wealthy conservative funders, and pushed through conservative channels of statehouse power.

The wildfire growth was sparked in 2013 when Mark Levin, the right-wing Fox News host, published *The Liberty Amendments*, which topped the *New York Times* best-seller list.[51] Levin's book made the case for an Article V convention and set out an agenda for such a convening.[52] Levin's proposed constitutional amendments might seem quite familiar, as they were a precursor to those passed by the Williamsburg mock convention in 2016: congressional and judicial term limits, state legislative override of federal actions, sweeping limitations on congressional regulatory power, onerous spending and taxing limitations, and elimination of the direct election of senators, among others.[53]

Levin's advocacy became the seed for a new enterprise. After *The Liberty Amendments* hit shelves and topped charts, Mark Meckler's multimillion-dollar conservative advocacy group, Citizens for Self-Governance, received a seed grant of $500,000 from the Mercer Family Foundation to form the Convention of States Project, a donation Meckler said was the necessary jump-start for the convention campaign.[54] The group aimed to advocate for calling a convention to advance conservative restructuring of the constitutional order.

As Levin's book, which one *National Review* article called "required reading," percolated through conservative circles in late 2013, Meckler launched the new campaign. Joining other activists at the annual meeting of the American Legislative Exchange Council (ALEC), the corporate-backed, conservative policy clearinghouse for state legislators, he pitched the plan to Republican politicians.[55] At a panel entitled "The Solution—A Convention of States to Restrain the Power, Scope and Jurisdiction of the Federal Government," Meckler provided a twenty-four-page dossier to Republican legislators outlining the action plan. The goal was "viable political operations," with district captains organizing in at least three thousand state legislative districts in forty states.[56] The convention need not take up just the specific topics debated by legislatures or discussed in promotional materials, the white paper made clear, because the convening would be called "for the purpose of limiting the power and jurisdiction of the federal government." That limitation is so vague and open that the convention could conceivably take up any topic.

The chances of success were "almost certain," the white paper declared. With enough money and support, the convention would be called.[57] Senator Ron Johnson, who attended the 2013 ALEC workshop to express his support for a convention, agreed: "We've got the drill and the Novocain to fix the cavity."[58]

Just a few days after the ALEC gathering, the Convention of States Project held its first war game meeting at Mount Vernon, one that predated the gathering in Williamsburg. This first four-hour mock convention was largely attended by legislators elected during the 2010 Tea Party sweep of Congress. "Over the last year and a half I've been studying Article V," Chris Kapenga, a new Wisconsin state senator elected in 2010 remarked. "I saw that hundreds of resolutions have been brought forth, by both parties, and always failed. Reason No. 1: The states are not used to working together. Reason No. 2 was the process. So, we worked on the process."[59]

This planning, and the use of ALEC as a networking hub, proved powerful. By the end of 2014, states had submitted sixteen conservative convention applications. By 2018, the Convention of States Project and Citizens for Self-Governance had a combined annual revenue of nearly $10 million, spurred by the support of conservative megadonors like Charles and David Koch and the Mercer family.[60] This influx of cash funded a massive ground game operation, with the project claiming to have support in every state legislative district in the country, a true feat. They also had developed grassroots efforts to foster popular support for a convention, creating training videos on the topic as part of their Convention of States University and frequently broadcasting material on the subject to over two million Facebook followers.

The rapid growth of this movement is impressive on its own account, a manifestation of concerted financial investment by donor interests and a radicalization of the hard-right edge of contemporary politics. This growing political strength can also be gauged by the widespread support it has garnered among conservative and hard-right leaders: Governor Ron DeSantis, Senator Marco Rubio, Senator Rand Paul, Mark Meadows, Sean Hannity, Sarah Palin, Ben Shapiro, Governor Mike Huckabee, Charlie Kirk, Jeb Bush, and Ken Cuccinelli have all endorsed the project's sweeping convention proposal.[61] In a 2016 law review article entitled "The Myths and Realities of Article V," Texas governor Greg Abbott likewise supported forging ahead with convention applications despite the long-standing "myths" of its danger.[62] In October 2021, the group took on as a "senior advisor" former senator Rick Santorum.[63]

In addition to the Convention of States Project, two other conservative Article V advocacy organizations have worked to pass applications. One group, U.S. Term Limits, pushes an Article V application restricted to congressional term limits. The other, Let Us Vote on a Balanced Budget Amendment, focuses on marrying balanced budget amendment applications from the 1980s with the last few necessary to cross the threshold today.

The rapid-fire growth of convention fervor over the last decade might appear at first glance to be splintered among these three groups. Because each operates under a different banner and has proposed slightly different draft application text, one might think of each of these movements as distinct. Yet it would be imprudent to view the conservative efforts as wholly siloed operations with unrelated aims. They are not. While spearheaded by different organizations, these conservative movements cannot be considered distinct efforts because, once a convention is called, it is likely impossible to limit the convening to the stated purposes of the applications. This legal reality demands that citizens consider the conservative convention movement as a monolithic whole.

A mainstay of the now-dominant Republican establishment in statehouses, ALEC has proved to be an essential element in the Article V push. The group functions as an idea clearinghouse for conservative legislators, convening conservative legal and policy professionals to draft model legislation and set a national agenda for Republican state legislatures. ALEC provides these model bills (over one thousand to date) to

Republican legislators at no extra cost, writes talking points to support the bills, and then helps legislators pass the draft legislation into law, including providing expert witnesses to testify. Recent political science research has examined millions of lines of legislative text and shown that state legislatures usually adopt ALEC's model bills unchanged, down to the last comma.[64] This system has allowed ALEC to exert outsized influence on state law. And ALEC does this all on a relatively small budget. This is the genius of its success—the recognition that it is inexpensive to influence state politics at a dramatic scale with the right mix of community building and know-how.

The organization ramped up its convention advocacy shortly after the Republican Party gained control of twelve state governments in the Obama-backlash midterm elections of 2010. Since that time, the effort has taken an even more hard-right turn. First introduced in 1995, the model language for Article V conventions ALEC provides to the states called for a convention "limited to proposing" a balanced budget amendment.[65] By 2015, ALEC's array of potential model applications had expanded significantly, one adopting the Convention of States Project's formulation: a convention to propose "amendments to the Constitution of the United States that impose fiscal restraints on the federal government, limit the power and jurisdiction of the federal government, and limit the terms of office for its officials and for members of Congress."[66]

Now the organization is helping plan for the impending event. In 2018, ALEC joined a coalition of conservative groups in pushing then–vice president Mike Pence to lobby Congress to set a convention date (the letter proffered "July 4, 2019 in Indianapolis," Pence's home state capital, as one possibility).[67] The group made a similar request of House Speaker Paul Ryan and Senate Majority Leader Mitch McConnell, calling for Congress to support convention applications and an eventual call.[68]

THE MIRAGE OF A LIMITED CONVENTION

The growth of the conservative convention movement—almost fifty applications over just fourteen years—demonstrates a remarkable degree of political strength and a slow-burn resolve to induce massive constitutional change. This alone is cause for alarm. But the real problem with modern convention fervor is its full-on embrace of a dangerous and likely flawed core assumption: that a convention cannot run away, meaning it can be legally limited to the topics listed in state applications and the call.

For over a century, many concerned legislators and citizens have feared that once a convention is called, a more radical agenda long waiting in the wings—either shrouded from public view or perhaps simply the result of newfound goals—will come to the floor.[69] A convention supposedly called to consider a balanced budget amendment, for example, might advance more radical proposals, like alterations to the Bill of Rights or bans on same-sex marriage. Because a convention is so hard to convene, would not radical partisans try to co-opt the convening to meet their ends? One would not want the once-in-a-two-century opportunity to go to waste.

There are two interrelated considerations regarding the runaway risk: first, whether it is even constitutional to hold a limited convention, and second, whether a convention once convened would have the inherent authority to disregard limits stated in applications and the call to consider other topics. On both issues, a simple reading of the Constitution's plain text makes clear that a convention likely cannot be limited at all by Congress or the states. Consider again the text of Article V, in relevant part: "The Congress . . . on the application of the legislatures of two thirds of the several states, shall call a convention for proposing amendments, which . . . shall be valid to all intents and purposes, as part of this Constitution, when ratified by the legislatures of three fourths of the several states, or by conventions in three fourths thereof, as the one or the other mode of ratification may be proposed by the Congress." Notice what Article V does not include: there is no mention that a convention is called to consider a specific amendment or that applications can limit an agenda, no mention of the contents of state applications or their binding nature, nor even a claim that states can control a convention at all.

As Senator Heyburn, a conservative Idaho Republican, noted in the early twentieth century, the text of Article V "does not contemplate that any constitutional convention shall assemble with a limitation on it to deal with a particular question."[70] In the absence of a constitutional provision providing for a limiting mechanism, the default position must be the most logical, straightforward reading of the text—a convention with unlimited, plenary authority.[71]

This clear, textual reading of Article V is supported by over a century of legal opinion from across the political spectrum, including among former justices of the Supreme Court.[72] As Professor Michael Paulsen argued in a 1993 *Yale Law Journal* article, "If anything, the two textual checks of state ratification and congressional control over the mode of ratification tend to *negate* any inference of a further power of Congress or the states over the proposing power of the convention" (emphasis ours).[73] This means, as the constitutional scholar Professor Charles Black wrote in 1972, that Article V contemplates only one form of constitutional convening: "a convention for proposing such amendments as that convention decides to propose."[74] Chief Justice Warren Burger put it more bluntly: "There is no way to put a muzzle on a Constitutional Convention."[75]

That a convention must have unlimited authority is clear from Article V's text and is also central to the Constitution's spirit and the Founding ethos. As detailed in Chapter 1, a convention called to consider constitutional matters is, by its very nature, a meeting in the name of the People empowered to act on their behalf. A convention is arguably one of the purest manifestations of popular self-governance.[76] Just as congresspeople cannot be limited in which amendments they propose through the congressional route, the People's representatives at a convention likewise cannot be limited.[77] To do so would put asunder one of the most basic tenets of American constitutionalism: that the People are the source of all power.

Even Senator Everett Dirksen, the leading champion of the conservative convention cause in the mid-twentieth century, seems to have believed that a convention could not be limited. In a 1965 speech at a meeting of the National Grange, Dirksen remarked, "A constitutional convention, many sincere people believe, would, once unlocked, spread in every direction."[78] When pressed on the Senate floor two years later by Wisconsin senator William Proxmire on whether he agreed with that legal assertion, Dirksen responded in the affirmative. Consider the exchange:

Senator Proxmire:	So the Senator is not only saying that if this convention is called it can go in any direction, but is he now adding that in his judgment this is the way a constitutional convention of the people should develop?
Senator Dirksen:	That is right, and the States upon their applications have indicated an interest in one thing, which is the question of apportionment.

> *Senator Proxmire*:   Then, the Senator would entertain only those
> petitions which would specify that they are
> interested in apportionment; others would be
> considered invalid?
>
> *Senator Dirksen*:   I do not run the convention.[79]

The implication is clear: the convention decides its own mandate, rules, and agenda. Even though applications might purport to limit it to a certain topic, even though states might claim they are requiring certain rules for debate, those limitations expressed in the text of an application and a call are not *legally* binding on the convention.[80] They cannot be. As Professor Black put it, "No convention can be called that has anything to run away from."[81] Conventions, by their very nature, have no guide except what delegates desire.

A convention's amendment proposition authority is thus just like that of Congress. Members of Congress can propose any amendment they desire. The convention, once called, likewise also must have plenary authority. But the perceived reticence of Congress to propose amendments might not be a good indicator of what would occur in a convention. The reason is simple mathematics. The threshold for successful proposition is arguably lower in a convention—a majority of *states*, regardless of population, versus two-thirds of each house of Congress. Because a convention is more malapportioned than Congress, many believe the fear of a runaway is heightened because a minor majority of delegations at their own behest, or at the direction of their state legislatures, could alter the convention rules or agenda after it has convened. This is the core thrust of the runaway fear: that those representing a minority of the country could take the majority on a constitutional ride against their will.

Some spectators accept that a convention's agenda cannot be legally limited but argue that *political* realities and the Constitution's amendment procedures make a doomsday scenario unrealistic. In a 1968 article in the *Michigan Law Review*, for example, Senator Dirksen argued that the runaway risk was not as pronounced as commentators made it out to be, as the high three-quarters ratification threshold served as a "safeguard" against misstep.[82] A convention necessarily will only operate in an ideological middle ground, many argue, seeking to find workable solutions. For example, while Republicans might command the agenda through their control of a majority of the state legislatures, it would be hard for an amendment to be ratified without the support of state legislatures currently controlled by Democrats. Even if fringe amendments get through a convention, the thinking goes, they will never be ratified—the genius of Article V, the Framers' famed "middle way." This alone makes a convention both safe and worthwhile, providing a forum for constitutional reckoning at certain critical moments in the history of the country.

But this kumbaya view likewise could be a mirage. Political winds are fickle. Statehouses change hands, and even if a state votes to *not* ratify an amendment today, the state could later change its mind. One legislative session cannot bind another. And with the all-important role of partisan gerrymandering in controlling certain state legislatures, the very notion that state legislatures represent "the People's" true will might seem somewhat flawed. One unfortunate election cycle could lead to radical changes in partisan power—hastening rapid ratification of fringe amendments in states long thought to be moderate. Whether states can rescind their ratifications of amendments is a contentious open question; many scholars make the reasonable argument that ratification is a final, consummating legal act, one that cannot be undone by future meetings of a state legislature that disagrees. And since a convention held today would be able to propose amendments that stay alive for a century or more before they are finally ratified, the concern is even more pronounced.[83] The Twenty-Seventh Amendment, for example, lived for 202 years before ratification.

A "stayin'-alive" scenario, in which amendments can sit on the shelf until ratified, could radically transform state politics in purple states. Amendment ratification would become a key wedge issue and attract millions in dark super PAC spending to otherwise backwater races for mainly part-time state legislative positions. Such a protracted battle would not be new. Right-wing activists have proved they can play long legal games and fund them lavishly—one need only look at the groups currently pushing for a convention. Why would *ratification*—the last mile in the most important marathon of a century—be any different? This amendment realpolitik discourages many from supporting a convention. The status quo might be less than desirable, but it could get worse.

Without a sure, unquestionable legal consensus that a convention does *not* have the legal authority to run away, citizens cannot be sure a convention will proceed in a predictable course generally understood as appropriate and legitimate. And with the multitude of open questions about ratification time limits and rescission, many rightfully determine that an Article V convention poses far too many constitutional risks.

SOWING CONFUSION, LEADING CITIZENS ASTRAY

Conservative convention activists, well aware that the threat of a runaway convention is their greatest vulnerability to criticism, work on all fronts to construct a funhouse of legal mirrors to distract citizens. Within the last fifteen years, modern conservative activists have worked hard to downplay the foundational power of the People in an Article V convention and the runaway risk that popular authority necessarily creates. Responding to over a century of trepidation about the convention mechanism and the very real risk that the convention could go off course, they work hard to completely redefine Article V in the public psyche. A convention is not a pure manifestation of the popular will, they argue, but rather a mere clerical organ of interstate relationships. It is inherently safe because it is not really that powerful—more akin to a clerk filing paperwork than a supreme legislator drafting constitutional law.

The effort begins with vocabulary. Because Article V's text cannot support their claims, conservative convention advocates rarely reference the actual Constitution. Instead, they have devoted considerable resources to contriving an entirely new convention lexicon. This new vocabulary has become dominant in conservative discourse, obfuscating troubling legal issues and sowing confusion. Indeed the new vocabulary is so dominant that some state legislatures have used the concocted terms in official legislative instruments.[84]

Article V provides not for a constitutional convention or "a convention for proposing amendments," advocates insist. The new term is *convention of states*. The distinction is important, advocates assure us, supposedly making clear that such a convening is controlled by state legislatures and thus is safe. But this name was not routinely used until activists began pushing the term in 2010. It is a modern, ahistorical invention that distorts the meaning of Article V.

The phrase *convention of states* is nowhere to be found in the Constitution. It never appears in Madison's Notes from the debates at the 1787 Convention. And a review of Professor Max Farrand's authoritative 1937 volume of historical sources from the Convention yields *not one* instance where the Framers or their contemporaries used the phrase, or anything close to it, in their correspondence and diaries.

Later historical practice further underscores the error of the modern reimaginative approach. Early state applications used a variety of terms to refer to a convention held under Article V, none of which were dominant. Virginia's and New York's 1789 applications—the first in history—referred to an Article V convening as a "convention *of deputies from* the several states" (emphasis added). The difference between this historical usage and modern advocates' new term is considerable. How such deputies "from" the states (notably not "deputies *of* the states," a formulation with a very different meaning) would be selected, what their duties would be, and in whose stead those deputies would act remained undefined.[85] Underscoring the open nature of these foundational questions, Georgia's 1832 convention application—the fourth in history—called an Article V meeting "a convention *of the people* to amend the constitution" (emphasis added).[86] This formulation is consistent with the preamble to the Constitution and its ethos. The 1789 Constitution cast aside the Articles of Confederation's state-focused invocation "We the undersigned Delegates of the States" in favor of a more expansive understanding of constitutional sovereignty: "We the People." The states, as sovereign bodies, did not make the Constitution. The People did. And the Constitution remained the People's to change.

Even though they lack a historical or legal basis for the claims, activists continue to attribute their new phrase to the Constitution's drafters. "Our Founders put a Convention of States in Article V of the Constitution for a moment just like now," Senator Rick Santorum recently remarked to convention proponents.[87] But a "convention of states" is not in Article V at all, or in any other part of the Constitution, for that matter. One can draw that obvious conclusion by reading the text. And if those who wrote the Constitution never once used the term in their debates or contemporaneous writings, how could it be a wellspring of inferred meaning about the text that *is* in the document? That those who acted under the Constitution in the same year it was enacted and shortly thereafter used formulations with substantially different meanings makes the point even more plain. Article V does not provide for a "convention of states." It did not in 1789, and it most surely does not today.

Despite these errors, the vocabulary retooling does not end with the *convention of states* moniker now common in conservative parlance. Activists also insist with a particular fervor that convention members are not "delegates," as most scholars have called such individuals for well over a century. The new term is *commissioners*. The distinction is likewise important, advocates assure us, noting that those who attend a convention have no independent agency, merely serving on the orders of their state legislatures. Where delegates are quasi-legislators who can make their own decisions, activists claim that any action so-called commissioners make in contravention of their commission is void.[88] This makes a convention safe, advocates argue, because convention attendees have no real power.

But this new term likewise was crafted within the last two decades and has little historical significance in the Article V realm.[89] This reality is made plain by a review of the historical record of the 1787 Convention and early practice. The Confederation Congress specifically invoked the term *delegate* in its convention call: "Resolved, That in the opinion of Congress, it is expedient, that on the second Monday in May next, a *convention of delegates*, who shall have been appointed by the several states, be held at Philadelphia" (emphasis added).[90] Those at the Convention also consistently referred to their colleagues as delegates.[91] A review of Professor Max Farrand's extensive archival appendices relating to the Convention likewise shows that contemporary commentators almost exclusively referred to attendees as delegates. At least forty-seven letters and diary entries in Farrand's compiled appendix use the term *delegate*.[92] Among those writing or receiving these documents were a who's who of the Founding generation, including Washington, Jefferson, Madison, and others. Only one letter used another term.[93] So too did the Convention refer to those attending state ratifying conventions as delegates in its final report to Congress and citizens.[94] Virginia and New York's use of the term *deputies* in their 1789 Article V applications, a term that had a similar meaning as *delegate* at the Founding as it does today, further underscores the primacy of this understanding.[95]

That Article V convention-goers are called *delegates* is also clear from modern law. All states that have incorporated regulations regarding Article V conventions in their official codes use that historical term. None has used *commissioner*.[96]

These attempts to engineer small alterations to the vocabulary of Article V might seem innocuous, the stuff of overly intellectual quibbling. But in law, language is power. When legal provisions are confusing and contested, how one even *speaks* of the provision implies certain truths about what it means. Words matter. Advocates' attempts to devise small changes in convention parlance are part of their broader strategy to assert a new theory of Article V, hide the great power of a convention, and change how citizens conceive of the convention mechanism. Activists achieve this goal by recasting the convening not as a meeting in which "We the People" exercise sovereign authority but rather as a meeting created by, and under the direct control of, state legislatures. The work of constitutional change is reserved to the states, not the People, conservative activists claim. The distinction is subtle but, if successfully executed, changes one's entire conception of Article V, reframing the process of constitutional change.

Under this new thinking, an Article V convention is like any other meeting held under the auspices of an interstate compact, like those of the Atlantic States Marine Fisheries Commission, the Washington Metropolitan Area Transit Authority, or the Education Committee of the States. This makes an Article V convention not an august gathering for grand law-drafting but a group of functionaries undertaking clerical tasks. The runaway risk is not real, advocates claim, because the convention is merely a bureaucratic organ. Just as the Midwest Interstate Passenger Rail Commission drafts long-range plans for infrastructure growth for eight states, so too does an Article V convention outsource state legislative clerical work to a group of experts. The convention has no real independent power. And it surely cannot set its own agenda.

Reading Article V's plain text demonstrates the fallacy of this new approach. The term *convention of states* never appears in Article V, or anywhere else in the Constitution for that matter. Nor does Article V even imply that the convention is a functionary, bureaucratic organ intended to ease cooperation between statehouses in doing the work of constitutional drafting. That Congress can prescribe ratification through state conventions, and not state legislatures, further underscores the clear reality that the People, and not state legislatures alone, are the intended locus of the amendment power. As discussed in Chapter 1, conventions and state legislatures have always been two separate mechanisms for harnessing the People's power. Conventions are not *subservient* to the power of a legislature. They are a different kind of body altogether, another kind of legal forum in which the People speak.

Amid the many open questions regarding Article V, the text does provide some clear truths. Among them is this: the only role of the states provided in the *text* of Article V is to apply to Congress for a "convention for proposing amendments." Once that convention is called and its delegates are seated (how they are selected is unclear), the states arguably have no role until the time for ratification. The convention is the People's work, effected through the People's representatives meeting in convention. Those representatives can chart their own course.

This reading of Article V is in accord with over a century of mainstream scholarly opinion. Nonetheless, the work of obfuscation continues. The Convention of States Project buoys their convention fervor with conservative lawyers' assertions that the Project's approach to Article V is legally sound. Despite over a century of legal opinion to the contrary, eleven pro-convention lawyers signed a 2014 document (with the lofty title "The Jefferson Statement") declaring that "Article V provides the states with the opportunity to propose constitutional amendments through a process called a Convention of States."

The document claimed a convention is "safe" because a "Convention is limited to considering amendments on these specified topics" in states' applications.[97] Among those eleven signers was John Eastman, a lawyer pivotal in Donald Trump's attempts to block the Electoral College's count in January 2021.[98] Michael Farris, the organizer of the 2016 mock convention in Williamsburg and a lawyer also involved in efforts to challenge the 2020 election, likewise signed.[99] Notably absent from the statement was any reference to the actual text of the Constitution, which includes no provision for a "convention of states" nor for a convention limited to considering topics in states' applications. On what other legal authorities the signatories reached their conclusion remains unclear.

The view that a convention is "safe" is also promoted to citizens on opinion pages and in letters to the editor nationwide. Emblematic of this tack, one citizen writing in an April 2021 letter in Nebraska's *Grand Island Independent* corrected those who would believe the runaway fallacy: "A convention of states is bound to follow a strict protocol and cannot deviate," the author argued. (Notice the subtle change of terms?) "It is time to stop this monster [the federal government] from destroying our country," the letter-writer concludes, before providing contact information for the area's legislators.[100] Despite its rousing rhetoric, the letter never outlined those strict protocols a convention was supposedly required to follow or what procedure or law would prevent a convention from "deviating." This is perhaps because the author could not cite such authorities. There is no protocol, let alone a "strict" one. And there is no legally binding assurance a convention could not consider other topics. It is all made up.

While convention advocacy groups work to discount the runaway risk in the public sphere, ALEC has attempted to muddy the Article V legal waters for unsuspecting state legislators, holding out as legal fact remarkably tenuous claims about their ability to control an Article V convention. Rather than noting the open legal questions and plumbing their uncertainties, the group has provided state legislators documents that are riddled with half-truths and clear error.

In 2011, ALEC published the first version of its *Article V Handbook for State Lawmakers*. The most recent version was published in 2016 and authored by convention activist and former University of Montana law professor Robert Natelson.[101] The *Handbook* claims to provide state lawmakers with a summary of "the fundamentals of the procedure by which state legislatures apply for a convention" and "what a convention would look like today."[102] In reality, the document makes bold claims of legal certainty about topics on which there is little consensus. And in its consideration of the runaway risk, ALEC's *Handbook* reads at times more like a work of fiction.

Despite the breadth of scholarly and political discussion on these questions over more than a century, the *Handbook* simply refers to the runaway risk as a "myth" used by "liberal activists, legislators and academics to defeat application campaigns."[103] To debunk this so-called myth, the document entirely ignores the Constitution's text and the dispositive legal question—a convention's *inherent* powers under the Constitution. Rather, the document discusses certain political veto points that could maybe, hopefully, stop runaway proposals.[104] But such veto points are cold comfort, missing the point entirely. A simple majority of state delegations could arguably change a convention's agenda, leaving the remaining twenty-four behind in the dust. So too could these renegade delegations refuse to set time limits for ratification, leaving proposed amendments active for many decades. The runaway fear raised for over a century is not a political question, as ALEC's advocacy makes it out to be. The concern is a legal one.

The question is the inherent authority of conventions and the dangerous risk that a simple majority of states, likely supported by their state legislatures, would seek to end-run the meeting for more radical purposes.

When the *Handbook* does venture to make legal claims about the runaway risk, it offers to state legislators as settled legal fact the remarkable, indeed shocking, theory that courts could disregard as "void" *ratified* amendments that exceeded a convention's ambit.[105] (Consider the implications of such a claim: If a procedurally valid ratification by the People's representatives can be invalidated by the courts, who are "the People," anyway? Are the People subservient to the courts, who can decide whether their sovereign action was acceptable? And even if the courts had such authority—they do not—on what body of law would they ground their decision? There is no relevant law.) So too does the *Handbook* claim that Congress could choose not to accept an amendment that contravened a convention's call. But Congress's role in Article V is purely ministerial, save its choice of ratification method—this is one of the core truths of the Hamilton-Mason compromise and clear in the text of Article V.

What textual grant of power to Congress or the courts could justify such radical actions, which the *Handbook* claims are the last-stop proof that the runaway possibility is a myth? One cannot be sure, as the document cites no legal or scholarly authority to substantiate any of the claims beyond the author's own writings.[106]

Perhaps this argumentative approach was out of necessity. One cannot legitimately dispel "the myth" of a runaway convention because it is not a myth. Were ALEC to provide a true recitation of the state of Article V's legal play, it would—at the very least—note the widespread and historical divergence of opinion and lay out the various approaches to the hard legal questions involved. It would note that Article V's text clearly does not provide for limits on a convention's powers.[107] So too would the *Handbook* note that Senator Dirksen himself—the champion of the mid-twentieth-century conservative convention cause—likely believed it was within the power of conventions to consider topics beyond the formal call. It would also cite other leading conservatives, including Phyllis Schlafly and Justice Antonin Scalia, who shared those conclusions. Schlafly remarked that calling a convention would be "playing Russian Roulette with the Constitution."[108] Scalia was even more blunt: "I certainly would not want a constitutional convention. Whoa! Who knows what would come out of it?"[109] Hardly a "myth" spun by "liberal activists, legislators and academics."[110]

Some state legislators likely have cast votes in favor of Article V applications based on the *Handbook*'s assurances and related ALEC testimony. In the absence of necessary context, a state legislator, trusting the document and ALEC's reputation as an arbiter of conservative opinion, would never know that over a century of legal opinion and multiple near-miss convention debates in Congress and statehouses—in the 1910s, 1960s, and 1980s—had reasoned through to a very different conclusion based on a clear reading of plain constitutional text.

ALEC has also helped lawmakers try to address (or perhaps hide) the runaway risk through state law. In response to the legitimate runaway concern, many state legislatures have gone to great lengths to regulate the actions of convention delegates. These restrictions prevent the runaway risk, proponents argue, because they place delegates under the strict control of the state legislature.

In Florida, a delegate who votes in contravention of the state legislatures' commands commits a felony.[111] The same is true in Tennessee, Indiana, and Utah.[112] In Wyoming, it is a felony with a specific punishment prescribed by law: up to five years in prison.[113] In South Dakota, delegates who violate their oath, which includes a voting restriction, are liable for civil fines of up to $5,000.[114] A recent bill passed in both houses of the West Virginia legislature goes to even further extremes: a delegate voting to consider an "unauthorized amendment" commits a felony punishable by up to a $500,000 fine and ten years in prison.[115] Other states have taken a less draconian tack. Wisconsin, for example, allows the state's delegation to remove one of their own who votes to support an "unauthorized amendment."[116]

But these legislative attempts at assuaging runaway fears are toothless. They pose no real impediment for two simple reasons: first, the laws assume that the runaway risk comes from renegade *delegates*, not renegade states. Each faithless-delegate law requires the delegates to follow the instructions of the legislature. But what if it is the state legislatures that change course once a convention is called, suddenly desiring a much more radical program of constitutional reformation than they had previously let on? Such a scenario is permitted under even the strictest delegate-control laws. Second, the laws regulate only *that state's* delegates, not the convention itself. It is possible, although not a legal certainty, that only twenty-six state delegations would need to support proposals outside the agenda specified in the call.[117] Even if delegates from states with delegate-restricting laws did not support these actions, it is possible those proposals still would succeed.

Rather than inherently limiting a convention, these legal efforts—the core thrust of ALEC and activists' attempts to convince citizens that a convention is safe—actually *amplify* runaway concerns. Faithful delegate laws would require delegates to make a convention run away if some states desired that result. And who is to say whether state legislators (or, in reality, hyperpartisan state legislative leadership) would not desire such an outcome? Careful observers can see beyond the mirage.

State legislatures have become a hotbed of right-wing radicalism in recent years. One need only look at many state legislators' attempts to throw out their own citizens' votes in the 2020 election to support Donald Trump's failed scheme to stay in the White House. Were state legislators to have the opportunity to tinker with the country's motherboard, would they really act with self-restraint? There is little reason to trust that, once called, legislatures would not demand delegates expand the scope of a convention.

Forceful statements, toothless legal provisions, and pleasing page layout do not make constitutional claims true. Yet ALEC and the contemporary convention movement forge forward, telling thousands of unsuspecting state legislators and citizens that "those who promote the runaway scenario are either uninformed of Article V law and convention history or are preying on those who are."[118] Those who argue otherwise cannot be trusted, as ALEC's *Handbook* outlines in its introduction, because "one reason [the convention mechanism has not been used] has been misinformation spread about the process by opponents, academics and other writers who failed to do their homework."[119]

For the public servants who have spent considerable time studying the topic and the tenured scholars, many of whom hold conservative legal and political views, who have published contrary views in the nation's leading law journals, hearing that they have "failed to do their homework" or were peddling "misinformation" would be surprising news.

Convention proponents' oftentimes fanciful, aggressive tack is symbolic of their hard-right approach to the Article V debates. In the absence of settled law, and in the face of the very real dangers a convention would pose, activists choose to muddy the waters. Ignoring over a century of contravening thought, they divine legal rules—some seemingly from thin air—and vigorously assert their supposed age-old truth. But such certainty is a fantasy. No matter how emphatically one makes the claim, merely saying something is fact cannot make it so.

Summarizing this prevailing, reckless approach, ALEC's *Handbook* provides telling advice for Republican state legislators: "Move fast. . . . Do not allow alarmism to dissuade you."[120] Perhaps it should have substituted Facebook's ill-fated slogan: "Move fast and break things."[121]

* * *

"WHAT TRUMP AND THE TEA PARTY COULDN'T DO"

The law of Article V is remarkably opaque, the list of important and unanswered questions long. Amid this uncertainty, concerned citizens ask the reasonable question: How should one respond to the growing possibility of a twenty-first-century convention? What could such a convention actually do? Can activists' legal claims be trusted?

The most prudent approach to these questions is to look to the constitutional text: What does Article V say, and how does its internal structure reveal a convention's power and meaning? As most legal commentators have argued for over a century, Article V does provide at least one certain answer: a convention cannot be limited by state applications or Congress's call. Neither have constitutional authority over a convention. Despite contemporary conservative activists' fervent claims to the contrary, a convention is not merely an outgrowth of state legislatures. Nor can Congress try to control a convention through legislation. The convention is a distinct, freestanding constitutional body—one that sets its own rules and agenda.

So too are the political safeguards that many claim ameliorate convention risk not a sure protection. Proposals pushed through the convention by a bare majority of state delegations could sit dormant for decades before ratification, polarizing state-level politics and creating troubling new constitutional uncertainty.

Confronted with the clear risk of a runaway convention, many commentators sound the alarm by arguing a convention could redraft the whole Constitution. Others fear that the Bill of Rights would be in play, that modern constitutional reframers would, for example, take it upon themselves to fashion new approaches to the free-speech guarantee. Others raise even more dire concerns, arguing that a convention might take up again the question of slavery.[122] Such a runaway is, as a legal matter, in the realm of the possible. Because a convention cannot be legally limited, *any* proposal could be entertained. Amendments adopting a parliamentary legislative system, joining a world federal government, making international law binding on national law, or fashioning ours into a "monarchical constitution" have been proposed within the last century and could be fair game.[123] For many, the extent of this great constitutional unknown makes a convention an inappropriate path for change. The risk is too high.

In this view, a runaway convention is always brazen in its redrafting exuberance. It commits constitutional surgery with an unholy hatchet, never with a scalpel. The runaway stomps, never tiptoes.

Conservative convention advocates often use these fears of blatant, carte blanche constitutional reframings as a foil to discount the runaway risk. Convention naysayers live in a fantasy world, activists argue. No convention would ever entertain such extreme proposals. The runaway risk is thus, as ALEC's *Handbook* remarks, "alarmist." Even if legally permissible, a runaway can be easily discounted as a political impossibility. It simply will never happen, they claim.

This argument is convincing when the runaway is framed in such stark, exaggerated terms. But the runaway risk has never only been about the extreme proposals. The real runaway—ultimately the scarier one—would be the runaway of a lawyer, not a revolutionary. It would feel reasonable, correct, and likely mundane.

Convention delegates engineering the run would insist their approach is cautious, reverential, and wholly legal. Picking up political breadcrumbs already being laid today in statehouses nationwide, delegates or renegade state legislatures would define the convention's mandate as limited to an allegedly discrete and popular issue like federalism. Delegates would know that whether that agenda topic "limitation" was included in state applications or the call is of no matter. Modern conservative activists rarely claim that a convention can be legally limited by state or congressional actions occurring prior to the convening, opting to obfuscate the runaway issue by focusing on supposed control *during* the convening or political veto points *after* a convention adjourns. Partisan state legislators are trustworthy, conservative activists claim. When they say they will limit themselves, they mean it. But such a claim is the stuff of folly. Even under conservative activists' theory, the door is wide open for bait-and-switch tactics in which some states seek to move the goalpost after the game has started. Once a convention is called, who is to say whether a group of radical legislatures— bodies that likely would include different members from when an application was made—would not get a bit too giddy, hoping not to waste the opportunity.

Yet even after such a run is executed, delegates would proceed with an air of decorum and humility. Under the guise of a supposedly limited mandate, albeit a new one, the convention could draft and push through seemingly technical changes that fit within their discreet agenda area. These changes would have foundation-altering impact. But they would seem to be small and legalistic, some maybe not even making headlines.

Such a wonky runaway is the real risk, coming like a thief in the night. Few would give rousing speeches announcing its arrival or paint their endeavor as one meant to eclipse the work of the 1787 Convention. Many citizens might not even see the dangerous impacts of the runaway's proposals. The whole affair would be painted as normal, legitimate, and within a fair reading of a convention's *perceived* mandate. Indeed, most runaway proponents would likely contest the very notion that the convention was running away. The theme would be pious patriotism and constitutional fidelity.

One can already see glimpses of this play gaining steam. In politics, where there is money, there is usually a viable plan. As the Williamsburg gathering and the rapid flow of cash to modern conservative convention efforts demonstrate, many are betting on, or at least willing to invest large sums in, Article V. They see it as the ultimate path to neutering modern government, or, as contemporary activists put it, "do[ing] what the Tea Party and Trump couldn't."[124] While a convention is made palatable to the unsuspecting public through legal obfuscation and vague discussions of contemporary ills, troubling proposals wait quietly in the wings.

Limitations expressed in an application must be treated as what they are: nonbinding *claims* of limitation. Yet even these claims have remark- able communicative power, expressing possible agenda items that could be considered once a convention is called and sparking political discussion of the contours of such change. To see the full range of futures, we need only look at recent Article V applications. The Convention of States Project's model Article V application, for example, allows for *any* amendments that "limit the power and jurisdiction of the federal government." It has already been passed in nineteen states as of this writing.

The breadth of this stated goal is remarkable, allowing almost any policy to fit within its scope. The Project's founder has even claimed that fixing the number of Supreme Court justices at nine would be germane.[125] How exactly such a proposal would "limit the power and jurisdiction of the federal government" is unclear; if anything, it could *increase* the power of the federal government. Yet the true purpose of such a broad so-called limitation is clear.

Under the seemingly pleasant guise of "limiting federal power"—a rebranding of the troubled "states' rights" rallying cry of yesteryear—activists hope to achieve their dream of disassembling the New Deal consensus. First, the federal government would be starved of most of its revenue by repealing the income tax. This would be a death knell to most social safety net programs like Medicare, Medicaid, Social Security, and food programs for children and the poor. Then Congress would be stripped of most of its power, forbidden from setting national policy on nearly any important national issue. Alterations to Congress's lawmaking authority would likely ban national environmental regulatory regimes long vilified by conservatives, like the Clean Air Act and Clean Water Act. Small, legalistic changes would ban outright or drastically hamper the federal civil rights framework that sets national antidiscrimination policy. So too would new powers for state legislatures to nullify f ederal law and regulations, like the Court of the Union first proposed during the Dirksen era, become a decisive backstop against national policy.

Also on the chopping block could be congressional authority to protect voting rights and outlaw discrimination in elections, as well as essential yet technical governmental safety standards, like those for food, drugs, consumer goods, cars, and hazardous conditions in the workplace. Federal protection of workers' rights to unionize would almost certainly go. Efforts to strip the federal courts' ability to hear civil rights claims, a sly but decisive move to destroy a half-century of civil rights advancements, would also be perfectly acceptable as they would "limit the power and jurisdiction of the federal government." Wonky changes to federal judicial jurisdiction might also be able to erode areas of settled law relating to free speech, religious liberties, marriage, procreation, health rights, and the rights of criminal defendants and prisoners.

By fashioning Article V's convention route as the means to secure a new conservative vision for American federalism, convention activists have laid bare their true aim. Regardless of the textual grant in state applications or Congress's call, it is likely that a hard-right faction of delegates—supported and spurred on by their state legislatures and buoyed by conservative legal opinion leaders and deep-pocketed donors—would work to ram through provisions altering the very nature of modern American government. This should be cause for alarm for those of most political persuasions. But how close activists are to their goal remains unclear, an inquiry riddled with murky, unanswered questions.

6

COUNTING TO
THIRTY-FOUR

Constitutional Mathematics and Its Dangerous Flaws

"This concept [of an Article V convention] is almost like a Lord of the Rings movie where some ancient giant beast or some sort of secret is unlocked and suddenly it's the greatest power, but nobody knew about it or it was lost for a long time."

—Ohio senate majority leader Matt Huffman (July 2020)[1]

IF YOU VISIT THE CAPITAL OF NEBRASKA, two names might come to mind: Abraham Lincoln (after whom the city is named) and William Jennings Bryan, the trail-blazing progressive congressman and later presidential candidate. Neither Lincoln nor Bryan grew up in Nebraska. They were Illinoisans. Yet both remain revered by Nebraskans today. The statue of Lincoln on the grounds of the art deco–style state capitol shows a modest figure in scale and demeanor. Lincoln's head is bowed, connoting a humble plea for national unity rather than the bravado of a victorious commander in chief.

Bryan, on the other hand, who came from Illinois to Nebraska in search of new opportunity, is remembered as a great prairie progressive who rose to national fame advocating for a new role for the federal government to correct the nation's ills. In the early twentieth century, it was Nebraska—at Bryan's urging—that began the nearly successful effort to force a constitutional convention concerning the direct election question.[2]

And as discussed in Chapter 4, many historians believe that these applica-tion efforts were the final catalyst that led Congress to propose what became the Seventeenth Amendment.[3]

Neither of these figures nor the state's historical liberal pedigree would suggest the deep "red" nature of contemporary Nebraska politics. Governor Pete Ricketts is as conservative as any in the nation and an avid supporter of Donald Trump. Both current United States senators representing Nebraska are deeply conservative as well. As early as 1992, Democrats did not seriously contest Nebraska's electoral votes, and the state was famously last in line on Bill Clinton's presidential visit list. Yet not that long ago, Nebraska had two Democratic senators, including the charismatic Bob Kerrey, who, like Bryan, was a presidential candidate.

Considering this hard-right turn in Nebraska state politics, one might assume that the unicameral state legislature would go the way of Bryan: leading the charge to approve Article V convention applications proffered by contemporary conservative activists. After all, the policy objectives of such a convening align well with policies advanced by many of the state's elected leadership. But the story is more complicated. In 2021, attempts to move a convention application to the floor of the state's unicameral legisla-ture failed by a vote of twenty-three to fourteen, trapping the application in committee, where it had been voted down.[4] Proponents had introduced applications in previous years, each of which was likewise defeated. Among the concerns raised by naysayers was the runaway potential and the possi-bility that special interests would corrupt the gathering. Attempts months later to resurrect the bill were successful, though, and Nebraska passed a renewed application in January 2022.

The Nebraskan experience is not unique. In deep-red Montana, the state senate likewise voted down an application twenty-six to twenty-four, with seven Republicans joining all Democrats in their opposition.[5] There, opposition was fostered by the John Birch Society and its worries of a left-ward convention run as well as the opposition of gun rights groups and the far-right Oath Keepers militia.[6] But the application will be resubmitted in the new legislative session and has a chance of success.

Far from finding greased skids to success, contemporary convention proponents have hit roadblocks. State legislatures, even conservative ones, have rebuffed activists' arguments and defeated proposed applications. To some, it seems like a crisis never has loomed. The arithmetic is clear, they say: the nation is nowhere near the two-thirds threshold. But as recent experience demonstrates, how one does such constitutional mathematics is a topic of debate and intrigue.

FAILED EFFORTS, RADICAL CLAIMS

In July 2020, former Wisconsin governor and presidential candidate Scott Walker launched the convention wars' opening salvo. Joining other convention activists at the annual meeting of ALEC, Walker and his colleagues made a bold and exciting claim: the number of applications necessary for a successful call had already been reached. Next it was up to Congress—or for the courts to force Congress—to issue a call.[7] The day for a modern constitutional convention had come.

Ohio senate majority leader Matt Huffman, a Republican, expressed excitement at Walker's claim: "This concept [of an Article V convention] is almost like a Lord of the Rings movie where some ancient giant beast or some sort of secret is unlocked and suddenly it's the greatest power, but nobody knew about it or it was lost for a long time."[8] And even if a call is not issued, Walker's claim could still have remarkable political consequences. As Huffman noted at the ALEC gathering, "The force of this concept of an Article V convention called by the states has been used before." When state convention calls during the Progressive Era "got sort of to a critical mass, Congress said 'you know we were gonna do that the whole time anyway. We'll pass the resolution.'"[9] The plan was worth pursuing in any event.

Far from a decisive blow, Walker's claim might have seemed like a misfire. The perplexing announcement, seemingly made out of the blue, presented more troubling questions than certain answers. How had a successful convention application movement gained such steam without public notice? Was Walker's count even right? Had the threshold been met? But perhaps the most obvious and problematic question was not about the content of Walker's announcement but rather the forum.

If the constitutional threshold for a convention uncontrovertibly were satisfied, would not such a claim be made on the floors of Congress, or at least at a news conference flanked with a small army of mainstream, generally respected constitutional scholars? Would not the claim be meticulously substantiated, perhaps with a dossier at hand for the press? A convention call is one of the last remaining constitutional firsts. How one begins the process is of substantial political importance.

Yet Walker made his claim at a meeting of an advocacy organization notorious for manipulating the levers of statehouse power to support monied conservative interests. The organization operates as a coalition of politicians, conservative thinkers, corporate interests, and wealthy donors aimed at reshaping American law. Just under a third of all state legislators are dues-paying members—providing enormous organizational strength. But only these Republican state legislators, and the retinue of lobbyists that fund ALEC to push their policies, take the organization seriously.[10] Many ALEC workshops occur in private, and the organization has a history of threatening journalists who attempt to report on their activities.[11] Were it not for the COVID-19 pandemic, and ALEC's decision to host the gathering online, it is possible Walker's comments would have never become public. What should one make of this choice of forum? Might it be a sign of a deeper motive? The Associated Press article reporting the gathering implied as much in its headline: "Budget Hawks Hatch Plan to Force Constitutional Convention."[12]

As explained below, Walker's application count—his "constitutional mathematics"—is deeply flawed, grounded in a theory with little to no basis in our constitutional and legal tradition. So too can his claimed victory no longer stand according to its own logic; his math included applications from Colorado and New Jersey that legislators have since rescinded.

But this opening salvo should be taken seriously. Even if Walker's count is wrong, it is Congress that determines whether the constitutional two-thirds threshold for a convention call has been satisfied. In our fraught political environment, where one of the two major parties grows ever more comfortable with conspiracy theories, delusional lies, and power-at-all-costs politics, wrongheaded and dangerous ideas have been shown to enter the mainstream. The past decade has proved not only that such errors can take quick hold but also that they can have disastrous consequences.

If one accepts Walker's highly suspect theory, then a few successful applications from the likes of deep-red South Carolina, Idaho, or Montana could push the country over the threshold.[13] Activists have been hard at work to secure these supposedly final states, with a bill recently introduced in the South Carolina Senate.[14] More action is likely.

Were these efforts successful, it is quite possible Congress would entertain activists' arguments and issue a call, a momentous and reckless action that would thrust the country into a constitutional crisis. An arguably illegal convention purporting to wield the ultimate power to draft sweeping changes to our fundamental law would seem to be given legitimate sanction. The magnitude of such a crisis is difficult to overstate.

CONSTITUTIONAL MATHEMATICS AND ADVOCATES' TENUOUS GAMBIT

Between 2009 and 2021, at least twenty-three states made forty-seven separate applications proffered by conservative groups calling for a constitutional convention under Article V.[15] While this success is remarkable, calling to mind the rapid convention application movement during the late nineteenth- and early twentieth-century Progressive Era, the number can be misleading. These twenty-three applications do not get Walker to the magic thirty-four threshold. One might think the country is far off from a potential convention call—at least eleven states away. And even that analysis depends on a thorny legal question: if and how an application's subject-matter limitations, disparate between the different states' applications, are assessed. Yet Walker still claimed success. Congress must issue a call, he argued. A convention was imminent. How could he make such a claim?

In addition to the applications passed within the last decades, some states have still-active applications from a movement for a convention in the 1980s to consider a balanced budget amendment. If one can combine these with current applications that also mention a balanced budget amendment (an open legal question), there were (in July 2020) twenty-eight valid applications, still six states short of the threshold.

To continue in Walker's logic and reach his dramatic conclusion, one must enter murky waters. Recall James Madison's prescient observation at the 1787 Convention that Article V was flawed due to the lack of clear "constitutional regulations" regarding its operation. How one does "convention mathematics," figuring out whether thirty-four applications have satisfied the constitutional threshold, quickly becomes confusing and obtuse. Amid this uncertainty lies opportunity for dangerous subterfuge—a glimpse of future legal turmoil likely to reach the courts and the halls of Congress as activists forge ahead with their plans.

Walker's mathematical magic—getting those last six states—employs a tenuous legal theory first sketched in 2011 and later developed in a 2018 article in the *Federalist Society Review* by Robert Natelson, the author of ALEC's *Handbook on Article V* provided to Republican state lawmakers and discussed in Chapter 5. Natelson argues that "plenary" applications, meaning applications that purportedly do not express a topic limitation in their legally operative text, can be added to any other topic-limited applications.[16] So the twenty-eight (at the time) balanced-budget-amendment applications can be combined with any "general" or no-topic applications. Activists claimed there were six purportedly "plenary" applications, just the right number to reach the two-thirds mark—enough to clear the outfield wall. A home run.

The part that convention proponents do not say too loudly is that their theory's simplicity is manufactured. Their claims of a successful count rest not on settled premises but rather on fraught legal assumptions with questionable bases in our constitutional tradition. The claims are so shaky many might believe their error is self-evident. But in the unsettled world of Article V, where established principles are rare, it is important to lay bare the theory's errors lest a fallacy gain traction. And because presumably *Congress*, not the courts, has the ultimate say on whether the Article V threshold has been met, the danger of such fallacies is particularly pronounced. Erroneous theories must be engaged head-on, disproved, and dismissed.

First consider the so-called plenary applications themselves. Two were unrescinded applications from Illinois and Kentucky that petitioned for a convention to avert the Civil War. This purpose is clear from their texts.

Illinois's application went so far as to claim in its legislative text that "the people of the State of Illinois do not desire any change in our Federal constitution" but that if an Article V convention would avert war, the state should be considered as having applied.[17] Kentucky's resolution was likewise animated by questions of slavery, a fact substantiated by the inclusion in the application of a list of proposed amendments on the topic.[18]

Next, the theory relies on multiple Progressive Era applications from Oregon and Washington, which likewise state clear purposes in their prefatory language.

The final application that proponents claim to be plenary—Walker's home run—was from New York, passed in *1789*, calling for a second convention to draft the Bill of Rights.[19] The text of the application itself makes this aim clear: the New York legislature declared a convention was necessary to "secure to ourselves and our latest posterity, the great and unalienable rights of mankind." New York ratified the Constitution, the memorial remarked, "in the fullest confidence of obtaining a revision of the said Constitution by a General Convention."[20]

Each application expresses clear purposes in its text of the state legislature's intentions for a convention.[21] But these clear purposes pose problems for modern convention proponents. They have not been able to secure the requisite number of applications themselves, so they must seek historical companions to help from beyond the grave. To cleanse these century-old applications of their historical animating purposes and thus use them to advance their own contemporary aims, convention advocates purport to look *only* to the applications' supposedly legally operative text.[22] This allows them to ignore all stated purposes for the application.

DANGEROUS COUNTING ERRORS

Contemporary convention activists' amalgamation theory has little to no foundation in the American constitutional tradition. The theory is flawed on its face for at least three reasons. First, the theory erroneously equates convention applications with statutes, a distinct form of legal text read in unique ways. Applications are not statutes and should not be read like them. Second, even if the applications are statutes (and they are not), the theory misstates and misapplies American canons of statutory construction, fashioning an incredibly strict interpretive method forbidden by long-established legal doctrines. Finally, and perhaps most obviously, the theory belies basic common sense.

First, the theory considers convention applications to be statutory instruments that should be interpreted according to a (very) strict statutory interpretive canon—what the theory's author claims to be "a basic rule of *legal* interpretation" (emphasis ours).[23] Yet convention applications are not statutes but rather a form of text unique to themselves.[24] The Constitution does not set forth the form of an application under Article V, and the records from the Convention do not anticipate a format for such documents. Applications thus should not and cannot be treated as though they must conform to a supposed standard format and be interpreted according to canons unique to that format.

Applications are more appropriately treated like a formal letter or petition from a legislative body, approved by official act, informing Congress of the legislature's intentions. This unique type of missive might happen to speak in a form and voice common to legislative instruments (using "whereas," "resolved," and the like), but it need not do so to be legally valid and binding. That applications have text that might appear to be prefatory or operative is of no real legal significance. New York's 1789 application underscores both this unique format and the formal-letter nature of applications. The New York legislature provided: "Resolved, That an application be made . . . to the Congress . . . in the words following, to wit."[25] The application contained no preambulatory language whatsoever; rather, the legislative instrument simply dictated the text of a letter to Congress.[26]

All applications, regardless of their particular form, undertake the same basic task. If legislatures choose to use a certain format for that missive, that is their prerogative. But the legislature's choice of format is not legally binding and need not and should not be used after the fact by those who would subvert legislative intentions, to invite or require a strict construction doctrine foreign to the instrument being interpreted. Importing modern interpretive canons from another inapt area of application to interpret idiosyncratic documents over a century old just does not make sense. As would any reasonable person reading a formal letter, Congress must read applications *in their entirety*, gleaning important context from all written text. If some text in an application can be ignored, why would the legislature have seen a need to include it?[27]

Second, even if one interprets the so-called plenary applications as statutory texts (they should not), there is no reason to ignore preambulatory language.[28] As William Blackstone, the preeminent authority on English law for the Founding generation, remarked in his *Commentaries,* "the proeme, or preamble, is often called in to help the construction of an act of [the legislature]."[29] The respected 1871 Dwarris Treatise, cited by justices of the Supreme Court as recently as 2008, likewise provides that "if any doubt arise on the words of the enacting part [of a statute], the preamble may be resorted to, to explain it."[30] Modern authorities take a similar view.[31]

Contemporary conservative convention proponents thus hang their entire theory on the argument that the plenary applications are unambiguous, that there is *no doubt* the legislatures that enacted them intended their applications to remain active forever and to be counted with any other application for any other purpose. Surely no reasonable observer could, with a straight face, argue that there is unambiguous certainty that the New York legislature in 1789 or Illinois in 1861 desired such an outcome, especially when the instruments themselves make plain their purposes to the contrary.

Like those who undertake serious, intellectual interpretation of religious texts, American interpretive canons assume that legal texts are internally consistent, that they must be interpreted as part of such a consistent whole (rather than cherry-picked), and that the interpreter must always show humble deference to the intention of the author—in the case of legislative enactments, the People's representatives. Such interpretive approaches are a bedrock of our legal system.[32]

So pronounced are these structural and purposive canons that twenty-two states have adopted them into their state codes, requiring courts to use them when interpreting legislative acts.[33] Among the states that have explicitly required a purpose-focused reading of state legislative enactments are New York and Kentucky—two states with so-called plenary applications essential for Walker's count.[34] Illinois, another of Walker's necessary states, has mandated a holistic, "whole act" approach to interpreting the legislature's actions.[35]

By their own law, these states' applications must be interpreted in a way that gives authoritative weight to their stated purposes. These purposes are clear in the applications' text and necessarily limit the applications to those purposes. If one treats the applications like statutes, then they must also look to the states' own binding interpretive methods, which plainly answer the question. And when one considers the long-held acceptance of these canons in the American legal tradition, interpreters should—*must*—likewise read the remaining so-called plenary applications in the context of their purposes, finding them to be necessarily limited to the purposes clearly stated in the instrument.[36]

Ironically, convention proponents have argued elsewhere that Congress could look to an application's preamble to *nullify* and *ignore* application rescissions that commit a "material mistake," a bizarre, concocted doctrine that would deny legislatures the ability to control their own applications when their rescissions are animated by understandings of Article V that differ from those of contemporary activists.[37] Yet these same activists also argue that one should completely ignore preambulatory text when determining an application's subject-matter purpose and limitation.[38] Which is it? Do preambles matter or not? For modern convention advocates, it seems to depend on whatever is beneficial to their cause. They have no consistent approach.

Finally, the plenary application aggregation theory defies basic common sense. It is outlandish to think an application from 1789 (or the 1860s or 1900s) could or should be used to bind unwitting states to the dangerous convention efforts of today's activists. How can modern convention proponents legitimately argue that legislators centuries ago should have known their applications—in the case of New York, the *second* application in history—must conform to strict, idiosyncratic drafting rules dubiously crafted within the last decade?[39]

And if this theory were so self-evident, why did advocates not employ it in 1967, when the nation was indisputably one state away from a call,[40] or in 1987, when the nation was two states away? The theory's mathematical magic would have been equally or more advantageous to convention proponents then as it is today. These two near-miss moments sparked the largest flourishing in public discussion and scholarship on Article V in the country's history. Yet the argument was never raised, let alone taken seriously. The proposition is made even more preposterous by contemporary convention proponents who argue that states should not be allowed to *rescind* applications in certain circumstances.[41] How can a state be bound by their forbears with no opportunity to change course?

A GLIMPSE AT FUTURE TROUBLE: WHY CONVENTION MATHEMATICS MATTER

There is an old joke that goes something like this: An engineer, a mathematician, and a lawyer are all called in for a test. Each is asked to solve the equation "two plus two equals what?" The engineer, after a short pause, answers, "Four." The mathematician answers without skipping a beat: "Four point zero." Finally, the lawyer takes the test. Answering even more quickly than the mathematician, he responds, "Well, what do you want the answer to be?"

Constitutional mathematics—how one counts to thirty-four—should be a hard science. But in reality, it is a political game that could, if Congress embraces the charade, allow for number fudging and backward, answer-getting theories. Scott Walker's dramatic claim in July 2020 that the convention threshold had been satisfied laid bare one of the most troubling elements of Article V: the Framers left no rules. As detailed in Chapter 2, the only constitutional guidance is Article V's requirement that Congress exercise a ministerial role in counting applications and issuing a call once the requirement has been met. This role is one in which Congress has no discretion; the text is clear and unambiguous: "Congress . . . *shall* call."

Even if the role is ministerial, however, the Constitution still provides no guidance on how to actually do the work of counting applications. Despite many attempts at reform, all the major questions—Do applications go stale? Can they be "plenary"? How are they aggregated? Must they be lodged with the Congress or merely passed by a legislature? Can states rescind? and so on—remain unanswered.

Convention proponents' current attempts at mathematical magic take advantage of this lack of "constitutional regulations," crafting new, dubious theories in hopes they will help their goals. But whether the theories are at all legitimate as a legal or constitutional matter might be beside the point. How to properly count applications has been a topic of intense debate for at least seventy years and is the subject of many law review articles and legislative reports.[42] No consensus has been reached. In this vacuum of confusion lies opportunity for gamesmanship, a phenomenon that constitutional scholar Russell Caplan has artfully called "the politics of uncertainty."[43] If contemporary activists' amalgamation theory proves unworkable, new ones will likely be brewed up in constitutional cauldrons. "Well, what do you want the answer to be?" the lawyer asks. "There! Thirty-four!"

Another problem, one that could very possibly become an enticing ingredient in a new counting-magic brew, also looms on the horizon. Multiple conservative groups—the Convention of States Project, U.S. Term Limits, and proponents of a balanced budget amendment—aim to call a convention. Several states have passed applications drafted by these different groups (some just one, others two, some states have passed all three). But the terms of the applications overlap. The Convention of States applications, for example, call for consideration of amendments imposing term limits and a balanced budget. Does this mean that a state that has passed the Convention of States Project's application but not the balanced budget amendment application can be counted toward the more limited budget threshold? And even if one believes that a convention can be limited (which, as discussed in Chapter 5, it likely cannot), then how would delegates interpret the array of disparate applications to determine a subject-matter limitation? Can one be sure that the least common denominator (budget issues, for example) would prevail? Some argue that only a simple majority of states is required to set an agenda.[44] Is the *true* subject-matter limitation threshold really twenty-six—a majority of the state delegations?

The clear grant of authority to Congress and the lack of any constitutional rules guiding that authority make Article V an inherently political process. Article V lives in the fraught world of faux constitutionalism, where the dispositive legal argument is not necessarily the one that is *right* as a matter of law but rather the one that delivers the appropriate outcome. Legal argumentation does not necessarily win the day in Congress. Rather, the important inquiry is what the political class desires. The recent debacles over Congress's role in certifying the 2020 election, the impeachment process, and Congress's attempts to investigate the January 6 attack on the Capitol underscore the point. When constitutional questions reach Congress, they are merely political issues painted with a thin veneer of gravitas. As Senator Lindsey Graham famously remarked during the first impeachment trial of President Trump, "I'm not trying to pretend to be a fair juror here," despite his oath to "do impartial justice according to the Constitution and laws."[45] For many legislators duty and settled principles of law are no matter. The concern will always be political ends. If a slim majority of Congress (50 percent plus one in each chamber) desired a convention, they could call one using tenuous theories or problematic math. It is Congress's prerogative.

For years, many have seen Article V's unique stew of ambiguity and required congressional action as the reason convention movements fail. Professor Michael Rappaport has called the phenomenon an "effective veto that Article V confers on Congress."[46] But in a hyperpartisan world where *Congress* has more political diversity than many state legislatures, it might be easier for hard-right activists to use the convention route for their aims, as it requires only a slim majority of Congress to approve a call, rather than the top-down congressional route, which requires two-thirds of each house to propose an amendment. And with large, well-funded advocacy organizations helping coordinate convention efforts between statehouses, the former challenge of corralling state legislatures and keeping them in line is simplified. The convention dam might be breaking.

Erroneous convention mathematics are gaining surprising traction. The "plenary" amalgamation theory has been repeated again and again, held out to legislators, governors, and citizens as established truth.[47] When a former governor and presidential candidate touts the theories, one should take notice. When the movement grows, and other prominent individuals on the far right of national politics—like Florida governor Ron DeSantis—openly endorse organizations that give comfort to these theories, one should pay even closer attention.

And it is quite possible that there are no safeguards outside the political process for determining whether the Article V threshold has been satisfied. Whether the courts can hear any cases regarding Article V procedures is an open, contested question.[48] Many argue that such issues are nonjusticiable "political questions." In 1939, the Supreme Court held thus in *Coleman v. Miller*, writing that amendment procedures committed to "the ultimate authority in the Congress" were beyond the courts' authority.[49] Four of the nine justices—the plurality—endorsed an even more expansive rule, arguing that courts must never engage *any* issues relating to Article V: "The [amendment] process itself is 'political' in its entirety, from submission until an amendment becomes part of the Constitution, and is not subject to judicial guidance, control, or interference at any point."[50] Under either understanding, whether the constitutional threshold has been satisfied would seem to be a question that cannot be raised in court.[51]

The *Coleman* holding has been criticized by scholars for many decades.[52] A treatise on the amendment process, published three years after the Court's decision, noted that it was "uncertain" to which phases of the Article V process the political question doctrine applied.[53] A contemporary scholar has gone so far as to call the decision "bad law."[54] Yet *Coleman* remains the law of the land, the centerpiece in a confusing legal quilt enveloping Article V. Scholars and legal commentators have arrived at no settled answers about the judiciary's authority to regulate the thorniest issues raised by claims of a successful call or a constitutional convention itself. Some district courts in the decades following *Coleman* have dismissed its holding and found Article V questions justiciable, including recently in relation to questions regarding whether the Equal Rights Amendment was successfully ratified. But those cases considered ratification issues, an area in which *Coleman* can be distinguished on its own facts.[55]

Legal disputes regarding a *convention* held under Article V, however, would be completely new, invoking questions of a constitutional gravitas never before considered by the federal courts. These issues are foundational, cutting to the core of our constitutional system, and are possibly ones in which courts would—and, some would argue, *should*—struggle to find "judicially discoverable and manageable standards" with which to weigh claims, an important component of the political question analysis.[56]

Professor Erwin Chemerinsky has called the political question doctrine one of "the most confusing" elements of the courts' role in the constitutional system.[57] Professor Martin Redish deems it "an enigma."[58] And the jurisprudence regarding the doctrine's role in Article V questions is perhaps the most confusing and enigmatic of all. Convention proponents fervently claim the courts can police convention procedures to protect against missteps, a reasonable third-party referee to constitution redrafting. But the claims have no foundation in settled law. No settled law exists.[59]

Convention activists' claims that a court could *force* Congress to issue a call once they have secured the requisite number (on whatever theory)— a judicial act called a "writ of mandamus"—are likewise flawed. The argument has been made since at least the 1950s.[60] Legal scholars considered it illegal then, and it is likely still so today.[61] Such an order would not only run afoul of *Coleman* on its own terms but would also be a direct affront on the most basic understandings of the separation of powers.[62]

The nation has approached the convention precipice before, in 1913, 1967, and 1987. The question now is whether there is political will to jump off the ledge or whether the *supposed* success of a convention movement— or near success—will spark meaningful formal constitutional change through the Article V congressional route. Both are reasonable and foreseeable possibilities, ones that must be taken seriously.

COUNTING TO THIRTY-FOUR

The question of how likely it is that the thirty-four-state threshold will be met, or even how many states have already validly applied for a convention under the strictures of Article V, is difficult to answer. This requires responsible analysis and reasonable approaches to legal uncertainties that neither unduly minimize nor recklessly exaggerate the exercise of the People's amendment power. Many groups exhibit a tendency to confidently predict one outcome or the other: claiming either that a convention will never happen or that it is indisputably imminent. But both approaches are inappropriate.

A comprehensive review illustrates that the ultimate outcome is a close question, full of variables and uncertainties that could tip the balance in either direction. Without clear, generally accepted guidelines, Article V remains a multifaceted political process, one that could suddenly be pushed in a decisive direction by one legislative session in a number of states or even a renegade Congress that engineers its own theory for a call.

The counting issue, and the array of troubling questions it presents, must be engaged with a dispassionate search for a rational, consensus-focused approach. Constitutional mathematics should not be a witch's brew, where lawyers make up a new formula when the old one does not yield the proper result. Counting should be a hard science, one that puts all actors on notice as to the procedures *before* applications are adopted and counted, ensuring that the intentions of legislators are properly assessed and given appropriate meaning. This is the essence of fair and clear procedure, which in the context of Article V is both desirable and necessary.

Congress, in whom the ministerial task of counting applications is vested, should take up this process and implement legislation clearly delineating the structure by which applications are to be counted.[63] While we believe that Congress has little power to regulate a *convention*, enabling legislation that provides guidelines for the application procedure would be an appropriate exercise of its counting authority. Some approaches to this exercise, many discussed above, are clearly off-the-mark attempts to reverse engineer a desired result and must be discarded as erroneous. But many scholars over at least sixty years have presented reasonable theories to resolve the counting problems, theories that should be intently considered and debated.

Some guiding principles are already clear. Congress should take a holistic approach when reading applications to determine whether the legislature desires a subject-matter limitation to a convention. So too should Congress construe those limitations narrowly to ensure that a legislature's intended limitation is both honored and not counted in union with other applications with varying purposes. Whether or not these limitations are binding *on the convention* is of no matter in the counting question; legislators have long believed their limitations matter and therefore that intent should, at the very least, be considered in the counting process. So too should the notion of a "plenary" application be quite narrowly construed, requiring an explicit invocation of the theory.

But until such legislation is adopted, the specter of bad math looms. Citizens should remain attentive to the upward creep of convention applications, noting at every turn that Congress could use applications against states' will to begin a process of constitutional reformation. And such a moment could be closer than many care to admit.

7

"WE THE PEOPLE" IN PERILOUS TIMES

A Constitutional Convention in an Era of Faction

"[The] domination of one faction over another, sharpened by the spirit of revenge, natural to party dissension, which in different ages and countries has perpetrated the most horrid enormities, is itself a frightful despotism."

—George Washington (1796)[1]

"An Article V convention? Yikes."

—Joseph Kearney, dean of Marquette University Law School, email to authors (2021)

D RIVING BETWEEN LINCOLN, Nebraska, and the small town of Ironwood in Michigan's Upper Peninsula, one passes through four contiguous midwestern states with active Article V applications: Nebraska, Iowa, Wisconsin, and Michigan. A person making this journey during the summer of 2021 would likely have been troubled by what they saw. Each of these states certainly has its own distinct political culture. According to a current political cliché, two are very red, and the other two are now purple after having been blue for a fair stretch of time. But in mid-2021, the highways of all these states shared a similar phenomenon: the glaring presence of homemade, brightly painted signs and flags broadcasting support for Donald Trump.

People typically remove political signs soon after an election. But eight months after Trump's November 2020 defeat, the signs still stood and the flags still waved. Some proud owners had even replaced "2020" with "2024."

A particularly striking example of these displays was at the main crossroads in Hurley, Wisconsin, a small town of about fifteen hundred a few hundred yards from the Michigan border. From the New Deal until recently, Hurley was a solid Democratic stronghold, home to many miners of Italian and Finnish descent. Now it is Trump country and recently has voted overwhelmingly Republican in almost all down-ballot races.

Hurley is emblematic of a hard-right political turn common in many communities across the heartland. Electoral results report this partisan change as a cold, statistical matter. But when visiting Hurley, one encounters a stark reminder of how far the country's political divisions have changed the way people think, relate, and react to the realities of the world. On the ground, one can see and feel how fractured the country has become.

What was this almost startling crossroads display seen in Hurley in summer 2021? An overturned, beat-up old rowboat on which was scrawled in red paint, "TRUMP WON! GOD BLESS US ALL!"

This contemporary bout of factional fervor is not limited to one politician or election cycle. It cuts to the very core of our national life, causing one to question the strength of our constitutional institutions and mechanisms. The pernicious lie that Donald Trump somehow won the 2020 election is not only the stuff of a weird counterculture, confined to the bowels of the internet or conspiracy theorists. The falsehood was endorsed in the halls of Congress by 147 elected congresspeople who voted to ignore the will of the voters, subvert the nation's democratic system, and overturn a presidential election.[2] As detailed in Chapters 5 and 6, many individuals involved in the contemporary conservative convention movement had a firsthand, active role in perpetuating this lie. The audacity of it all remains shocking. Over a *quarter* of the country's national leadership was seemingly willing to go down the road of despotism for quick partisan gain. Rather than stand up for what was factually accurate and morally right, these leaders cast aside the most basic belief that here, in America, the law and the People reign supreme, not one person or one party.

As of this writing, a possible second Trump presidency and the cult of personality it would empower looms as a dangerous prospect. For many of

A scene from Hurley, Wisconsin. August 2021. Photo taken by author.

all ideological stripes, the Trump era sounded an alarm. Perhaps for the first time in their lives, many now question whether the nation's institutions are as strong and stable as once thought. Many wonder whether the constitutional order that has undoubtedly formed and guided the greatest experiment in democratic self-rule in the history of mankind might somehow be faltering. Might the country have come to a turning point, veering toward a new, precarious future in which strongmen and their partisan lackies rule the country through fear, intimidation, violence, and deception?

The refrain that these are "not normal times" is now so commonplace that some have forgotten what normal really is. The constant upheaval has caused some to become numb, consumed with an omnipresent anger, fear, or, worse yet, apathy at the magnitude of the rot. But the extreme shift in our politics over the last few years is not new. Trump is but one manifestation of deeper fault lines that have been growing in the nation's body politic, emblematic of a dizzying growth of far-right trends that have accelerated throughout the past decade.

Many if not most Americans regard the current nature of our national politics, and the politics of many states, as hyperpartisan. The data back up the claim. Party-line voting in Congress has increased at a precipitous rate in the last forty years. In the early 1970s, the average legislator in Congress voted with their party on party-line votes about 60 percent of the time. But starting in the 1980s, voting patterns began to diverge. One 2015 study found the current rate at around 90 percent.[3]

This pattern has been particularly noticeable in the United States Senate, which has devolved into a strikingly more partisan body than it was thirty years ago. The filibuster in that body has become a nearly crippling partisan tool that bears no resemblance to the *Mr. Smith Goes to Washington* image of one senator speaking on principle against the wishes of a bipartisan opposition to his position until he drops from exhaustion. Today, the so-called silent filibuster is used merely as a partisan tactic to hinder and delay.

These developments are sharply at odds with the Framers' admonition to avoid a national public life animated by partisan division and oppressive majoritarian rule. The Founders greatly feared the rise of political parties, which they referred to as "factions." James Madison expounded on these concerns in *Federalist* No. 10: "Among the numerous advantages promised by a well-constructed union, none deserves to be more accurately developed than its tendency to break and control the violence of faction."[4]

Yet whether the Constitution and the strengthened union it fashioned had achieved such a goal was not certain. In his farewell address, George Washington warned that "the alternative domination of one faction over another, sharpened by the spirit of revenge, natural to party dissension, which in different ages and countries has perpetrated the most horrid enormities, is itself a frightful despotism."[5] So too did John Adams, who served as Washington's successor, echo the theme. "There is nothing I dread So much, as a Division of the Republick into two great Parties, each arranged under its Leader, and concerting Measures in opposition to each other," Adams wrote. "This, in my humble Apprehension is to be dreaded as the greatest political Evil, under our Constitution."[6]

It is hard to imagine that these same Framers envisioned Article V's convention mechanism would be deployed as one of those partisan "concert[ed] Measures." Yet that is precisely what contemporary activists desire. Unlike every formidable convention movement in history, the current effort has eschewed any pretense of broad-based, bipartisan support. The *point* of the effort is almost entirely partisan, inspired by and organized through one of the nation's two major political parties. Article V is seen as just another playing card in the contemporary blue-red wars (albeit a very powerful one), with applications approved in statehouses along stark partisan lines on the celebrated premise that the convening could likewise be controlled along partisan lines.

AN ERA OF FACTIONALISM

The Framers desired an amendment mechanism insulated from the organizational power of parties. Article V's other option for constitutional amendment proposal in Congress was designed specifically to avoid purely partisan proposals being sent to the states by requiring two-thirds vote in both houses. Yet if the current movement can succeed with principally simple party-line majority votes in Congress, and be controlled by hyperpartisan legislatures similarly voting on a simple-majority basis, the Framers' worst fears of the dangers of hyperpartisanship would be realized.

Despite the news media's obsession with federal politics, Congress, and the White House, the most harmful and long-lasting danger posed by the growing factionalist trend over the last four decades is not necessarily confined to Washington. An equally problematic and potentially much more consequential story is unfolding in plain sight across the land—in statehouses.

The cause is both ideological and procedural. State legislators today often identify more with their national party than with their fellow colleagues, a trend that has caused a troubling nationalization of local politics. This is precisely the phenomenon the Founders feared, the total control of partisan factions over the entire architecture of American government. Far from "break[ing] and control[ing] the violence of faction," as Madison put it in *The Federalist*, the infection of state-level politics by the machinery (and—no doubt—money) of national parties has created a federal system rife with factions' ill effects.

But this ideological turn in statehouses is about more than an insidious nationalization of our politics. Procedural problems have also spurred the change. Aggressive, conservative-led gerrymandering operations have built barricades around state legislatures, some of the nation's most important institutions, insulating them from popular control.

Such concerns regarding representation in state legislatures are not new phenomena. Prior to the Supreme Court's malapportionment decisions in the 1960s, discussed in Chapter 5, many state legislature districts were skewed—often toward rural areas, at the expense of urban voters (many of whom were people of color). Nor is the act of politicians picking their voters, and not the other way around, a one-sided partisan phenomenon. Democrats engage in the same kind of behavior.

But in recent years, such gerrymandering has grown more targeted, sophisticated, and consequential for our politics. In fewer states is this new bent toward factionalist, win-at-all-costs state politics more evident than in the two purple states on the drive from Michigan's Upper Peninsula to Nebraska.

In Wisconsin, for example, radically gerrymandered state legislative maps have allowed conservative Republicans to keep control of the legislature even when Democrats win statewide elections.[7] In 2020, Democratic candidates for the state senate received 47 percent of the total votes cast but only won 38 percent of the seats. In 2018, the disparity was even more stark: Democrats won *all* statewide races and 53 percent of votes cast for the state assembly but only garnered 36 percent of the seats.[8] As Anthony Chergosky, a political scientist at the University of Wisconsin–La Crosse, remarked, "It's plain as day that this was not just a gerrymandered map, but a very effective one."[9] The *Guardian* put it more bluntly, remarking that Wisconsin is "the state where democracy went to die."[10]

Wisconsin's gerrymander was part of a nationwide program for legislative capture, complete with a telling name—REDMAP.[11] In 2009, Republicans controlled only fourteen of the fifty state legislatures (meaning they controlled both houses). Democrats controlled twenty-seven. Midterm election losses during President Obama's first term dealt a pivotal blow, ushering in a wave of firebrand Republicans to increase control to twenty-five statehouses. This win had consequential, long-lasting effects as state legislatures elected in those midterms were able to draw legislative maps following the decennial census.

Aided by high-tech capabilities, legislatures engineered drastically skewed maps with one goal—winning.[12] "When I started doing this in the mid-70s, we were using handheld calculators, paper maps, pencils, and really big erasers," Republican districting operative John Ryder remarked in 2011. "It was pretty primitive."[13] But now it is the work of highly paid consultants with expensive equipment, flown into state capitals for marathon map-making sessions.

By 2018, Republicans controlled thirty-three statehouses. In 2021, Republicans controlled thirty-one, with chambers narrowly split in two states formerly controlled by Republicans—Alaska and Minnesota. We shall see how the Democrats fare in the first midterm elections under President Biden and if the high-water mark of thirty-three statehouses under one-party rule is once again achieved.[14] Nevertheless, the number of legislatures under one-party rule is venturing closer and closer to the thirty-four-state threshold for a successful convention call.

The sad fact about gerrymandering is that it is a self-perpetuating problem. Now that the Supreme Court has held that regulating gerrymandering is beyond its mandate, once a party wins the game, they get to write the rules, possibly forever.[15] The impact on our democracy is staggering. As districts become safer for a certain party, successful candidates need only worry about the *primary* elections, not the general. This breeds a turn toward extremes, as candidates must appeal not to the median voter but to a smaller, more extreme base. Perhaps as Madison, Washington, and Adams foresaw, over time, faction begets even starker factional division—a process that will continue until the country reaches some kind of breaking point.

This radical transformation of state politics makes plain the troubling struggle between popular and partisan control of the machinery of constitutional change. Even when the People speak authoritatively on an issue, state legislatures often try to put their finger on the scales to alter the outcome—finagling districts, changing rules, and even subverting the manifest democratic will.

Again, take Wisconsin for example. As we write in 2021, the legislature is actively considering dismantling the state's bipartisan elections commission to centralize authority in the legislature after Donald Trump narrowly lost the state. Lawmakers have also supported pursuing felony charges against the election commission's members.[16] These election commissioners' supposed crime? Issuing guidance to local elections officials regarding voting during a global pandemic, guidance that went unchallenged until *after* the November 2020 election and President Biden's win.[17] The commissioners committed no error; legislative leaders simply did not like who their constituents had elected. The partisan rancor runs so deep that the state senate refused to vote to affirm Biden's victory.[18] Some legislators were still trying to decertify the state's electoral vote count almost a year after the new president took office.[19]

Likewise in Michigan, Republican legislators spurred by Donald Trump's anger at losing the state are pursuing legislation to overhaul the state's election code. Among the more bizarre provisions is a ban on local elections officials using community space like churches and public libraries as polling places.[20] The law—which the legislature is passing over a gubernatorial veto—would require cash-strapped governments to pay for precinct rentals even when civic organizations are willing to provide them for free. The goal is clear: limiting the number of precincts will create long lines and discourage voters, especially in urban areas.[21]

This recent trend toward a scorched-earth destruction of democracy's core mechanisms for factional gain is but a symptom of a greater ill that has taken hold in our body politic. Politics, for many, has become a game, one that must be won simply for the sake of winning, regardless of the damage the game does to our shared democratic community. To pursue what Washington called "domination of one faction over another, sharpened by the spirit of revenge," seeking advantage even when it hurts our institutions and shared values, is an unqualified good for many today. Winning is all that matters. This is why our rhetoric has become so bitter, the reasoned search for truth disregarded, bipartisan compromise nearly nonexistent, and dislike between those of different views so pronounced. Some who like playing the game just do not care.

The ill effects of this trend in our politics on the national and state levels are well documented. But the prospect of a constitutional convention animated by such bitter factionalism would pose new troubles for our Constitution and political life.

THE DANGER OF A FACTIONAL CONVENTION

Perhaps unsurprisingly, the vast majority of the Article V applications focused on conservative topics adopted over the last decade have passed on strict party-line votes, albeit with a few aisle-crossers here and there. Yet data on Article V application votes over the last decade indicate that the most bipartisan thing about the current convention movement is *opposition* to the convening. In almost every state, a sizable number of Republicans have voted against the measure, often following the John Birch Society's sound advice regarding runaway concerns. In Utah, for example, almost 30 percent of the Republican house and senate caucuses voted against the application. It still passed.[22] In Montana, as discussed in the prologue, convention activists undertook an aggressive campaign to harass a Republican who cast the decisive vote against the proposal, actions that caused that legislator to consider resigning.

The aggressive, one-sided nature of the contemporary convention movement is disconcerting, rendering it different in kind. The former convention movements of the Progressive Era, the Dirksen era, and the balanced budget amendment effort of the 1980s were all broad in their appeal. Yet today, the core thrust of amendment fervor is defined by its appeal to party and faction. The movement operates through partisan networks, is funded by partisan megadonors, receives almost exclusively partisan support in legislatures, and cultivates a popular base using the aggressive, factious political rhetoric common among the modern hard right. And as proponents gleefully proclaim, empowering faction is the supposed great gift of Article V: it is possible that only a bare minimum of states would be needed to control a convention were it to be called. Far from mediating difference and channeling debate to the higher plane of constitutional lawmaking, a convention at this time would allow the further entrenchment of factionalist elements at the convening.

The rise of hyperpartisanship in the Article V realm raises a question that goes beyond the electoral fights of the present era to the core of our national life. Might the Constitution itself, through Article V, be the next field on which the Founders' fear of the divisive effects of factionalism comes to fruition? Might our present factious moment, and the terrible ills it has brought to our politics and society, become hardwired in our fundamental law through a slow-burn effort to radically transform our founding document?

The constitutional amendment mechanism was designed to be challenging so as to correct against the factious ills of electoral politics. The Framers, for example, required amendments proposed in Congress to achieve a two-thirds vote before being referred to the states. Yet as recent efforts show, the new organization of statehouses along nationalized partisan lines and the orchestration of policy through well-funded partisan networks have created a political environment in which the convention route could pose *fewer* checks against factionalism and simple majoritarian rule. This reality is true, in part, due to the array of unanswered questions regarding convention procedure.

Some argue that a convention could propose amendments on a simple majority vote, meaning only twenty-six state delegations would be needed to push proposed amendments to the states. This is—like most Article V legal questions—a contested proposition. But if that were the case, a constitutional convention would be more malapportioned than even the Electoral College, giving those who represent a small minority of the population the power to shape the contours of our constitutional debates.

The possibility also looms that the same twenty-six-state threshold could be used to throw out subject limitations altogether, vastly expanding a convention's mandate. The prevailing conservative movement is already pushing us toward that dangerous territory. It is quite possible that this is the true plan: solicit state applications with a supposed limited agenda and change course later—a bait-and-switch agenda.

Even if some states vehemently oppose such a move, trying to invoke their (likely toothless) delegate-control laws or perhaps even engineering a boycott and recalling delegates, a convention could continue its work. All that is required is a quorum. This is a clear teaching of the 1787 Convention—many delegates came and went throughout the convening, and Rhode Island never even showed up! As James Madison remarked in his Notes, we do not know the requisite quorum (as he put it, "difficulties might arise as to the form [and] the quorum").[23] But at the very least, the quorum might be said to be twenty-six.

Such a scenario poses no problem, some think, because the ultimate three-quarters ratification threshold remains a bulwark against radical proposals. While the threshold does indeed pose a high bar for final approval, as discussed in previous chapters, one should not discount the profound power that amendment *proposal* alone can have on our law and politics. As with the Equal Rights Amendment, which many argue spurred change in judicial doctrine, proposed amendments can have a very real impact on our politics and law even if they are never ratified.[24] And even if proposed amendments have an opaque, informal impact on our law and politics, as public attention moves on, it is possible that amendments proposed today could find new political salience far into the future. This is the lesson of the Twenty-Seventh Amendment (proposed in 1791, ratified in 1992), one that should loom large in the public's consideration of the Article V convention mechanism. What looks crazy today could seem reasonable to some tomorrow.

The problem with these questions is that there is no clear way to reach a resolution. As discussed in Chapter 6, the courts will likely shy away, invoking the political question doctrine and relevant precedent to avoid this hornet's nest. And even if the courts were to wade into the fray, from what body of law would they weigh litigants' claims? There is no body of law, and the records of the 1787 Convention provide little insight.

How then would these many uncertainties be resolved? Commentators can engage in respectable academic debate about these questions, and the previous chapters began to lay out our own arguments regarding some of the finer details. But as seems to be the rule for our current political epoch, raw partisan power will likely settle the matter. And in this simple truth lies the deepest trouble of Article V.

For better or worse, we live in a legalistic, litigious society. Regardless of the moral fortitude of a movement or the strength of its advocacy, success or failure almost always turns on the rules. Without clear procedures, determined by disinterested parties *before* a convention, the predictable result will be legal chaos. A small, factionalist minority could claim control, and few legal rules could discount their power grab. The possibility is profoundly troubling. A convention deemed illegitimate by some states would usher in a particularly dangerous and unprecedented constitutional crisis.

* * *

WHETHER TO HOLD A TWENTY-FIRST-CENTURY constitutional convention is not and should not be a partisan proposition. Rather, concerned citizens must consider the facts, weighing with cool heads the potential risk of such a convening.

The most important question is this: Can we trust the process? In the absence of clear rules guiding debate and controlling the nefarious influence of partisanship and special interests, can we trust the political class to respect the gravitas of a constitutional convention? Would a convention held today without such procedures in place spark the kind of respectful, deliberative debate regarding fundamental law to which we should aspire?

Law, history, and common sense make clear that the answer is no. Today's convention activists have cast their lot with the whims of faction, embracing and fomenting partisan division rather than attempting to forge broad-based support. And they have tossed aside most legal norms regarding Article V, creating fictitious new rules and theories to meet their ends. To believe that the factionalism and legal subterfuge would subside once a convention is called is wishful thinking. It would be emboldened.

These realities should spark both concern and action. But we cannot allow the need to stop a convention movement today to foreclose permanently the possibility of formal constitutional change. Rather than merely a political threat to be quashed, the contemporary convention movement lays bare a deeper problem in our democracy—the disheartening failure of our politics to adequately address the high questions of constitutional change. We need a new path forward.

Part IV

A WAY FORWARD

8

THE CONSTITUTION IN JEOPARDY

Article V in the Twenty-First Century

THE EVENTS OF THE LAST decade have laid bare fissures in American public life. For some, the troubling rise of hyperpartisan politics and the potential that a once-august American political party is eschewing long-held values for the ideologies of reactionary, strongman politics raises legitimate concerns about the future.[1] Many worry that our institutions are not strong enough and that our shared beliefs—long the bedrock of communities and a bulwark against extremism—are fading. The country is changing, and it is difficult to tell just where it is headed.

Such troubling phenomena are not limited to traditional electoral politics. So too have new efforts, defined and animated by factious desires, set their sights on our fundamental law. A radical right-wing movement is working with great speed to move the levers of constitutional amendment and is finding remarkable success in statehouses. These activists are readily aware that Article V's procedures are opaque and have war-gamed how to take advantage of the uncertainties for their gain.

That these actors are pursuing formal constitutional change through an established mechanism cannot be faulted. The overall effort is legitimate. But the dangers Article V's array of unanswered questions pose to our constitutional law and national life are real. And contemporary convention activists' bewildering attempts to resolve these uncertainties through

The Supreme Court under construction. (1934)

subterfuge and new legal theories, made to order every few months as needs change, make plain that the current movement must be stopped and its legal errors refuted. Despite the myriad false claims of these groups, there are not yet adequate guardrails on this constitutional road to protect our fundamental law from extreme proposals brought forth amid a historic moment of political tumult. The Constitution is in jeopardy, and swift action must be taken to protect it.

But Americans cannot allow attempts to block a convention today to place the Constitution into another troubling jeopardy: the slow death of stagnation and ossification. Constitutions must change through time to meet new needs; otherwise, they grow brittle and ineffective. While the stabilizing force of our Constitution is one of its many gifts, it is not and cannot be treated as immutable holy writ.

The power of law ultimately rests in citizens' belief that it has legitimacy, that it has a right to govern. If the Constitution does not or *cannot* change when extraordinary need arises, some might begin to consider the document merely a piece of paper—an irrelevant historical artifact that can be ignored. Such a turn of events would sound the death knell for the American experiment in self-government.

As those Americans in Roxbury, Massachusetts, remarked in 1778, such constitutional stability cannot be assumed. Only through fair, open, legitimate, and democratic processes that allow the People to "recur to first principles in a Regular Way" can a community avoid "hazarding a Revolution in the Government."[2] We must, as the Essex town delegates argued the same year, be able to "rectify the errors that will creep in through lapse of time, or alteration of situation."[3] Without a workable amendment mechanism that allows the People to craft changes to constitutional law through settled procedure and a deliberative, democratic process, we venture further into a dangerous legal world foreign to the ethos of the Founding and of the American way. We either remain content with a dysfunctional status quo or we embolden new and potentially troubling ways to address perceived errors—some legal and, as we saw on January 6, some violent. As the Lexington town delegates remarked in 1778, without a reasonable method for bloodless revolution, that "happy means, under providence, of preventing popular commotions, mobs, bloodshed and civil war," other nefarious elements might begin to exert influence on public life.[4]

The country thus faces two interwoven jeopardies. First, that a hard-right faction will contort Article V to open its Pandora's box, recklessly steering the country into the unknown in search of their far-right dream. And second, that if reasonable citizens are successful in averting this danger, the country will—as it did in 1913, 1967, and 1987—simply move on, accepting that Article V has no real power. Many might congratulate themselves for averting catastrophe; a few law review articles likely will be written, as many were during the last flourishing of Article V scholarship in the 1960s and 1980s; and perhaps an academic symposium or two will be held. But for most, the news will leave the front page, and the country will quickly forget that trouble ever loomed. New election cycles and new political crises will consume the popular attention. And the conventional wisdom that Article V is dead will be confirmed with newfound certainty.

THE CONSERVATORSHIP CONSTITUTION

This second jeopardy—the People's acceptance that Article V has no real power—is as dangerous as the first. Allowing the Constitution to continue

without a workable means for change would reinforce the accepted narrative that formal amendment is functionally irrelevant, a way of thinking
that has warped citizens' understanding of the American constitutional
system and the very essence of our shared democratic life.

Many today intuitively believe that the Constitution can only survive
frozen in a strange vegetative state, kept alive under the close palliative
care of judges and the legal establishment. Constitutional law, they
believe, is the domain of judges, lawyers, and academics, not the People.
And because Article V seems to be unworkable, or just too challenging,
many accept this state of affairs as right and proper.

Under this now-dominant view, ours can be viewed as a conservatorship
Constitution. Fundamental law is held and cared for by guardian-
judges for the People's benefit but without their direct engagement. The
Constitution must adapt to modern events; otherwise, over time it will
fail. And because Article V is dead, as many believe, the only method for
such change is through the conservatorship: battles over judicial nominations and constitutional interpretation.

Today the conventional wisdom that Article V is dead has metasta-
sized beyond the halls of universities, courts, Congress, think tanks, and
law firms into the public psyche—with troubling effect. Rather than discussing *formal* constitutional change as a first-order inquiry, mainstream
public debate regarding the Constitution has devolved into a fixation on
an important and related yet second-order inquiry: what one might call
the interpretation debates. Public and academic discussion of the Constitution and its future is now mainly focused on the work of conservatorship,
on the interpretative theories that help guide judges in deciding discrete
cases. Living constitutionalism and its sister theories, which hold that
judges should interpret the Constitution considering present needs in
light of its text, structure, and tradition, are pitted against the various
strands of originalist theory, which claim to argue that the Constitution
should be interpreted as it was understood either by its drafters or by the
long-ago public that accepted it.

Debates regarding constitutional interpretation are important, good,
and necessary. The role of the judiciary in the American constitutional system requires them. Even if the use of amendment is frequent and powerful,
even if the Supreme Court is reformed to correct for what many see as
structural failure, judges will still be called on to apply constitutional

meaning to cases and controversies that come before them. This requires using tools of judicial craft—processes, interpretive canons, and habits of mind—seen as legitimate by the public. Many of the various constitutional interpretive theories provide compelling arguments and raise important points regarding judicial legitimacy, the meaning of legal text, and the Constitution's enduring role in public life. Without such intellectual debate, the courts and Constitution suffer.

Yet it is important to ponder a deeper reality that the contemporary fixation on the interpretive debates lays bare, an unsettling truth that should inform one's consideration of Article V. The interpretive debates, which used to be confined to academic symposia and law review articles, have seeped onto the front pages of our newspapers of record. Dueling interpretive theories are openly debated on the floors of Congress, on news shows, and on leading opinion pages. Many nonlawyers, who previously might have had little engagement with the finer details of constitutional jurisprudence and adjudication, are keenly aware of the prevailing debates among legal scholars, lawyers, and judges regarding how and why judges interpret the Constitution's text. Many know the names of theories and the jurists who espouse them and can paint with a broad brush the theories' core tenets. Authors have even written picture books to teach children about certain interpretive theories.[5]

Increased public awareness and understanding of the workings of the judicial branch is a good thing. The common nonlawyer citizen should know and understand how and why judges decide the cases that come before them. Such is the essence of a judiciary that acts not with the capricious whims of authority and office but with the legitimate force of law, reason, and justice.

But what does this change in popular focus say about the state of the Constitution and constitutional law? Over the last five decades, constitutional change in the public's eye has seemingly become synonymous not with constitutional amendment but with the machinations of the Supreme Court: nomination fights, partisan gamesmanship, and the baroque dance of interpretation-turned-politics. The shift is subtle and has taken hold over time. But it is noticeable and troubling. Where the People, as the absolute sovereign and source of all power, *should* be debating the Constitution's meaning and purpose as a first-order inquiry, public discussion has devolved into debates about judicial craft, judicial selection, and other minutiae of the judiciary's functioning. The everyday work of the Supreme Court—its decisions, its justices, even its "shadow docket" (the wonkiest of wonky topics)—is front-page news.[6] The country has become obsessed with the Court in a way that is both strange and unhealthy for a functioning constitutional democracy.

Why do so many assume the courts maintain a monopoly on constitutional meaning? Why is it that the public has become so fixated on the second-order interpretive questions? And perhaps most troubling of all, why is it that constitutional politics—that highest form of discourse to which a self-governing democracy can call itself—has all but accepted the People's abdication of their inherent constitutional authority?

Many would argue that the Court's hold on constitutional meaning has been a near monopoly for more than a few decades. Some would point to the Court's 1803 decision in *Marbury v. Madison* and the establishment of a theory of judicial review as the true genesis point. Others might argue that the linkage has been functionally true since the Sixteenth Amendment, the last time the People overturned a decision of the Court (there, regarding the federal income tax).[7] Some others still might point to the compromises of the New Deal and the "switch in time that saved nine," which engineered a tenuous truce between the judiciary and the executive, thus cementing a new constitutional order.[8]

The existence of this supposed monopoly has long been troubled. *Marbury* itself was controversial. Thomas Jefferson famously remarked that "the opinion which gives to the judges the right to decide what laws are constitutional, and what not, not only for themselves in their own sphere of action, but for the legislature and executive also in their spheres, would make the judiciary a despotic branch."[9] As detailed in Chapter 5, the contemporary conservative movement to call a constitutional convention, which began in the 1960s, was inspired by frustration with the Supreme Court's apportionment and civil rights decisions. Other notable examples abound.

The intention here is not to debate high constitutional theory but rather to raise a simple observation. The *public* perception of constitutional change has become surprisingly narrow, myopically focused on procedural machinations far removed from the first-order questions. Within the last half decade, after multiple tumultuous and troubling Supreme Court nominations and sad episodes of partisan gamesmanship over judicial vacancies, public discontent has reached a new height. The present moment is defined by frustration not with a few landmark cases but rather with our system of making constitutional meaning. Where the Constitution and the courts that interpret it used to be seen by many as a relatively neutral arbiter of politics, maybe with a few missteps here and there, today the veneer of impartiality appears to be falling away.[10] For many, the very essence of *fundamental* law seems to be changing as electoral and legislative politics become more hopelessly intertwined with the work of constitutional law.

In few places is this clearer than in the interpretive battles themselves. In the beginning, originalism and other competing theories primarily aimed to add legitimacy to judicial review and to articulate a cohesive structure allowing judges to interpret and advance constitutional meaning within the People's grant of authority. In the face of an unused and arguably *unusable* Article V, the goal of the theory debates was to articulate a manner of thinking about the Constitution that had inherent legitimacy. Heated ideological disagreements arose, but the aim was noble, and many on all sides of the issue engaged with goodwill. In this first manifestation, theory was theory. The debates were a discussion of the inherent problems Article V's disuse and possible demise had wrought on the constitutional system and an earnest attempt to find a workable way forward. One might think of this period as the conventional wisdom's salad days.

Over time, however, the debates left the relatively reasoned and collegial realm of the academy and entered the rough-and-tumble world of politics. With the backing of wealthy anti-regulation interests, private advocacy organizations transformed the academic debate about theory into a political project. The goal was to reclaim the courts and to remake them as a new bastion of entrenched power. The endeavor was outcome focused, informed by base impulses of partisan politics, and aimed at ensuring the courts would provide certain results.

This turn has crafted a peculiar new reality. Constitutional interpretation has taken on an intense partisan bent, with Republicans and conservatives reflexively adopting and supporting one theory and Democrats and liberals supporting others. For many, the idea of a Democratic originalist or a Republican living constitutionalist seems oxymoronic, a troubling indictment of the state of the country's politics and judicial debates. So prevalent is this partisan approach to interpretive theory that a reasonable observer might question whether the country cares much about *theory* at all anymore.

They might wonder whether the intellectual approach, consideration of legal text, or the balancing of often-counterpoised values such as consistency, predictability, impartiality, justice, and legitimacy really matter. The whole game, the reasonable observer might ascertain, is about outcomes.

If one opposes abortion, many citizens believe, then one must espouse a particular intellectual theory not necessarily because that theory is right as a jurisprudential matter but because it will bring about the "right" political result. If one supports the rights of racial, sexual, and other "discrete and insular minorities," others believe, then one must support a different theory.[11] No gray area, no nuance, no legal complexity is allowed. The menu of assumed theory-policy matchups is long. But the very notion of such correlation betrays what many citizens see as a deeper truth: theory has become proxy for policy, constitutional interpretation a forum for politics.

In recent years, the overtly policy-focused turn in our public debates regarding constitutional theory has taken center stage. The response to Justice Neil Gorsuch's majority opinion in *Bostock v. Clayton County* perhaps best exemplifies the turn.[12] In *Bostock*, the Court employed strict textualist theory to hold that the Civil Rights Act of 1964's prohibition of employment discrimination "because of . . . sex" protected lesbian, gay, bisexual, and transgender people from similar discrimination. Following the opinion, one Republican senator, himself a highly pedigreed lawyer and member of the Senate Judiciary Committee, declared on the Senate floor that *Bostock* marked "the end of the conservative legal movement." Why? Because the supposedly "pro-Constitution religious liberty judges" the Republican Party supported were not following through on their alleged mandate—to import by judicial fiat conservative sexual mores into the country's statutory law.[13]

The "conservative legal movement" was dead not because the legal theories it long advanced had proved ill formed as intellectual or jurisprudential matters. Some of the supposedly conservative theories have become dominant. As Justice Elena Kagan famously remarked, "We're all textualists now."[14] The death knell for the conservative legal movement was the failure of judges employing a supposedly neutral theory to reach the "right" political conclusion. Never mind that *Bostock* involved a *statutory* issue relating to a congressional act, not a constitutional question implicating the First Amendment's religion clauses—a crucial legal distinction. The interpretive games, the senator seemed to imply, were not delivering.

Other commentators on the reactionary far right have made even more strident and dangerous advances into outcome-focused theory retooling, ones that have no basis in the Constitution's text or history, or in our national tradition. In a widely discussed series of articles, noted Harvard constitutional scholar Adrian Vermeule argues originalism "has met the political and rhetorical needs of legal conservatives" and "has outlived its utility." Judges should thus eschew the pretense of interpreting constitutional text, he argues. Such a focus is "an obstacle to the development of a robust, substantively conservative approach to constitutional law and interpretation." In its stead, he argues, judges should read into the Constitution's "majestic generalities and ambiguities" a Christian understanding of the "common good."[15] Among the supposed dictates of such a "common good" is the rejection of the thoroughly American understanding of personal autonomy and freedom. Writing in the *Atlantic*, Vermeule argued "that each individual may 'define one's own concept of existence, of meaning, of the universe, and of the mystery of human life' should be not only rejected but stamped as abominable, beyond the realm of the acceptable forever after." That proposition that his theory seeks to destroy, perhaps unsurprisingly, is a quote from the Supreme Court's 1992 decision in *Planned Parenthood v. Casey*, which upheld *Roe*'s right to abortion.[16]

Whatever else Vermeule's understanding of a binding, judicially enforceable "common good" contains is open to debate. Giving some clues, the phrase "better conception of liberty" in his article was hyperlinked to a digital copy of Pope Leo XIII's 1888 encyclical *Libertas*, "On the Nature of Human Liberty."[17] Devotees of the theory have also shared some insights into how it might function. Likewise criticizing *Bostock*'s finding that gay people are protected by antidiscrimination laws, other supporters of "common-good constitutionalism" remarked that the opinion proved a new tack is required. Again disregarding the essential distinction between constitutional and statutory interpretation, these proponents argued that the decision "evinces the folly of a morally neutered, overtly positivist approach to interpreting legal texts."[18] The courts, it would seem, should get into the business of deciding cases not through the nuanced consideration of legal text and meaning but with the full-bore imposition of a conservative moral system using the machinery of the state—a proposition completely foreign to our American understanding of liberty.

How Vermeule's theory finds sanction in the People's grant of authority to their government remains unclear. Constitutional text, history, and accepted tradition do not support it. Many conservatives, including leading scholars and jurists, have raised similar concerns.[19] But perhaps such an inquiry is beside the point. In the second-order world of the interpretive debates, common-good constitutionalism can prove to be as legitimate as any other theory if enough judges, legal elites, and academics buy into the project. Such is the trouble of the conservatorship Constitution and the country's constitutional debates when the conventional wisdom that Article V is dead has reached its ascendance, when fundamental law becomes more and more removed from the People, and when the work of changing constitutional meaning is vested solely in a ruling elite insulated from the popular will.

In the realm of judicial institutions, the popular perception that ideology and party are proxy for outcomes becomes dangerous. Judicial interpretive theory should espouse neutral values, ones that are legitimate, based in the People's authority, and unbiased toward the case and litigants to which they are applied. Even if the perceived truth that all judging is political is not born out in actual practice all the time, which it certainly is not, the public *perception* of a partisan, outcome-driven hold on the judicial process is cause for alarm.

Article V's onerous and opaque procedures did not create the need for interpretive theory, nor did the procedures wholly fashion ours into a conservatorship Constitution. The nature of judicial review and its legal foundations are more complex, forming an important and necessary component of our constitutional system.[20] There are essential areas in which judicial review plays a crucial role in ensuring the Constitution's enduring values are made real in a democratic society. As the late constitutional scholar John Hart Ely argued in his magnum opus *Democracy and Distrust*, one of the judiciary's essential duties is to ensure that the democratic principles of participation and representation remain alive in the face of countervailing, majoritarian instincts. Such interbranch checks are important.[21]

Yet the legal establishment's insistence, and popular acceptance, that Article V is unusable has created a system rife with bad incentives. Relying on the conservatorship to do the work of constitutional upkeep runs the risk of turning fundamental law into a charade of intellectualized legal philosophizing that allows outcomes-based interpretive approaches to contravene the People's grant of authority. While most judges ignore the impulse, the conservatorship provides ready opportunity for some to read into the Constitution theories wholly distinct and unmoored from any semblance of constitutional authority.

Such is the ultimate trouble with the conventional wisdom about Article V. As the People abdicate their amendment responsibilities, the courts and the president will fill the void out of necessity. Yet however good-willed the initial impulse might be, emboldened by a logic that gives normative weight to historical practice, this shift of authority over constitutional meaning can become entrenched in a few institutions far from the People.

If the People accept this shift, over time they might come to believe the amendment provision need not, or even should not, have any power. They begin to believe its disuse is not a failing but is rather a bonus—maybe even good, correct, and proper. Ours *is* a conservatorship Constitution, and the People are content with the results, however imperfect they might be. This turn toward embracing the conservatorship—the natural result of the conventional wisdom—is profoundly dangerous.

*   *   *

THE CONSTITUTION'S TWO INTERWOVEN JEOPARDIES—the dangers posed by contemporary attempts to awaken Article V's convention mechanism, and the possibility that the People will accept that the provision need not or should not have any real power—are of foundational significance. While each threatens to inflict different kinds of harm on our fundamental law, the two jeopardies share a common source: an amendment mechanism not fit to meet the needs of the twenty-first century.

Article V provides inadequate guardrails to foster and guide the dialogue of constitutional change and places ultimate constitutional authority in the hands of institutions too far removed from the popular will. While constitutional amendment should be rare and difficult, requiring sufficiently broad support to render it a solemn act of the sovereign People, the current mechanism has missed the mark. And into the void has rushed a slew of troubling phenomena.

But rather than bemoaning the state of Article V, throwing up our hands, and declaring defeat, the time has come to begin a serious national conversation regarding the future of the Constitution in American public life. We must reclaim the Founding generation's belief in bloodless revolution, reforming Article V to provide an amendment procedure fit for a modern, democratic society. We must fashion a new kind of constitutional politics.

9

REVOLUTION, REVISITED

Toward a New Constitutional Politics

"It is for the peace and good of mankind, that a solemn opportunity [for constitutional change] every nineteen or twenty years, should be provided by the constitution; so that it may be handed on, with periodical repairs, from generation to generation, to the end of time, if anything human can so long endure."

—Thomas Jefferson to Samuel Kercheval (July 12, 1816)[1]

IN MAY 2021, Chileans cast ballots in a history-making poll, electing 155 delegates to sit in a convention tasked with redrafting the country's forty-year-old constitution. Among those chosen were midwives, a mechanic, teachers, and students.[2] By law, half were women, and 11 percent represented indigenous communities.[3] "The convention is a much better reflection of Chile than Congress," Juna Pablo Luna, a political scientist at the Catholic University of Chile, remarked.[4] The election had begun a truly national, representative process of constitutional reimagination, what President Sebastián Piñera called "the beginning of a path that we must all walk together."[5]

Chile's 1980 constitution, approved under the watchful eye of dictator Augusto Pinochet, commenced a stunted transition to democracy. In a resulting 1988 plebiscite, 56 percent of Chileans voted to boot Pinochet from power—a clear vindication for the famed "No!" campaign.[6] Yet the 1980 constitution's relationship with the bloody dictatorship and its

The Constitution is "a layman's document, not a lawyer's contract," President Franklin Roosevelt declared from the foot of the Washington Monument, commemorating Constitution Day on September 17, 1937.

hardwiring of unpopular Pinochet-era policies continue to cast a long shadow on Chilean society. In 2019, growing disillusionment with party politics, corruption, and economic disparity led to civil unrest, leaving at least thirty dead.[7] The following year, Chileans overwhelmingly approved the government's plan to start the constitutional process anew, opting in two separate ballot questions both to draft a new constitution and to do so in a convention with elected citizens rather than in a mixed assembly, which would have included members of parliament.[8] "The country is like a pressure cooker that's exploded," one Chilean remarked after casting her vote. "This is our chance to make things right."[9]

While only 44 percent of voters turned out for the delegate election in 2021, the results caught worldwide attention due, in part, to their oddity. The majority of the new delegates were independents, with Chile's main political parties faring poorly. "People wouldn't talk to us about our campaign until we said we were independents," Cristina Dorador, a biologist elected as an independent from the Antofagasta mining region, remarked.[10] The stark, anti-establishment fervor that animated the initial plan for constitutional reframing had created a new uncertainty in the convention's drafting process. As the convention takes up important social issues like pensions, education, and water rights (currently privately held, in perpetuity), how such a new experiment will fare in an independent-delegate-led constitutional drafting remains an open question. The Chilean convention raises worries on both ends of the political spectrum: either that the convention will be wildly successful, crafting a troubling, radical future for the country, or that it will be a total failure.

The possibility that the convention may be *too* successful might, in and of itself, doom the whole project. Some fear that the convention will go down the path of other citizen-led constitutional conventions that have crafted laundry lists of new rights with no plan to make them real.[11] The Ecuadorian constitution's 494 articles, drafted by a constituent assembly in 2008, contains the most enumerated constitutional rights in the world: ninety-nine.[12] Among them are rights to "a safe and healthy habitat" and "a decent life," as well as "to have goods and services of the highest quality."[13] Bolivia's (2009) and Serbia's (2006) constitutions rank second, with eighty-eight enumerated rights each.[14]

Rather than an actionable, legally enforceable fundamental law, many of these rights become merely aspirational—a statement of what should be rather than what *must* be. Legal text by itself cannot change reality. The people must make legal guarantees real through a robust constitutional culture, fair courts empowered to adjudicate and vindicate rights, and well-managed government programs that provide a necessary structure for rights to flourish.[15] Many fear that Chile might go down the same path, crafting a plethora of new rights the government will ignore.[16]

Others fear a fizzle, that because the convention will be governed by unaligned independents, it will be unable to reach sufficient consensus. Impasse would make the whole process worthless, emboldening the Pinochet-era system most citizens see as broken.[17] Failed reform now would chill future attempts, many worry.[18]

Neither a rights frenzy nor outright failure is desirable. And like the United States' 1787 Convention in Philadelphia, the Chilean gathering will be closed-door, so it is possible the public will not know precisely how the convening proceeds. Yet in this recent example of constitutional fervor abroad, one can catch a glimpse of what truly democratic constitutional change can look like.

Like those new Americans in the 1770s and 1780s, democratic communities *can* debate constitutional change in newspapers, in public meetings, at the ballot box, and in citizen assemblies. The People *can* engage in the work of constitution crafting of the highest order. And with the right procedures to guide debate, guard against misstep, and cool passions, such a flourishing of popular constitutional authority *can* embolden and enliven a shared national life.

BLOODLESS REVOLUTION, TWO CENTURIES ON

We have yet to achieve the Founding generation's aspiration of a new constitutional system in which fundamental law provides both a means for steadfast order and a forum for peaceful, periodic reform. There have been moments of great triumph, such as the amendments of Reconstruction and the Progressive Era, among others. While contemporary convention movements make clear that Article V is a potent force, one that must be critically engaged with a sober mind, the paucity of amendments remains a problematic element of our constitutional system. And the recurring necessity to stifle amendment movements out of legitimate concerns regarding procedure and the power of factional interests, as must be done in the present moment, underscores the trouble the amendment mechanism has caused. Article V is not wholly defunct, but it has missed the mark.[19]

That the Framers made missteps in drafting Article V—the first attempt in world history to craft a national amendment mechanism not premised on unanimity—is not surprising.[20] However inspired and well studied one might like to consider them to have been, those present at the 1787 Convention were not clairvoyant. The Framers, understandably, may have not foreseen the trouble the provision would create. Madison's Notes recount little debate regarding Article V, and *none* regarding the convention route's technical mechanics. Madison's single unrebutted argument that the provision was flawed due to its lack of procedure, a comment potentially added to the Notes long after the convention adjourned, is itself a telling admission.[21] Amid the new flurry of constitutional drafting, the Framers likely assumed that Article V would function well, perhaps like the new constitutional amendment mechanisms in the states. Yet their procedure was simultaneously too strict and too undefined.

Or as detailed in Chapter 2, perhaps other factors, such as Hamilton's desire to protect the federal government from encroachment, contributed to the formation of a purposefully opaque amendment procedure. If bloodless revolution was to be the new norm, and the procedure for such revolution was overly difficult, the new constitutional system could remain undefiled. Many anti-federalists argued as much even prior to ratification. Today, exacerbated by the troubling rise of nationalized politics over the last fifty years in which citizens have become less wedded to state or geographic region than they are to partisan faction, it is no wonder the mechanism has not functioned well.

Whatever the case may be, over two centuries of lived experience, accentuated by recent troubling attempts to capitalize on procedural uncertainties for factional gain, make plain that reform is needed. Article V provides underdetermined procedures and too few guardrails to be appropriately workable, and it vests authority in institutions too far removed from the popular will to claim the legitimacy a modern, twenty-first-century democracy should require for constitutional reform.

The Framers knew that humans are fallible but capable of slow improvement, of learning from missteps and starting anew.[22] As George Washington remarked, such an understanding of both fallibility and improvement is baked into our founding document: "The warmest friends and the best supporters the Constitution has do not contend that it is free from imperfections; but they found them unavoidable and are sensible if evil is likely to arise there from, the remedy must come hereafter." Compromise at the Convention was necessary, Washington made clear, and some mistakes would have to be remedied later, work that would be done by the community at large. The "People (for it is with them to Judge) can, as they will have the advantage of experience on their Side, decide with as much propriety on the alteration[s] and amendment[s] which are necessary. . . . I do not think we are more inspired, have more wisdom, or possess more virtue, than those who will come after us."[23]

Washington's core contention that the Constitution is a work in progress, one improved through the deliberative process of amendment, should be an inspiration for us today. With "the advantage of experience on [our] Side," we must acknowledge and address the Constitution's prime imperfection: its own manner of curing imperfection. Only through a reform of Article V can we be sure that the Constitution can survive and flourish in its third century and beyond.

TOWARD A NEW CONSTITUTIONAL POLITICS

We need a new constitutional politics, a new procedure and culture of constitutional change that allows the People to undertake the work of correcting imperfection themselves, to "recur to first principles in a Regular Way."[24] Rather than relying on the power of courts and the executive to shift the tides of constitutional meaning, we should aspire to kindle a rebirth of constitutional imagination and of first-order debate about fundamental law.

Such a rebirth can only be achieved through an amendment mechanism that provides clear procedure, fosters open and democratic debate, and places final authority for constitutional change in the hands of the People, not partisan intermediaries like state legislatures. As the artisan and mechanics guilds of New York City expressed in the summer of 1776 after the state legislature had both written and ratified New York's first constitution, constitutional power belongs to the "inhabitants at large" as a "right which *God* has given them, in common with all men."[25]

The amendment mechanism drafted by the 1787 Convention, and the troubling constitutional politics its disuse has inspired, need not and should not be understood as the sole, sacrosanct manifestation of the American conception of bloodless revolution. In discerning the values and culture of American constitutionalism, commentators too often look only to the 1787 Convention. The work of the Framers meeting in Philadelphia, many believe, provides *the* authoritative statement of American thinking about fundamental law.

But such a view ignores the important historical and contemporary development of American constitutionalism.[26] Citizens have worked over two centuries to make the ethos of the Founding and its constitutional values real through the creation, re-creation, and amendment of state constitutions.[27] In the states, the People have experimented, learned from previous mistakes, and implemented new ways of making and changing fundamental law that worked to apply and embolden the ideals of the Founding.

·The United States has not one constitution but fifty-four—those of the federal government, the fifty states, and three territories (Guam and the U.S. Virgin Islands are governed by congressional organic acts, not constitutions). These many attempts to craft workable theories of American constitutionalism share a common theme: amendment mechanisms that make constitutional change more democratic and provide clear procedural safeguards to foster and guide debate. Far from a defunct ideal, the Founding generation's notion of bloodless revolution has been emboldened in the states.

On the most important point of any constitutional amendment mechanism, how to harness the People's power, the federal Constitution is a clear outlier. In all cases (save one, Delaware) the phrase "We the People" has a literal meaning. Rather than a process undertaken in statehouses, oftentimes behind closed doors, or merely the work of interpretation-turned-politics, in 96 percent of all American constitutions, the People—gathered at the ballot box—make constitutional law themselves.

As detailed in Chapter 1, the first attempts at constitutional imagining occurred at the local level even before the federal Constitution was drafted, as citizens debated how to formulate their new governing charters. Some of these early attempts at the Founding worked to give the People at large a direct role in crafting constitutional meaning. Massachusetts and New Hampshire, for example, ratified their constitutions in 1778 and 1779 by popular vote.[28] Other states followed suit in the country's first century, with direct popular votes on constitutional questions becoming the norm. By 1876, at least thirty-four states provided for constitutional plebiscite mechanisms.[29] Soon direct popular votes were required for constitutional amendments as well. Connecticut's 1818 constitution, for example, was the first to apply this plebiscite approach to amendments, requiring a popular vote to ratify legislature-drafted changes.

Today, forty-nine of the fifty states require popular ratification of constitutional amendments; only Delaware lacks a plebiscite mechanism.[30] The same is true for altering the constitutions of all United States territories as well as the District of Columbia's Home Rule Charter.[31] The finer details of popular ratification vary; most states require a simple majority to ratify, with the highest bar being two-thirds, as required in New Hampshire. Nine states have more complex ratification thresholds; Illinois's 1970 constitution, for example, provides different thresholds depending on voter turnout in the election versus the number of voters that respond to the amendment ballot question, requiring, in effect, that the public be sufficiently engaged in the constitutional question to render a legitimate public sanction.[32]

During the Progressive Era, many states also expanded the People's constitutional amendment power to allow citizens to circumvent the legislature altogether, making popular constitutional authority one of not only passive approval but also active initiation. In 1902, Oregon was the first state to apply the Progressive democratic reform triptych—the initiative, referendum, and recall—to constitutional matters, allowing the People to put proposed constitutional amendments on the ballot themselves.[33] Eighteen states now allow the People to propose amendments through initiative without support from elected officials.[34] Fourteen others automatically put the question to voters whether a state should hold a constitutional convention at certain intervals, allowing the People to determine for themselves whether the constitutional regime should be revised.[35]

In New York, for example, the voters are asked every twenty years: "Shall there be a convention to revise the constitution and amend the same?"[36] If a majority of voters support the proposition, the voters will then elect convention delegates in the next general election, three from each state senate district and fifteen elected at large statewide.[37] New York voters have directly called a convention three times, in 1866, 1886, and 1936. But in 1957, 1977, 1997, and 2017, the voters overwhelmingly rejected the question, most recently by a vote of 83 to 17 percent. Most New Yorkers voting no raised concerns about runaway risk and the power of special interests to control the convening.[38] So too did the voters in Iowa, Alaska, Missouri, New Hampshire, Rhode Island, Connecticut, Illinois, and Hawaii vote down holding a convention within the last two decades.[39]

Voters' displeasure with convention calls is indisputable. Since 1992, no state has held a constitutional convention, despite fourteen putting the question to voters at a regular interval.[40] In some cases, as in New York, many fears raised in the Article V realm, like runaway concerns, are seeping into state debates about constitutional conventions.[41] But regardless of the voters' rationale, in all cases it has been the People who made that decision, not legislators, and it would have been the voters who selected the delegates, not legislators. The People acted in the first instance as the ultimate sovereign, taking up the question of constitutional change themselves.

The impact of placing constitutional questions within the direct reach of democratic authority, the clear norm in the American constitutional tradition, has been consistent and profound. The states have frequently returned to constitutional principles, amending their governing charters and, in some cases, replacing them entirely by popular vote. From 1776 to the present, Americans have held 233 state constitutional conventions, adopted 149 different state constitutions, and ratified over 8,000 state constitutional amendments.[42]

It would be imprudent to judge the fitness of a constitution merely by the number of times it has been changed. Constitutional amendment is not an unqualified good to be sought for its own sake. Indeed, frequent constitutional change can be quite problematic, prioritizing an often inapt forum to settle political debates and creating a fundamental law that is unwieldy, looking little different from ordinary statutes.

But these experiences of constitutional change in the states underscore just how unique the federal Constitution and its amendment mechanism are in the American constitutional tradition. As one study found, the *least* amended state constitution, as measured by the number of amendments divided by the age of the document, was that of Vermont: with fifty-four amendments since 1793, twice as many as the comparably aged federal Constitution.[43] Might there be a way to fashion a reformed Article V that protects against destabilization yet empowers more frequent, popular constitutional change?

RETHINKING ARTICLE V: SOME THOUGHTS ON REFORM

In 1913, the leading American Progressive and Wisconsin U.S. senator Robert "Fighting Bob" La Follette introduced a proposed reform of Article V in Congress. Reflecting widespread discontent with state legislatures, La Follette's reformed amendment mechanism aimed to democratize constitutional change.[44] His revision provided:

> The Congress, whenever a majority of both Houses shall propose amendments to this Constitution, or on the application of the legislatures of 10 States, or on the application of 10 States through the vote of the majority of the electors of each, voting upon the question of such application, shall propose amendments to this Constitution, to be submitted for ratification

in each of the several States to the electors qualified to vote for the election of Representatives. And the vote shall be taken at the next ensuing
election of Representatives in such manner as the Congress may prescribe. And if in a majority of the States a majority of the electors voting
thereon approve any proposed amendment, and if a majority of all the
electors voting thereon also approve any proposed amendment, it shall be
valid to all intents and purposes as part of this Constitution.[45]

La Follette's draft was but one of many proposed amid the amendment
fervor of the Progressive Era.[46] Other reforms sought to allow voters to
propose amendments by petition, require ratification in popularly elected
conventions, and lower the threshold for legislative proposal.[47] But these
early proposals, including La Follette's, died in committee. A decade later,
the Senate approved a provision providing for ratification by popular
referendum but then proceeded to quickly reject it.[48] This about-face, combined with the Supreme Court's 1920 ruling in *Hawke v. Smith* throwing
out Ohio voters' rejection of Prohibition in favor of the state legislature's
approval, chilled further attempts at reform.

Over the last century, calls to reform Article V have all but come to a
halt. A small cadre of scholars have tended the fire of reform, proposing
tweaks here and there. Professor Michael Rappaport, for example, has
proposed allowing direct state legislative drafting of amendments, allowing legislators to circumvent Congress and the convention mechanism
entirely.[49] But none has sought the necessary democratic-minded reforms
La Follette and his colleagues proposed in the first decades of the last century. That even *discussion* of such reform has waned is cause for a moment
of serious reflection.

The road to reforming Article V is long and arduous, in no small part
because such reform would require an amendment that itself satisfies the
strictures of Article V—no easy task. But like the Senate reform debates
during the Progressive Era a century ago, a time when most thought such
reform was also impossible, the effort must be made.

Such a revision to Article V should be proposed through the congressional route so as to avoid the runaway concerns posed by ill-formed
procedure. To begin this process, we propose the creation of a congressional
bipartisan commission on reforming Article V. Such a commission would
gather members of the public, constitutional scholars, state legislative leaders, and members of Congress to discuss the future of formal constitutional

change. Among its guiding principles, the commission should aim to craft a reform proposal that implements, at the very least, the following:

1. Ratification of proposed amendments by popular referendum, requiring both a majority vote in a sufficient number of states and—as did La Follette's proposal—a majority vote of all qualified voters nationwide. Provision could also be made, as Article V currently contemplates, that Congress can refer certain proposed amendments to state conventions for ratification. But such conventions should be regulated by constitutional rules rather than state statute, providing a mechanism for popular delegate selection. Such rules could, for example, provide for legislature-selected delegates approved by the voters in a manner akin to judicial retention vote (e.g., "Shall the delegate represent the People of this state in convention assembled?"). This would allow the People at large an opportunity to express their intention on the specific constitutional questions by direct proxy.

2. Lower vote thresholds for congressional constitutional amendment proposal, combined with other institutional safeguards—such as requiring approval in two separate Congresses, as do nine states, or a time-lock measure, as in Vermont.[50]

3. Constitutional provision of general convention regulations, including rules regarding application counting, topic limitations, and an explicit grant of authority to Congress to set forth general regulations for a convention by statute. This would settle key procedural questions long before a convening, helping guide debate.[51]

4. Requirement that convention applications under Article V must be referred by state legislatures to voters for approval by plebiscite at a general election at which federal officers are elected to be valid.

5. Requirement that Article V convention delegates be nominated by state legislatures or some other method yet receive their delegated authority through popular election, in a manner akin to a judicial retention vote (a yes-no vote) or by a contested race.

6. Explicit constitutional requirement that a call is binding on a convention and that delegates cannot contravene topic limitations expressed in a call, thus providing constitutional guarantees against a runaway convention.

Rather than a certain prescription, these proposals are intended to sketch a starting point for debate. Many essential components, such as proposal and ratification thresholds, are purposely undefined. These issues, the focus of considerable academic and political debate, require theoretical introspection, balancing often competing conceptions of popular sovereignty and federalism. They thus deserve more consideration than this short work can provide.

RECLAIMING "WE THE PEOPLE"

Many across the political spectrum worry about giving the People direct constitutional power. On the right, it has become fashionable for politicians to make the bold claim that the United States is not a democracy. The United States is a unique form of republic, they claim, one that legitimizes insulating institutions from the People in favor of partisan, antimajoritarian choke holds that empower insiders and elites.[52] On the left, many likewise fear the whims of popular power. Like Hamilton in his own day, they believe that the federal order has been essential to national flourishing and human equality. Frequent, direct popular elaboration of constitutional law might disrupt Hamilton's delicate handiwork, many argue, and should be avoided.[53]

Others would contest on theoretical grounds the argument that the Constitution should allow for more frequent and popular reform. It is a good thing that the document has not changed much, they argue. A tradition of limited change has inspired unparalleled stability, allowing the Constitution to endure as the oldest written national fundamental text in the world. A more democratic form of constitutional politics would be undesirable, creating a troubling new future where the Constitution becomes destabilized by the whims of popular desire. Far from a fluke, its challenging, undemocratic amendment mechanism is a blessing. While the Constitution we have is not perfect—as Washington himself believed—it is better than what we *could* have.

These discussants might point to Alabama as a prime example of the trouble amendment-happy voters can make. With 977 amendments and 388,882 words (almost four times as long as Harper Lee's *To Kill a Mockingbird* and just a tad longer than Tolstoy's *Anna Karenina*), Alabama's 1901 constitution is not only the longest in the country; it is the longest in the world. The document provides particularly specific constitutional limitations. In 2020, for example, two separate amendments were approved by voters providing protection in two counties for anyone who kills another while defending church property (each passed with 72 percent of the vote).[54] In 2011, Alabama chief justice Sue Bell Cobb reflected on the trouble the state constitution had made for her work: by "any reasonable test, it is high time for constitutional reform in Alabama."[55]

California, where the state constitution has been amended 516 times, also poses a thorny counterexample.[56] There, a system for citizen-initiated constitutional amendment proposals crafted during the Progressive Era to guard against special interests has yielded a constant barrage of amendment ballot questions on complicated issues, often, perhaps ironically, funded by special interest groups.[57] Sometimes such a citizen-empowered process can prove decisive in checking the state legislature. As discussed in Chapter 5, the contemporary conservative convention movement was itself born in California by Howard Jarvis's citizen-initiated constitutional limitation on property taxes. But overall, many commentators argue that the California system has proved problematic.[58] One proposal in 2018, funded by venture capitalist Tim Draper, sought to dissolve the state, erecting three new sovereign states in its stead.[59] The state Supreme Court yanked the question from the ballot on procedural grounds.[60]

Others too might point out the troubling history of voter-supported constitutional amendments and referenda that explicitly aimed to discriminate against racial, religious, and sexual minorities.[61] The federal Constitution has helped remedy these discriminatory acts, empowering a countermajoritarian logic that supersedes even direct, popular sanction when the acts of the sovereign People are animated by animus or deny equal protection of the law.[62] Might more popular, democratic constitutional change infect this laudable component of our constitutional tradition?

Determining whether constitutional stability requires a certain degree of stagnancy was controversial even in the country's earliest days. James Madison argued in *Federalist* No. 49 that a constitution should be entrenched from change, fixed in time and binding on future generations until rare moments for revision presented themselves. Were constitutions to undergo more frequent revision, he argued, "the PASSIONS, therefore, not the REASON, of the public would sit in judgment. But it is the reason, alone, of the public, that ought to control and regulate the government. . . .

Occasional appeals to the people would be neither a proper nor an effectual provision."[63]

Thomas Jefferson disagreed, remarking that "the earth belongs in usufruct to the living." Drawing from actuarial tables, he concluded that constitutions and laws should expire every nineteen to twenty years, the average duration of a generation. "If it is enforced longer, it is an act of force, and not of right." Each successive generation should be empowered to craft the governing regime anew, he believed.[64]

Perhaps both Madison and Jefferson were right. The ideal constitutional system should chart a course between the Scylla of populist fervor and the Charybdis of ossification, seeking a middle way in which amendment is legitimately feasible but infrequent. Constitutional change should be not so hard as to bind current generations without any reasonable ability for reform, but also not so easy as to empower passion and not reason.

George Washington expressed such a middle path in his farewell address. "The basis of our political systems is the right of the people to make and to alter their constitutions of government," Washington declared. Therefore "the Constitution which at any time exists, till changed by an explicit and authentic act of the whole people, is sacredly obligatory upon all." Such an explicit and authentic act should not be undertaken lightly. But in certain circumstances, it is both proper and good. "If, in the opinion of the people, the distribution or modification of the constitutional powers be in any particular wrong," Washington continued, "let it be corrected by an amendment."[65]

Over the last half century, the country has been drifting from this Washingtonian middle way, venturing into uncharted waters where the Constitution could, over time, lose both its vitality and claim to legitimacy. Yet Article V can provide sufficient procedure to allow balance between stability and change, should the country choose to allow it.

EPILOGUE

O N FEBRUARY 11, 1861, Abraham Lincoln boarded a train at Springfield, Illinois, setting off with his wife and three sons for his inauguration in Washington. "A duty devolved upon me which is, perhaps, greater than that which has devolved upon any other man since the days of Washington," he remarked in an emotional farewell address on the train platform. "I now leave, not knowing when, or whether ever, I may return."[1]

Just three days before, a provisional constitution of the Confederate States had been ratified and a spirit of violence was in the air. Widespread rumors of plans to assassinate Lincoln while en route to Washington gripped the nation. The *New York Daily Herald* reported that an investigative committee of the House of Representatives had recently heard testimony recounting a "widespread and intricate conspiracy" to seize the District of Columbia and install the former vice president, proslavery Kentuckian John Breckenridge, as president following the assassination.[2] The federal Constitution did not provide clarity on what happens when a president-elect dies after the Electoral College balloting yet before inauguration.[3]

Despite the concerns of his advisors, Lincoln insisted on keeping to his schedule. His journey to Washington took over two weeks and charted a circuitous route, allowing him to make short stops in many towns and cities. In Baltimore—the rumored site of the assassination—he changed trains under cover of darkness and made for the capital unannounced. Arriving at six in the morning wearing a simple overcoat and wool hat, he took up residence at Willard's Hotel to prepare for his new administration.

Lincoln's critics ridiculed him for sneaking into the city in disguise— hardly an act of a commander in chief. And his reception into official Washington's social circles left even his supporters unimpressed. He was awkward, lacked social grace, and is said to have taken a bit too much joy in

President Lincoln delivers his first inaugural address. (1861)

telling long-winded stories. To many, it seemed that the prairie lawyer's initial foray into national politics was more provincial than presidential.[4]

Inauguration Day on March 4 was overcast. But by noon, when the outgoing president James Buchanan arrived at the Willard to escort Lincoln to the ceremonies, sunlight had started to peek through the clouds. Lincoln donned a new black suit and ventured toward the Capitol still under construction. After taking the oath from Chief Justice Roger Taney, whom Lincoln had long criticized for his opinion in *Dred Scott v. Sandford*, which held that the Constitution granted neither citizenship nor protection to those of African descent, he began his inaugural address.[5]

Following a recitation of present threats against the Union, Lincoln reflected on the nature of authority in a constitutional democracy. "This country, with its institutions, belongs to the people who inhabit it," Lincoln declared. "Whenever they shall grow weary of the existing Government, they can exercise their constitutional right of amending it." But the Union must remain inviolable, he continued. "A majority, held in restraint by constitutional checks, and limitations, and always changing easily, with deliberate changes of popular opinions and sentiments, is the only true sovereign of a free people." It was thus incumbent on citizens to pursue legal, constitutional means for the redress of their grievances rather than resorting to the "anarchy" of violence, secession, and rebellion.

"I cannot be ignorant of the fact that many worthy and patriotic citizens are desirous of having the National Constitution amended," he continued. "While I make no recommendation of amendments, I fully recognize the rightful authority of the people over the whole subject, to be exercised in either of the modes prescribed in the instrument itself; and I should, under existing circumstances, favor rather than oppose a fair opportunity being afforded the people to act upon it." And it would be a convention that could best provide for such popular action, Lincoln believed. "I will venture to add," he remarked, "that, to me, the convention mode seems preferable, in that it allows amendments to originate with the people themselves, instead of only permitting them to take, or reject, propositions, originated by others, not especially chosen for the purpose, and which might not be precisely such, as they would wish to either accept or refuse."[6]

Lincoln's overtures for constitutional reform were quickly rebuffed, and for good reason. As discussed in Chapter 4, most efforts to avert the Civil War through Article V aimed to constitutionally codify the status of slavery in the United States. These proposals were fundamentally untenable, and attempts for peaceful constitutional resolution failed. But it was also Article V's procedures that had been troublesome, with convenings held outside its ambit and Congress deadlocked on a myriad of convention applications. At a critical juncture, constitutional amendment had proved unworkable. Far from a conduit for bloodless revolution, Article V had failed to quell a bloody one.

Yet in that inaugural moment, standing beneath scaffolding and an open Capitol dome, one can see a leader—poised to save the Union and commence a new epoch in the American story—trying to reconcile the nation's Founding ethos with its flawed fundamental law. How was it that the Constitution could mend a country in crisis?

Through the Civil War and his response to slavery and secession, Lincoln effectuated a rebirth in American constitutional thought—a Second

Founding—through the three Reconstruction Amendments that he set in motion but also through a conceptual reframing of the nature of the Constitution itself. His work was to reaffirm the principles of the Declaration of Independence, to make good on its claims that "all men are created equal and endowed by their creator with certain unalienable rights." This transformation in American constitutional thinking was thus one of both reformation and restoration, of reconciling our fundamental law with a purer manifestation of our deepest ideals. As Professor Mark Tushnet put it, Lincoln "worked to restyle the silver frame, the Constitution, around the apple of gold, the Declaration's principles."[7]

It was in this vein that Lincoln's initial, perhaps naive, attempt to resolve national conflict through the convention mechanism likely found its roots. In his framing, Article V was not merely a forum for the People to check the federal regime, as George Mason argued at the 1787 Constitutional Convention. Rather, the Constitution envisioned a conduit through which the national community could gather again and return to first principles on its own accord. Article V, in Lincoln's conception, was an embodiment of the Declaration's radical claim that it is the "Right of the People to alter" their government.

As he soon discovered, however, Article V was not as he thought it to be. Despite his fervent hopes, the mechanism was not a wellspring of popular governance, a means of empowering "the people themselves," as he remarked. The prelude to the Civil War had made clear that Article V's inherent inconsistencies and tensions were debilitating. Like today, its convention procedures were too unsettled, the risk of misstep too great, and its constitutional power placed in the wrong hands.

Yet Lincoln's belief that Article V could be a means for popular constitutional reform persists in our time. The moment has come to reclaim the Declaration's assertion that the People constitute their government and are empowered to alter its fundamental law. We must pay keen attention to antidemocratic elements attempting to capitalize on ill-formed convention procedure. But we must also pursue reform that rekindles those high aspirations of the Founding, refashioning Article V to ensure that the Constitution's hallowed invocation "We the People" means what it says.

ACKNOWLEDGMENTS

We are grateful to the many individuals who helped with this project. Thanks to Dean Paul Brest, Professor Sanford Levinson, Drew Cunningham, Ryan Nees, Miles Unterreiner, and Morgan Weiland for reading the manuscript and offering insightful feedback. Special thanks also to Mary Ellen Prindiville and Christine Ferdinand, who were incisive copy editors. Gratitude as well to Carole Sargent, who provided useful advice in the project's nascence, and Ben Adams, our editor, who was a helpful guide as we completed the manuscript.

The Stanford Constitutional Law Center, its faculty director Professor Michael McConnell, and its executive director, Morgan Weiland, offered us a welcome academic home as we undertook this research. Thanks also to Dean Joseph Kearney of the Marquette University Law School and Elana Olson, director of the Eckstein Law Library at Marquette, for providing access to library and research resources. The staff of the Robert Crown Law Library and the Green Memorial Library at Stanford also were very helpful in tracking down some hard-to-find sources.

Finally, a note of admiration for the late David Kyvig, a prolific historian of constitutional amendment at Northern Illinois University. Kyvig's decades-long study of Article V, including his exceptional book *Explicit and Authentic Acts* (University Press of Kansas, 2016), is an emblematic example of how focused scholarship can and should inform our public debates about important civic matters and is to be commended.

RDF

I am so grateful to my former Stanford Law student and now coauthor Peter Prindiville for proposing that we embark on this project. Peter was a brilliant first-year law student in my seminar on Article V and Amending the Constitution, which I first taught at Stanford in the spring of 2019. He then became my teaching assistant at the law school during the 2019–2020 academic year. His work was flawless, including skillfully adapting to the virtual, COVID-19-induced teaching environment required in the spring of 2020 as I taught the course again. Near the end of that quarter, Peter suggested that I write a book about Article V, in part due to my concern that a first-ever Article V constitutional convention could be called in the not too distant future.

I explained that the demands of my new role at the time as president of the American Constitution Society precluded me from writing a book on my own but that we could maybe do it together. He agreed, and we proceeded to pitch the idea to publishers until we had the good fortune to be introduced through my former editor at Crown, Sean Desmond, to Ben Adams at PublicAffairs and Hachette. Over about five months, while completing law school, studying for and passing the Illinois bar exam, and preparing for his associateship at Latham & Watkins, Peter took a deep dive into this subject, ensuring what I hope will be viewed as the high quality of scholarship in this book. The project was too compelling for me to simply passively encourage, so I ended up putting significant time into this collaboration. Having said that, much more than the lion's share of the writing and effort was done by Peter after we carefully mapped out each step of our approach. Our weekly (or more) conversations about this topic over about a year and a half were not only fruitful but a true pleasure. Peter combines first-rate intellectual rigor with an unfailingly pleasant and enthusiastic personality. I feel deeply fortunate to have partnered with him in this endeavor.

Thanks as well to Yale Law School, which first supported my teaching this subject when I was a visiting professor of practice there in the 2017–2018 academic year. Special thanks to Professors Harold Koh, Bruce Ackerman, and Akhil Amar for their advice and guidance as I developed this unique course.

At Yale, my excellent teaching assistant Jeff Zalesin was instrumental in helping develop the syllabus the first time I taught Article V. And thanks to Stanford Law School, where Professors Paul Brest and Barbara Fried encouraged me to teach the seminar again and where I was able to present my work on the topic at the Stanford Law Faculty workshop, gaining useful ideas from the comments made there. Zachary Bleckner was a marvelous teaching assistant there as well, providing innovative ideas to improve the course.

I also wish to thank my friend Dean Joseph Kearney of the Marquette University Law School, who first suggested to me late in 2010 that I try teaching law. Not only did I need a job at the time, but Joe and his then associate dean Matt Parlow provided the support to allow me to start a completely new and rewarding phase of my career—teaching law students all over the country.

I would be remiss in not thanking my wonderful staff colleagues, the board of directors, and all the members of the American Constitution Society for their tremendous collaboration during these very challenging years. We have made great strides together, and many of us share the concerns about the prospect of a far-right-driven constitutional convention that this book details.

Finally, I want to thank my delightful wife, Dr. Christine Ferdinand, for her belief that this book was worth writing and for her able editing and substantive advice. She could have said I had too much to do already, but she clearly grasped the potential gravity of this issue and encouraged me to move forward. She also took the intrepid step of personally attending, along with my brother-in-law Doug Green, a rally in favor of a constitutional convention at the Wisconsin State Capitol and then coming home with a terrific firsthand account of what these folks are up to.

PAP

Writing a first book poses many new challenges, especially when the topic is legally, historically, and politically complex. I could not have asked for a better companion on this journey. Working with Russ has been a true joy, one full of great conversation, deep thinking, and a lot of laughter. His intellect, wisdom, patriotism, strong moral character, and many decades of admirable public service have long been an inspiration to me and many others. I am happy we have been able to share this book with those also concerned about the future of the Constitution and our democracy.

I am especially indebted to Professor Michael McConnell, who encouraged me to pursue this project when it was in its early stages. His courses on constitutional history and theory and my work with him as a research assistant helped sharpen my own thinking on many of the topics considered in this book. I am grateful for his mentorship and support. Thanks also to Professor Anne Joseph O'Connell, with whom I had the privilege of studying constitutional and administrative law, for her guidance.

I wish to also express my gratitude for the many other educators in my life, each of whom in their own way and over many years had a hand in shaping this work. I am deeply thankful for their continued influence in my life. Among them: Penny Cichucki, the Reverend David Collins, S.J., Anthony DelDonna, Rebecca Gilmore, John Glavin, Diane Haleas, Matt Sparapani, and Lauren Tuckley. Thanks also to Pietra Rivoli, Trina Vargo, and John Tierney for their support and guidance.

I also would like to acknowledge my grandmother, Agnes Tierney Prindiville, whose tenacity, grace, wit, and deep faith remain a constant inspiration. After a successful career as a teacher and mother of seven, she decided in retirement to pursue her childhood desire to become an attorney, a path that had been foreclosed by the social norms of her youth. She was sworn in to the bar one month before her eighty-second birthday and at the young age of ninety-four continues her pro bono work, remaining (to our knowledge) the oldest person ever admitted to legal practice in Illinois. The special bond we have shared over the law and our many conversations and text message exchanges throughout the process of writing this book have been a source of great happiness.

Finally, thanks to my parents, to whom this book is dedicated. You have my eternal admiration and love.

APPENDIX

The Constitution of the United States

* * *

We the People of the United States,
in Order to form a more perfect Union,
establish Justice, insure domestic Tranquility,
provide for the common defence,
promote the general Welfare, and secure the Blessings of Liberty
to ourselves and our Posterity,
do ordain and establish
this Constitution for the United States of America.

* * *

Article. I.

Section. 1.

All legislative Powers herein granted shall be vested in a Congress of the United States, which shall consist of a Senate and House of Representatives.

Section. 2.

The House of Representatives shall be composed of Members chosen every second Year by the People of the several States, and the Electors in each State shall have the Qualifications requisite for Electors of the most numerous Branch of the State Legislature.

No Person shall be a Representative who shall not have attained to the Age of twenty-five Years, and been seven Years a Citizen of the United States, and who shall not, when elected, be an Inhabitant of that State in which he shall be chosen.

Representatives and direct Taxes shall be apportioned among the several States which may be included within this Union, according to their respective Numbers, which shall be determined by adding to the whole Number of free Persons, including those bound to Service for a Term of Years, and excluding Indians not taxed, three fifths of all other Persons. The actual Enumeration shall be made within three Years after the first Meeting of the Congress of the United States, and within every subsequent Term of ten Years, in such Manner as they shall by Law direct. The Number of Representatives shall not exceed one for every thirty Thousand, but each State shall have at Least one Representative; and until such enumeration shall be made, the State of New Hampshire shall be entitled to chuse three, Massachusetts eight, Rhode-Island and Providence Plantations one, Connecticut five, New-York six, New Jersey four, Pennsylvania eight, Delaware one, Maryland six, Virginia ten, North Carolina five, South Carolina five, and Georgia three.

When vacancies happen in the Representation from any State, the Executive Authority thereof shall issue Writs of Election to fill such Vacancies.

The House of Representatives shall chuse their Speaker and other Officers; and shall have the sole Power of Impeachment.

Section. 3.
The Senate of the United States shall be composed of two Senators from each State, chosen by the Legislature thereof, for six Years; and each Senator shall have one Vote.

Immediately after they shall be assembled in Consequence of the first Election, they shall be divided as equally as may be into three Classes. The Seats of the Senators of the first Class shall be vacated at the Expiration of the second Year, of the second Class at the Expiration of the fourth Year, and of the third Class at the Expiration of the sixth Year, so that one third may be chosen every second Year; and if Vacancies happen by Resignation, or otherwise, during the Recess of the Legislature of any State, the Executive thereof may make temporary Appointments until the next Meeting of the Legislature, which shall then fill such Vacancies.

No Person shall be a Senator who shall not have attained to the Age of thirty Years, and been nine Years a Citizen of the United States, and who shall not, when elected, be an Inhabitant of that State for which he shall be chosen.

The Vice President of the United States shall be President of the Senate, but shall have no Vote, unless they be equally divided.

The Senate shall chuse their other Officers, and also a President pro tempore, in the Absence of the Vice President, or when he shall exercise the Office of President of the United States.

The Senate shall have the sole Power to try all Impeachments. When sitting for that Purpose, they shall be on Oath or Affirmation. When the President of the United States is tried, the Chief Justice shall preside: And no Person shall be convicted without the Concurrence of two thirds of the Members present.

Judgment in Cases of Impeachment shall not extend further than to removal from Office, and disqualification to hold and enjoy any Office of honor, Trust or Profit under the United States: but the Party convicted shall nevertheless be liable and subject to Indictment, Trial, Judgment and Punishment, according to Law.

Section. 4.
The Times, Places and Manner of holding Elections for Senators and Representatives, shall be prescribed in each State by the Legislature thereof; but the Congress may at any time by Law make or alter such Regulations, except as to the Places of chusing Senators.

The Congress shall assemble at least once in every Year, and such Meeting shall be on the first Monday in December, unless they shall by Law appoint a different Day.

Section. 5.
Each House shall be the Judge of the Elections, Returns and Qualifications of its own Members, and a Majority of each shall constitute a

Quorum to do Business; but a smaller Number may adjourn from day to day, and may be authorized to compel the Attendance of absent Members, in such Manner, and under such Penalties as each House may provide.

Each House may determine the Rules of its Proceedings, punish its Members for disorderly Behaviour, and, with the Concurrence of two thirds, expel a Member.

Each House shall keep a Journal of its Proceedings, and from time to time publish the same, excepting such Parts as may in their Judgment require Secrecy; and the Yeas and Nays of the Members of either House on any question shall, at the Desire of one fifth of those Present, be entered on the Journal.

Neither House, during the Session of Congress, shall, without the Consent of the other, adjourn for more than three days, nor to any other Place than that in which the two Houses shall be sitting.

Section. 6.
The Senators and Representatives shall receive a Compensation for their Services, to be ascertained by Law, and paid out of the Treasury of the United States. They shall in all Cases, except Treason, Felony and Breach of the Peace, be privileged from Arrest during their Attendance at the Session of their respective Houses, and in going to and returning from the same; and for any Speech or Debate in either House, they shall not be questioned in any other Place.

No Senator or Representative shall, during the Time for which he was elected, be appointed to any civil Office under the Authority of the United States, which shall have been created, or the Emoluments whereof shall have been encreased during such time; and no Person holding any Office under the United States, shall be a Member of either House during his Continuance in Office.

Section. 7.
All Bills for raising Revenue shall originate in the House of Representatives; but the Senate may propose or concur with Amendments as on other Bills.

Every Bill which shall have passed the House of Representatives and the Senate, shall, before it become a Law, be presented to the President of the United States; If he approve he shall sign it, but if not he shall return it, with his Objections to that House in which it shall have originated, who shall enter the Objections at large on their Journal, and proceed to reconsider it. If after such Reconsideration two thirds of that House shall agree to pass the Bill, it shall be sent, together with the Objections, to the other House, by which it shall likewise be reconsidered, and if approved by two thirds of that House, it shall become a Law. But in all such Cases the Votes of both Houses shall be determined by yeas and Nays, and the Names of the Persons voting for and against the Bill shall be entered on the Journal of each House respectively. If any Bill shall not be returned by the President within ten Days (Sundays excepted) after it shall have been presented to him, the Same shall be a Law, in like Manner as if he had signed it, unless the Congress by their Adjournment prevent its Return, in which Case it shall not be a Law.

Every Order, Resolution, or Vote to which the Concurrence of the Senate and House of Representatives may be necessary (except on a question of Adjournment) shall be presented to the President of the United States; and before the Same shall take Effect, shall be approved by him, or being disapproved by him, shall be repassed by two thirds of the Senate and House of Representatives, according to the Rules and Limitations prescribed in the Case of a Bill.

Section. 8.
The Congress shall have Power To lay and collect Taxes, Duties, Imposts and Excises, to pay the Debts and provide for the common Defence and general Welfare of the United States; but all Duties, Imposts and Excises shall be uniform throughout the United States;

To borrow Money on the credit of the United States;
To regulate Commerce with foreign Nations, and among the several
    States, and with the Indian Tribes;
To establish an uniform Rule of Naturalization, and uniform Laws on the
    subject of Bankruptcies throughout the United States;
To coin Money, regulate the Value thereof, and of foreign Coin, and fix
    the Standard of Weights and Measures;

To provide for the Punishment of counterfeiting the Securities and current Coin of the United States;

To establish Post Offices and post Roads;

To promote the Progress of Science and useful Arts, by securing for limited Times to Authors and Inventors the exclusive Right to their respective Writings and Discoveries;

To constitute Tribunals inferior to the supreme Court;

To define and punish Piracies and Felonies committed on the high Seas, and Offences against the Law of Nations;

To declare War, grant Letters of Marque and Reprisal, and make Rules concerning Captures on Land and Water;

To raise and support Armies, but no Appropriation of Money to that Use shall be for a longer Term than two Years;

To provide and maintain a Navy;

To make Rules for the Government and Regulation of the land and naval Forces;

To provide for calling forth the Militia to execute the Laws of the Union, suppress Insurrections and repel Invasions;

To provide for organizing, arming, and disciplining, the Militia, and for governing such Part of them as may be employed in the Service of the United States, reserving to the States respectively, the Appointment of the Officers, and the Authority of training the Militia according to the discipline prescribed by Congress;

To exercise exclusive Legislation in all Cases whatsoever, over such District (not exceeding ten Miles square) as may, by Cession of particular States, and the Acceptance of Congress, become the Seat of the Government of the United States, and to exercise like Authority over all Places purchased by the Consent of the Legislature of the State in which the Same shall be, for the Erection of Forts, Magazines, Arsenals, dock-Yards, and other needful Buildings;—And

To make all Laws which shall be necessary and proper for carrying into Execution the foregoing Powers, and all other Powers vested by this Constitution in the Government of the United States, or in any Department or Officer thereof.

Section. 9.

The Migration or Importation of such Persons as any of the States now existing shall think proper to admit, shall not be prohibited by the

Congress prior to the Year one thousand eight hundred and eight, but a Tax or duty may be imposed on such Importation, not exceeding ten dollars for each Person.

The Privilege of the Writ of Habeas Corpus shall not be suspended, unless when in Cases of Rebellion or Invasion the public Safety may require it.

No Bill of Attainder or ex post facto Law shall be passed.

No Capitation, or other direct, Tax shall be laid, unless in Proportion to the Census or enumeration herein before directed to be taken.

No Tax or Duty shall be laid on Articles exported from any State.

No Preference shall be given by any Regulation of Commerce or Revenue to the Ports of one State over those of another: nor shall Vessels bound to, or from, one State, be obliged to enter, clear, or pay Duties in another.

No Money shall be drawn from the Treasury, but in Consequence of Appropriations made by Law; and a regular Statement and Account of the Receipts and Expenditures of all public Money shall be published from time to time.

No Title of Nobility shall be granted by the United States: And no Person holding any Office of Profit or Trust under them, shall, without the Consent of the Congress, accept of any present, Emolument, Office, or Title, of any kind whatever, from any King, Prince, or foreign State.

Section. 10.

No State shall enter into any Treaty, Alliance, or Confederation; grant Letters of Marque and Reprisal; coin Money; emit Bills of Credit; make any Thing but gold and silver Coin a Tender in Payment of Debts; pass any Bill of Attainder, ex post facto Law, or Law impairing the Obligation of Contracts, or grant any Title of Nobility.

No State shall, without the Consent of the Congress, lay any Imposts or Duties on Imports or Exports, except what may be absolutely necessary for executing it's inspection Laws: and the net Produce of all Duties and Imposts, laid by any State on Imports or Exports, shall be for the Use of the Treasury of the United States; and all such Laws shall be subject to the Revision and Controul of the Congress.

No State shall, without the Consent of Congress, lay any Duty of Tonnage, keep Troops, or Ships of War in time of Peace, enter into any Agreement or Compact with another State, or with a foreign Power, or engage in War, unless actually invaded, or in such imminent Danger as will not admit of delay.

ARTICLE. II.

Section. 1.

The executive Power shall be vested in a President of the United States of America. He shall hold his Office during the Term of four Years, and, together with the Vice President, chosen for the same Term, be elected, as follows

Each State shall appoint, in such Manner as the Legislature thereof may direct, a Number of Electors, equal to the whole Number of Senators and Representatives to which the State may be entitled in the Congress: but no Senator or Representative, or Person holding an Office of Trust or Profit under the United States, shall be appointed an Elector.

The Electors shall meet in their respective States, and vote by Ballot for two Persons, of whom one at least shall not be an Inhabitant of the same State with themselves. And they shall make a List of all the Persons voted for, and of the Number of Votes for each; which List they shall sign and certify, and transmit sealed to the Seat of the Government of the United States, directed to the President of the Senate. The President of the Senate shall, in the Presence of the Senate and House of Representatives, open all the Certificates, and the Votes shall then be counted. The Person having the greatest Number of Votes shall be the President, if such Number be a Majority of the whole Number of Electors appointed; and if there be more than one who have such Majority, and have an equal Number of Votes, then the House of Representatives shall immediately chuse by Ballot one of them for President; and if no Person have a Majority, then from the five highest on the List the said House shall in like Manner chuse the President. But in chusing the President, the Votes shall be taken by States, the Representation from each State having one Vote; A quorum for this Purpose shall consist of a Member or Members from two thirds of the States, and a Majority of all the States shall be necessary to a Choice. In every

Case, after the Choice of the President, the Person having the greatest Number of Votes of the Electors shall be the Vice President. But if there should remain two or more who have equal Votes, the Senate shall chuse from them by Ballot the Vice President.

The Congress may determine the Time of chusing the Electors, and the Day on which they shall give their Votes; which Day shall be the same throughout the United States.

No Person except a natural born Citizen, or a Citizen of the United States, at the time of the Adoption of this Constitution, shall be eligible to the Office of President; neither shall any Person be eligible to that Office who shall not have attained to the Age of thirty five Years, and been fourteen Years a Resident within the United States.

In Case of the Removal of the President from Office, or of his Death, Resignation, or Inability to discharge the Powers and Duties of the said Office, the Same shall devolve on the Vice President, and the Congress may by Law provide for the Case of Removal, Death, Resignation or Inability, both of the President and Vice President, declaring what Officer shall then act as President, and such Officer shall act accordingly, until the Disability be removed, or a President shall be elected.

The President shall, at stated Times, receive for his Services, a Compensation, which shall neither be encreased nor diminished during the Period for which he shall have been elected, and he shall not receive within that Period any other Emolument from the United States, or any of them.

Before he enter on the Execution of his Office, he shall take the following Oath or Affirmation:—"I do solemnly swear (or affirm) that I will faithfully execute the Office of President of the United States, and will to the best of my Ability, preserve, protect and defend the Constitution of the United States."

Section. 2.
The President shall be Commander in Chief of the Army and Navy of the United States, and of the Militia of the several States, when called into the

actual Service of the United States; he may require the Opinion, in writing, of the principal Officer in each of the executive Departments, upon any Subject relating to the Duties of their respective Offices, and he shall have Power to grant Reprieves and Pardons for Offences against the United States, except in Cases of Impeachment.

He shall have Power, by and with the Advice and Consent of the Senate, to make Treaties, provided two thirds of the Senators present concur; and he shall nominate, and by and with the Advice and Consent of the Senate, shall appoint Ambassadors, other public Ministers and Consuls, Judges of the supreme Court, and all other Officers of the United States, whose Appointments are not herein otherwise provided for, and which shall be established by Law: but the Congress may by Law vest the Appointment of such inferior Officers, as they think proper, in the President alone, in the Courts of Law, or in the Heads of Departments.

The President shall have Power to fill up all Vacancies that may happen during the Recess of the Senate, by granting Commissions which shall expire at the End of their next Session.

Section. 3.
He shall from time to time give to the Congress Information of the State of the Union, and recommend to their Consideration such Measures as he shall judge necessary and expedient; he may, on extraordinary Occasions, convene both Houses, or either of them, and in Case of Disagreement between them, with Respect to the Time of Adjournment, he may adjourn them to such Time as he shall think proper; he shall receive Ambassadors and other public Ministers; he shall take Care that the Laws be faithfully executed, and shall Commission all the Officers of the United States.

Section. 4.
The President, Vice President and all civil Officers of the United States, shall be removed from Office on Impeachment for, and Conviction of, Treason, Bribery, or other high Crimes and Misdemeanors.

ARTICLE. III.

Section. 1.

The judicial Power of the United States, shall be vested in one supreme Court, and in such inferior Courts as the Congress may from time to time ordain and establish. The Judges, both of the supreme and inferior Courts, shall hold their Offices during good Behaviour, and shall, at stated Times, receive for their Services, a Compensation, which shall not be diminished during their Continuance in Office.

Section. 2.

The judicial Power shall extend to all Cases, in Law and Equity, arising under this Constitution, the Laws of the United States, and Treaties made, or which shall be made, under their Authority;—to all Cases affecting Ambassadors, other public Ministers and Consuls;—to all Cases of admiralty and maritime Jurisdiction;—to Controversies to which the United States shall be a Party;—to Controversies between two or more States;—between a State and Citizens of another State,—between Citizens of different States,—between Citizens of the same State claiming Lands under Grants of different States, and between a State, or the Citizens thereof, and foreign States, Citizens or Subjects.

In all Cases affecting Ambassadors, other public Ministers and Consuls, and those in which a State shall be Party, the supreme Court shall have original Jurisdiction. In all the other Cases before mentioned, the supreme Court shall have appellate Jurisdiction, both as to Law and Fact, with such Exceptions, and under such Regulations as the Congress shall make.

The Trial of all Crimes, except in Cases of Impeachment, shall be by Jury; and such Trial shall be held in the State where the said Crimes shall have been committed; but when not committed within any State, the Trial shall be at such Place or Places as the Congress may by Law have directed.

Section. 3.

Treason against the United States, shall consist only in levying War against them, or in adhering to their Enemies, giving them Aid and

Comfort. No Person shall be convicted of Treason unless on the Testimony of two Witnesses to the same overt Act, or on Confession in open Court.

The Congress shall have Power to declare the Punishment of Treason, but no Attainder of Treason shall work Corruption of Blood, or Forfeiture except during the Life of the Person attainted.

ARTICLE. IV.
Section. 1.
Full Faith and Credit shall be given in each State to the public Acts, Records, and judicial Proceedings of every other State. And the Congress may by general Laws prescribe the Manner in which such Acts, Records and Proceedings shall be proved, and the Effect thereof.

Section. 2.
The Citizens of each State shall be entitled to all Privileges and Immunities of Citizens in the several States.

A Person charged in any State with Treason, Felony, or other Crime, who shall flee from Justice, and be found in another State, shall on Demand of the executive Authority of the State from which he fled, be delivered up, to be removed to the State having Jurisdiction of the Crime.

No Person held to Service or Labour in one State, under the Laws thereof, escaping into another, shall, in Consequence of any Law or Regulation therein, be discharged from such Service or Labour, but shall be delivered up on Claim of the Party to whom such Service or Labour may be due.

Section. 3.
New States may be admitted by the Congress into this Union; but no new State shall be formed or erected within the Jurisdiction of any other State; nor any State be formed by the Junction of two or more States, or Parts of States, without the Consent of the Legislatures of the States concerned as well as of the Congress.

The Congress shall have Power to dispose of and make all needful Rules and Regulations respecting the Territory or other Property belonging to the United States; and nothing in this Constitution shall be so construed as to Prejudice any Claims of the United States, or of any particular State.

Section. 4.

The United States shall guarantee to every State in this Union a Republican Form of Government, and shall protect each of them against Invasion; and on Application of the Legislature, or of the Executive (when the Legislature cannot be convened) against domestic Violence.

ARTICLE. V.

The Congress, whenever two thirds of both Houses shall deem it necessary, shall propose Amendments to this Constitution, or, on the Application of the Legislatures of two thirds of the several States, shall call a Convention for proposing Amendments, which, in either Case, shall be valid to all Intents and Purposes, as Part of this Constitution, when ratified by the Legislatures of three fourths of the several States, or by Conventions in three fourths thereof, as the one or the other Mode of Ratification may be proposed by the Congress; Provided that no Amendment which may be made prior to the Year One thousand eight hundred and eight shall in any Manner affect the first and fourth Clauses in the Ninth Section of the first Article; and that no State, without its Consent, shall be deprived of its equal Suffrage in the Senate.

ARTICLE. VI.

All Debts contracted and Engagements entered into, before the Adoption of this Constitution, shall be as valid against the United States under this Constitution, as under the Confederation.

This Constitution, and the Laws of the United States which shall be made in Pursuance thereof; and all Treaties made, or which shall be made, under the Authority of the United States, shall be the supreme Law of the Land; and the Judges in every State shall be bound thereby, any Thing in the Constitution or Laws of any State to the Contrary notwithstanding.

The Senators and Representatives before mentioned, and the Members of the several State Legislatures, and all executive and judicial Officers, both of the United States and of the several States, shall be bound by Oath or Affirmation, to support this Constitution; but no religious Test shall ever be required as a Qualification to any Office or public Trust under the United States.

ARTICLE. VII.
The Ratification of the Conventions of nine States, shall be sufficient for the Establishment of this Constitution between the States so ratifying the Same.

AMENDMENTS TO THE CONSTITUTION

AMENDMENT I (1791)
Congress shall make no law respecting an establishment of religion, or prohibiting the free exercise thereof; or abridging the freedom of speech, or of the press; or the right of the people peaceably to assemble, and to petition the Government for a redress of grievances.

AMENDMENT II (1791)
A well regulated Militia, being necessary to the security of a free State, the right of the people to keep and bear Arms, shall not be infringed.

AMENDMENT III (1791)
No Soldier shall, in time of peace be quartered in any house, without the consent of the Owner, nor in time of war, but in a manner to be prescribed by law.

AMENDMENT IV (1791)
The right of the people to be secure in their persons, houses, papers, and effects, against unreasonable searches and seizures, shall not be violated, and no Warrants shall issue, but upon probable cause, supported by Oath or affirmation, and particularly describing the place to be searched, and the persons or things to be seized.

AMENDMENT V (1791)
No person shall be held to answer for a capital, or otherwise infamous crime, unless on a presentment or indictment of a Grand Jury, except in cases arising in the land or naval forces, or in the Militia, when in actual

service in time of War or public danger; nor shall any person be subject for the same offence to be twice put in jeopardy of life or limb; nor shall be compelled in any criminal case to be a witness against himself, nor be deprived of life, liberty, or property, without due process of law; nor shall private property be taken for public use, without just compensation.

AMENDMENT VI (1791)

In all criminal prosecutions, the accused shall enjoy the right to a speedy and public trial, by an impartial jury of the State and district wherein the crime shall have been committed, which district shall have been previously ascertained by law, and to be informed of the nature and cause of the accusation; to be confronted with the witnesses against him; to have compulsory process for obtaining witnesses in his favor, and to have the Assistance of Counsel for his defence.

AMENDMENT VII (1791)

In Suits at common law, where the value in controversy shall exceed twenty dollars, the right of trial by jury shall be preserved, and no fact tried by a jury, shall be otherwise re-examined in any Court of the United States, than according to the rules of the common law.

AMENDMENT VIII (1791)

Excessive bail shall not be required, nor excessive fines imposed, nor cruel and unusual punishments inflicted.

AMENDMENT IX (1791)

The enumeration in the Constitution, of certain rights, shall not be construed to deny or disparage others retained by the people.

AMENDMENT X (1791)

The powers not delegated to the United States by the Constitution, nor prohibited by it to the States, are reserved to the States respectively, or to the people.

AMENDMENT XI (1795/1798)

The Judicial power of the United States shall not be construed to extend to any suit in law or equity, commenced or prosecuted against one of the

United States by Citizens of another State, or by Citizens or Subjects of any Foreign State.

AMENDMENT XII (1804)

The Electors shall meet in their respective states and vote by ballot for President and Vice-President, one of whom, at least, shall not be an inhabitant of the same state with themselves; they shall name in their ballots the person voted for as President, and in distinct ballots the person voted for as Vice-President, and they shall make distinct lists of all persons voted for as President, and of all persons voted for as Vice-President, and of the number of votes for each, which lists they shall sign and certify, and transmit sealed to the seat of the government of the United States, directed to the President of the Senate;—The President of the Senate shall, in the presence of the Senate and House of Representatives, open all the certificates and the votes shall then be counted;—The person having the greatest Number of votes for President, shall be the President, if such number be a majority of the whole number of Electors appointed; and if no person have such majority, then from the persons having the highest numbers not exceeding three on the list of those voted for as President, the House of Representatives shall choose immediately, by ballot, the President. But in choosing the President, the votes shall be taken by states, the representation from each state having one vote; a quorum for this purpose shall consist of a member or members from two-thirds of the states, and a majority of all the states shall be necessary to a choice. And if the House of Representatives shall not choose a President whenever the right of choice shall devolve upon them, before the fourth day of March next following, then the Vice-President shall act as President, as in the case of the death or other constitutional disability of the President—The person having the greatest number of votes as Vice-President, shall be the Vice-President, if such number be a majority of the whole number of Electors appointed, and if no person have a majority, then from the two highest numbers on the list, the Senate shall choose the Vice-President; a quorum for the purpose shall consist of two-thirds of the whole number of Senators, and a majority of the whole number shall be necessary to a choice. But no person constitutionally ineligible to the office of President shall be eligible to that of Vice-President of the United States.

AMENDMENT XIII (1865)

Section 1. Neither slavery nor involuntary servitude, except as a punishment for crime whereof the party shall have been duly convicted, shall exist within the United States, or any place subject to their jurisdiction.

Section 2. Congress shall have power to enforce this article by appropriate legislation.

AMENDMENT XIV (1868)

Section 1. All persons born or naturalized in the United States, and subject to the jurisdiction thereof, are citizens of the United States and of the State wherein they reside. No State shall make or enforce any law which shall abridge the privileges or immunities of citizens of the United States; nor shall any State deprive any person of life, liberty, or property, without due process of law; nor deny to any person within its jurisdiction the equal protection of the laws.

Section 2. Representatives shall be apportioned among the several States according to their respective numbers, counting the whole number of persons in each State, excluding Indians not taxed. But when the right to vote at any election for the choice of electors for President and Vice President of the United States, Representatives in Congress, the Executive and Judicial officers of a State, or the members of the Legislature thereof, is denied to any of the male inhabitants of such State, being twenty-one years of age, and citizens of the United States, or in any way abridged, except for participation in rebellion, or other crime, the basis of representation therein shall be reduced in the proportion which the number of such male citizens shall bear to the whole number of male citizens twenty-one years of age in such State.

Section 3. No person shall be a Senator or Representative in Congress, or elector of President and Vice President, or hold any office, civil or military, under the United States, or under any State, who, having previously taken an oath, as a member of Congress, or as an officer of the United States, or as a member of any State legislature, or as an executive or judicial officer of any State, to support the Constitution of the United States, shall have engaged in insurrection or rebellion against the same, or given aid or comfort to the enemies thereof. But Congress may by a vote of two-thirds of each House, remove such disability.

Section 4. The validity of the public debt of the United States, authorized by law, including debts incurred for payment of pensions and bounties for services in suppressing insurrection or rebellion, shall not be questioned. But neither the United States nor any State shall assume or pay any debt or obligation incurred in aid of insurrection or rebellion against the United States, or any claim for the loss or emancipation of any slave; but all such debts, obligations and claims shall be held illegal and void.

Section 5. The Congress shall have power to enforce, by appropriate legislation, the provisions of this article.

AMENDMENT XV (1870)

Section 1. The right of citizens of the United States to vote shall not be denied or abridged by the United States or by any State on account of race, color, or previous condition of servitude.

Section 2. The Congress shall have power to enforce this article by appropriate legislation.

AMENDMENT XVI (1913)

The Congress shall have power to lay and collect taxes on incomes, from whatever source derived, without apportionment among the several States, and without regard to any census or enumeration.

AMENDMENT XVII (1913)

The Senate of the United States shall be composed of two Senators from each State, elected by the people thereof, for six years; and each Senator shall have one vote. The electors in each State shall have the qualifications requisite for electors of the most numerous branch of the State legislatures.

When vacancies happen in the representation of any State in the Senate, the executive authority of such State shall issue writs of election to fill such vacancies: Provided, That the legislature of any State may empower the executive thereof to make temporary appointments until the people fill the vacancies by election as the legislature may direct.

This amendment shall not be so construed as to affect the election or term of any Senator chosen before it becomes valid as part of the Constitution.

AMENDMENT XVIII (1919)

Section 1. After one year from the ratification of this article the manufacture, sale, or transportation of intoxicating liquors within, the importation thereof into, or the exportation thereof from the United States and all territory subject to the jurisdiction thereof for beverage purposes is hereby prohibited.

Section 2. The Congress and the several States shall have concurrent power to enforce this article by appropriate legislation.

Section 3. This article shall be inoperative unless it shall have been ratified as an amendment to the Constitution by the legislatures of the several States, as provided in the Constitution, within seven years from the date of the submission hereof to the States by the Congress.

AMENDMENT XIX (1920)

The right of citizens of the United States to vote shall not be denied or abridged by the United States or by any State on account of sex.

Congress shall have power to enforce this article by appropriate legislation.

AMENDMENT XX (1933)

Section 1. The terms of the President and Vice President shall end at noon on the 20th day of January, and the terms of Senators and Representatives at noon on the 3d day of January, of the years in which such terms would have ended if this article had not been ratified; and the terms of their successors shall then begin.

Section 2. The Congress shall assemble at least once in every year, and such meeting shall begin at noon on the 3d day of January, unless they shall by law appoint a different day.

Section 3. If, at the time fixed for the beginning of the term of the President, the President elect shall have died, the Vice President elect shall become President. If a President shall not have been chosen before the time fixed for the beginning of his term, or if the President elect shall have failed to qualify, then the Vice President elect shall act as President until a President shall have qualified; and the Congress may by law provide for the case wherein neither a President elect nor a Vice President elect shall have qualified, declaring who shall then act as President, or the manner in which one who is to act shall be selected, and such person shall act accordingly until a President or Vice President shall have qualified.

Section 4. The Congress may by law provide for the case of the death of any of the persons from whom the House of Representatives may choose a President whenever the right of choice shall have devolved upon them, and for the case of the death of any of the persons from whom the Senate may choose a Vice President whenever the right of choice shall have devolved upon them.

Section 5. Sections 1 and 2 shall take effect on the 15th day of October following the ratification of this article.

Section 6. This article shall be inoperative unless it shall have been ratified as an amendment to the Constitution by the legislatures of three-fourths of the several States within seven years from the date of its submission.

AMENDMENT XXI (1933)

Section 1. The eighteenth article of amendment to the Constitution of the United States is hereby repealed.

Section 2. The transportation or importation into any State, Territory, or possession of the United States for delivery or use therein of intoxicating liquors, in violation of the laws thereof, is hereby prohibited.

Section 3. This article shall be inoperative unless it shall have been ratified as an amendment to the Constitution by conventions in the several States, as provided in the Constitution, within seven years from the date of the submission hereof to the States by the Congress.

AMENDMENT XXII (1951)

Section 1. No person shall be elected to the office of the President more than twice, and no person who has held the office of President, or acted as President, for more than two years of a term to which some other person was elected President shall be elected to the office of the President more than once. But this Article shall not apply to any person holding the office of President, when this Article was proposed by the Congress, and shall not prevent any person who may be holding the office of President, or acting as President, during the term within which this Article becomes operative from holding the office of President or acting as President during the remainder of such term.

Section 2. This article shall be inoperative unless it shall have been ratified as an amendment to the Constitution by the legislatures of three-fourths of the several States within seven years from the date of its submission to the States by the Congress.

Amendment XXIII (1961)

Section 1. The District constituting the seat of Government of the United States shall appoint in such manner as the Congress may direct:

A number of electors of President and Vice President equal to the whole number of Senators and Representatives in Congress to which the District would be entitled if it were a State, but in no event more than the least populous State; they shall be in addition to those appointed by the States, but they shall be considered, for the purposes of the election of President and Vice President, to be electors appointed by a State; and they shall meet in the District and perform such duties as provided by the twelfth article of amendment.

Section 2. The Congress shall have power to enforce this article by appropriate legislation.

Amendment XXIV (1964)

Section 1. The right of citizens of the United States to vote in any primary or other election for President or Vice President for electors for President or Vice President, or for Senator or Representative in Congress, shall not be denied or abridged by the United States or any State by reason of failure to pay any poll tax or other tax.

Section 2. The Congress shall have power to enforce this article by appropriate legislation.

Amendment XXV (1967)

Section 1. In case of the removal of the President from office or of his death or resignation, the Vice President shall become President.

Section 2. Whenever there is a vacancy in the office of the Vice President, the President shall nominate a Vice President who shall take office upon confirmation by a majority vote of both Houses of Congress.

Section 3. Whenever the President transmits to the President pro tempore of the Senate and the Speaker of the House of Representatives his written declaration that he is unable to discharge the powers and duties of his office, and until he transmits to them a written declaration to the contrary, such powers and duties shall be discharged by the Vice President as Acting President.

Section 4. Whenever the Vice President and a majority of either the principal officers of the executive departments or of such other body as Congress may by law provide, transmit to the President pro tempore of the Senate and the Speaker of the House of Representatives their written declaration that the President is unable to discharge the powers and duties of his office, the Vice President shall immediately assume the powers and duties of the office as Acting President.

Thereafter, when the President transmits to the President pro tempore of the Senate and the Speaker of the House of Representatives his written declaration that no inability exists, he shall resume the powers and duties of his office unless the Vice President and a majority of either the principal officers of the executive department or of such other body as Congress may by law provide, transmit within four days to the President pro tempore of the Senate and the Speaker of the House of Representatives their written declaration that the President is unable to discharge the powers and duties of his office. Thereupon Congress shall decide the issue, assembling within forty-eight hours for that purpose if not in session. If the Congress, within twenty-one days after receipt of the latter written declaration, or, if Congress is not in session, within twenty-one days after Congress is required to assemble, determines by two-thirds vote of both Houses that the President is unable to discharge the powers and duties of his office, the Vice President shall continue to discharge the same as Acting President; otherwise, the President shall resume the powers and duties of his office.

Amendment XXVI (1971)

Section 1. The right of citizens of the United States, who are eighteen years of age or older, to vote shall not be denied or abridged by the United States or by any State on account of age.

Section 2. The Congress shall have power to enforce this article by appropriate legislation.

Amendment XXVII (1992)

No law varying the compensation for the services of the Senators and Representatives shall take effect, until an election of Representatives shall have intervened.

ILLUSTRATION CREDITS

Currier, N. *Destruction of Tea at Boston Harbor.* 1846. (New York: N. Currier). https://www.loc.gov/item/91795889/.

George Washington Papers, Series 4, General Correspondence: Constitution, Printed, with Marginal Notes by George Washington. 1787. https://www.loc.gov/item/mgw435950/.

Chassériau, Théodore, artist. *Alexis de Tocqueville.* 1901. Lithograph. https://www.loc.gov/item/96509612/.

Harris & Ewing, photographers. *George Washington Said.* 1932. https://www.loc.gov/pictures/item/2016879473/.

Shrine of Constitution in Cong. Library, Washington, D.C. 1924. https://www.loc.gov/item/2016848918/.

Greenleaf, Thomas, printer. James Madison Pamphlet Collection. *The Conventions of a Number of the States.* 1789. https://www.loc.gov/item/92838253/.

Shober, Charles, lithographer; Louis Kurz, artist; and Erik Shogren. *Behold Oh! America, Your Sons. The Greatest Among Men.* 1865. (Chicago: Chas. Shober). https://www.loc.gov/item/2003656573/.

Ottmann, J., lithographer; and J. Keppler, artist. The Bosses of the Senate. 1889. (New York: Puck Magazine). https://www.loc.gov/item/2002718861/.

Keppler, Udo J., artist. *Polly's Chance to Get Some Nice Crackers.* 1909. New York: Keppler & Schwarzmann, Puck Building. Photograph. https://www.loc.gov/item/2011647496/.

Allender, Nina, artist. *"The Spirit of '76!"—On to the Senate.* 1915. Sketch. https://www.loc.gov/item/2020635503/.

Beloit Daily News, September 12, 1963. On file with author.

"Trump Won God Bless Us All. Hurley, Wisconsin. August 1, 2021." Photo taken by author.

Horydczak, Theodor, photographer. *Front Facade of U.S. Supreme Court Under Construction, from Street.* Circa 1934. Photograph. https://www.loc.gov/item/2019674049/.

Harris & Ewing, photographers. *President Lashed Supreme Court in Constitution Address to Nation.* 1937. https://www.loc.gov/pictures/item/2016863109/.

Meigs, Montgomery Cunningham. *Inauguration of President Lincoln at U. S. Capitol.* 1861. Photograph. https://www.loc.gov/item/pin2104/.

NOTES

PROLOGUE

1. "Arkansas Senate Journal: 2019 Regular Session," Index of Proceedings, 92nd General Assembly Regular Session, 2019, 346–375, https://www.arkleg.state.ar.us/Bureau/Document?type=pdf&source=assembly%2F2019%2F2019R%2FSenate+Journal&filename=2019R+Senate+Journal.

2. Arkansas State Senate Livestream Archive, "Senate Convenes, Video," January 29, 2019, video, 1:26:00, https://www.arkleg.state.ar.us/Calendars/Meetings?ddBienniumSession=2019%2F2019R.

3. Arkansas State Senate Livestream Archive at 1:22:30.

4. Arkansas at 1:55:00.

5. Arkansas at 1:45:30.

6. Senators Jane English, Matthew Pitsch, Bill Sample, James Sturch—all Republicans—also voted against the resolution. Two senators did not vote. One senator was absent. See "Arkansas Senate Journal: 2019 Regular Session," 365.

7. Alex Newman, "Sen. Manzella: States Must Resist Federal Overreach, False Solutions," *New American*, March 11, 2021, video, 21:56, https://thenewamerican.com/sen-manzella-states-must-resist-federal-overreach-false-solutions/.

8. Sam Wilson, "Fiery Constitutional Debate Splits Senate Republicans," *Helena Independent Record*, February 11, 2021, https://helenair.com/news/state-and-regional/govt-and-politics/fiery-constitutional-debate-splits-senate-republicans/article_8ad20c76-e8c5-55af-aeb4-6a7f80859eb4.html.

9. See Montana State Senate Live Broadcast, "Senate Floor Session," February 20, 2021, video, 1:48:00, http://sg001-harmony.sliq.net/00309/Harmony/en/PowerBrowser/PowerBrowserV2/20210210/-1/41112.

10. Montana State Senate Live Broadcast at 13:59:00. See also Steve Byas, "John Birch Society Credited with Killing Constitutional Convention Call in Montana," *New American*, February 14, 2021, https://thenewamerican.com/john-birch-society-credited-with-killing-constitutional-convention-call-in-montana/. For more on the Oath Keepers' position, see Elias Alias, "Why the Article V Convention Must Be Opposed," *Oath Keepers* (blog), April 3, 2015, https://oathkeepers.org/2015/04/why-the-article-v-convention-must-be-opposed/.

11. Montana State Senate Live Broadcast at 13:59:15.

12. Montana at 14:00:57.

13. Montana at 13:53:45.

14. See also David P. Schneider, "Soros and Hillary Clinton Influence in Helena," accessed November 2, 2021, https://conventionofstates.com/news/senator-pushing-fear -and-status-quo. ("We need legislators in Helena that listen to James Madison, George Mason, and George Washington and follow the action plan they left for the states inside of the Constitution, Article V. We no longer can tolerate those proclaiming to be Constitutionalists, while repeating the talking points of Soros groups and Hillary Clinton.")

15. Montana State Senate Live Broadcast at 13:53:45.

16. Wilson, "Fiery Constitutional Debate."

17. Wilson.

18. Newman, "Sen. Manzella: States Must Resist Federal Overreach," at 3:50.

19. Convention of States Montana, "Senator Manzella Thanks Democrats for Help Defeating Convention of States," February 15, 2021, https://conventionofstates.com /news/senator-manzella-thanks-democrats-for-help-defeating-convention-of-states.

20. Ken Stone, "Santorum to ALEC: Convene States to Amend Constitution (but Sidestep Trump)," *Times of San Diego*, December 3, 2021, https://timesofsandiego.com /politics/2021/12/02/santorum-to-alec-convene-states-to-amend-constitution-but -sidestep-trump/.

21. This is a contested proposition, one on which we do not take a position.

22. See Robert Natelson, "Avoiding Secession Through an Amendments Convention," *Epoch Times*, September 26, 2021, https://www.theepochtimes.com/avoiding-secession -through-an-amendments-convention_4015435.html. Regarding the *Epoch Times*, see Seth Hettena, "The Obscure Newspaper Fueling the Far-Right in Europe," *New Republic*, September 17, 2019, https://newrepublic.com/article/155076/obscure-newspaper-fueling- far-right-europe; Jason Wilson, "Falun Gong-Aligned Media Push Fake News About Democrats and Chinese Communists," *Guardian*, April 30, 2021, https://www.theguardian .com/us-news/2021/apr/30/falun-gong-media-epoch-times-democrats-chinese-communists; Simon van Zuylen-Wood, "MAGA-Land's Favorite Newspaper," *Atlantic*, January 13, 2021, https://www.theatlantic.com/politics/archive/2021/01/inside-the-epoch-times-a -mysterious-pro-trump-newspaper/617645/.

INTRODUCTION

1. U.S. Constitution, Preamble.

2. George Washington to David Humphreys, October 10, 1787, in Max Farrand, ed., *The Records of the Federal Convention of 1787* (New Haven, CT: Yale University Press, 1937), 3:103–104, quoted in David E. Kyvig, *Explicit and Authentic Acts: Amending the U.S. Constitution, 1776–2015* (Lawrence: University Press of Kansas, 2016), 1.

3. Letter of George Washington to Bushrod Washington, November 10, 1787, in *The Origins of the American Constitution: A Documentary History*, ed. Michael Kammen (New York: Penguin, 1986), 83, quoted in Sanford Levinson, *Our Undemocratic Constitution: Where the Constitution Goes Wrong (and How We the People Can Correct It)* (New York: Oxford University Press, 2006), 21.

4. Michael Rozansky, "Amid Pandemic and Protests, Civics Survey Finds Americans Know More of Their Rights," *Penn Today*, September 16, 2020, https://penntoday
.upenn.edu/news/amid-pandemic-and-protests-civics-survey-finds-americans-know
-more-their-rights.

5. Compiled from the Article V Library. See http://article5library.org/apptable
.php?type=Application&sort=Y&order=A.

6. Farrand, *Records of the Federal Convention of 1787*, 2:630.

7. See James H. Hutson, "Creation of the Constitution: The Integrity of the Documentary Record," *Texas Law Review* 65, no. 1 (1986): 2.

8. Farrand, *Records of the Federal Convention of 1787*.

9. See generally Mary Sarah Bilder, *Madison's Hand: Revising the Constitutional Convention* (Cambridge, MA: Harvard University Press, 2015).

10. Hutson, "Creation of the Constitution," 34.

11. OED Online, s.v. "supply, v.1," last modified March 2022, https://www.oed.com
/view/Entry/194666?rskey=dHyIr6&result=2&isAdvanced=false.

CHAPTER 1: BLOODLESS REVOLUTION

1. See "A Little Rebellion Now and Then Is a Good Thing: A Letter from Thomas Jefferson to James Madison," *Early America Review* 1, no. 1 (1996). (In original, Jefferson spelled medicine as "medecine.")

2. Benjamin Woods Labaree, *The Boston Tea Party* (New York: Oxford University Press, 1964), 126–129. The weight and measurements are found in Robert J. Allison, *The American Revolution: A Concise History* (New York: Oxford University Press, 2011), 17. For an interesting discussion of the legal fight over the tea, including some quibbling over the definition of *importation*, see Labaree, *Boston Tea Party*, 126.

3. See generally Labaree, *Boston Tea Party*, 69–79; see also Allison, *American Revolution*, 16–29.

4. Labaree, *Boston Tea Party*, 7.

5. Labaree, 73.

6. See generally Labaree, chap. 1.

7. Lyman Henry Butterfield, ed., *Diary of John Adams*, vol. II (Cambridge, MA: Belknap Press of Harvard University Press, 1961), 85–86, quoted in Labaree, *Boston Tea Party*, 124.

8. See Gordon S. Wood, *The Creation of the American Republic, 1776–1787* (Chapel Hill: University of North Carolina Press, 1969), 4–5.

9. For a similar rendition of this argument, see David E. Kyvig, *Explicit and Authentic Acts: Amending the U.S. Constitution, 1776–2015* (Lawrence: University Press of Kansas, 2016), 20.

10. *A Letter to the Right Honourable the Earl of Hilsborough, on the Present Situation of Affairs in America* (London: George Kearsly, 1769). (Authorship is sometimes attributed to George Canning and Samuel Adams.)

11. Henry St. John (Viscount Bolingbroke), *A Dissertation upon Parties* (3rd ed., London, 1735), 108, quoted in Russell L. Caplan, *Constitutional Brinksmanship: Amending the Constitution by National Convention* (New York: Oxford University Press, 1988), 3.

12. William Blackstone, *Commentaries on the Laws of England*, ed. William Carey Jones, vol. 1 (San Francisco, CA: Bancroft-Whitney Company, 1915), 212 (at *126).

13. For further discussion regarding the constitutionality-legality distinction, see generally Wood, *Creation of the American Republic*; J. W. Gough, *Fundamental Law in English Constitutional History* (Oxford: Clarendon Press, 1955), 174–213.

14. The Declaration of Independence, para. 2 (U.S. 1776).

15. See generally Kyvig, *Explicit and Authentic Acts*, 15–18; Edward S. Corwin, *The "Higher Law" Background of American Constitutional Law* (Ithaca, NY: Cornell University Press, 1955), 1–5, 82–100; Andrew C. McLaughlin, *The Foundations of American Constitutionalism* (New York: New York University Press, 1932). But see generally Jonathan Gienapp, *The Second Creation: Fixing the American Constitution in the Founding Era* (Cambridge, MA: Harvard University Press, 2018) (arguing that the new idea of written fundamental law was still in flux during the Constitution's first decade and challenging the idea that a logic of constitutional and textual fixity had taken a firm hold).

16. Hobbes taught that, in the state of nature, every person was entitled by natural right to do anything she thought necessary for self-preservation. Life was, as he famously put it, "solitary, poor, nasty, brutish, and short." See Thomas Hobbes, *The Leviathan* (Oxford: Clarendon Press, 1909), 97. Locke painted a slightly rosier picture, theorizing that since people are "all equal and independent [in the state of nature], no one ought to harm another in his life, health, liberty or possessions." John Locke, *Second Treatise of Government*, ed. C. B. Macpherson (Indianapolis, IN: Hackett, 1980), 9 (§ 6).

17. There were many colonial institutions that enjoyed considerable local control. These were reconstituted swiftly, some with little change. But it is this reconstitution that matters; the right of former colonial institutions to govern had been vanquished by the Declaration. New constitutional arrangements were needed. See generally Forrest McDonald, *Novus Ordo Seclorum: The Intellectual Origins of the Constitution* (Lawrence: University Press of Kansas, 1985), 57–66.

18. Rhode Island's representatives did not see a need to amend their charter or assert its force. They merely affirmed the Declaration, replaced all royal references in colonial statutes, and banned public prayers for the king. In October 1776, the Connecticut General Assembly affirmed their charter as binding, stripped it of all references to the Crown, and declared Connecticut independent. See Willi Paul Adams, *The First American Constitutions: Republican Ideology and the Making of the State Constitutions in the Revolutionary Era* (Lanham, MD: Rowman & Littlefield, 2001), 64–65.

19. See Adams, *First American Constitutions*, 65.

20. The states adopted a diverse range of solutions to these problems. Virginia, Delaware, and others included a bill of rights; Georgia did not. Pennsylvania expanded the right to vote to elect constitutional convention delegates; Maryland refused. New York, South Carolina, and others adopted their constitutions by simple legislative action; Massachusetts put their constitution directly to the voters. See Adams, 66–90.

21. Thomas Paine, *The Rights of Man*, in Philip Sheldon Foner, ed., *The Complete Writings of Thomas Paine*, vol. 1 (New York: Citadel Press, 1967), 378. For a more recent examination of the appropriate role of legislative consideration of constitutionality, see Russ Feingold, "The Obligation of Members of Congress to Consider Constitutionality While Deliberating and Voting: The Deficiencies of House Rule XII and a Proposed Rule for the Senate," *Vanderbilt Law Review* 67, no. 3 (2014): 837–874; Russ Feingold,

"Upholding an Oath to the Constitution: A Legislator's Responsibilities," *Wisconsin Law Review* 2006, no. 1 (2006): 1–16.

22. See John R. Vile, *The Constitutional Amending Process in American Political Thought* (New York: Praeger, 1992), 1.

23. *Providence Gazette*, November 23, 1776, quoted in Adams, *First American Constitutions*, 138.

24. As quoted in Adams, 137–138.

25. See generally Donald Barr Chidsey, *The Siege of Boston: An On-the-Scene Account of the Beginning of the American Revolution* (New York: Crown, 1966).

26. See generally Mary Beth Norton, *1774: The Long Year of Revolution* (New York: Knopf, 2020), chap. 4.

27. See generally Adams, *First American Constitutions*, 135.

28. Martin Loughlin and Neil Walker, eds., *The Paradox of Constitutionalism: Constituent Power and Constitutional Form* (New York: Oxford University Press, 2007), 1.

29. Hobbes did not use the term *sleeping sovereign* in the context of popular sovereignty but rather more generally to note the idea that a sovereign, like a king, could delegate power to other officials yet retain their ultimate power. For a general overview of the historical development of popular sovereignty theory, including an examination of Hobbes's writing on the subject, see Richard Tuck, *The Sleeping Sovereign: The Invention of Modern Democracy* (Cambridge: Cambridge University Press, 2015). For a discussion of the development of the theory during the Founding Era, see generally Tuck, 181–248.

30. One particularly robust field of scholarly engagement with this question considers the relationship between popular sovereignty and judicial review. See, e.g., Alexander M. Bickel, *The Least Dangerous Branch: The Supreme Court at the Bar of Politics*, 2nd ed. (New Haven, CT: Yale University Press, 1986); John Hart Ely, *Democracy and Distrust: A Theory of Judicial Review* (Cambridge, MA: Harvard University Press, 1980). So too do scholarly and political debates regarding the veracity of different modes of constitutional interpretation ultimately find root in this foundational question. For a very general introduction, compare Stephen G. Breyer, *Active Liberty: Interpreting a Democratic Constitution* (New York: Oxford University Press, 2008) (articulating one approach within the "living constitutionalism" school of interpretive theory) with John O. McGinnis and Michael B. Rappaport, *Originalism and the Good Constitution* (Cambridge, MA: Harvard University Press, 2013) (providing an overview of the theory of originalism).

31. Loughlin and Walker describe these complexities as the "paradox of constitutionalism." We have opted to focus our examination of the general paradox on conceptions of the People as they relate to amendment, a distinct element of what Loughlin and Walker call "the paradoxical relationship between constituent power and constitutional form." See Loughlin and Walker, *Paradox of Constitutionalism*, 1–8.

32. See David Singh Grewal and Jedediah Purdy, "The Original Theory of Constitutionalism," *Yale Law Journal* 127, no. 3 (2018): 686–688.

33. See generally Tuck, *Sleeping Sovereign*, 181–248.

34. The 1660 Convention Parliament restored Charles II to the throne following the interregnum. The 1689 Parliament confirmed a Protestant monarchy. See Caplan, *Constitutional Brinksmanship*, 5–6.

35. Tuck, *Sleeping Sovereign*, 185; Caplan, *Constitutional Brinksmanship*, 3–7.

36. As quoted in Caplan, *Constitutional Brinksmanship*, 6.

37. J. Franklin Jameson, "The Early Political Uses of the Word Convention," *The American Historical Review* 3, no. 3 (1898): 479n3, quoted in Caplan, *Constitutional Brinksmanship*, 6.

38. See generally Wood, *Creation of the American Republic*, 310–319.

39. Caplan, *Constitutional Brinksmanship*, 7.

40. Pennsylvania, Delaware, New Hampshire, Massachusetts, and Maryland held special elections to select constitutional convention delegates. The legislatures of Virginia, Georgia, and North Carolina opted to forgo a convention and draft the document themselves. The other states followed similar paths.

41. See Tuck, *Sleeping Sovereign*, 197n20.

42. Adams, *First American Constitutions*, 82; see also Wood, *Creation of the American Republic*, 308 (emphasis in original).

43. The first draft failed 9,972 to 2,083. The second draft arguably passed, but we can't be sure as town meetings voted provision by provision rather than up or down on the entire document. After spending weeks attempting to tally the confusing mix of votes, the convention gave up and declared the constitution ratified. See generally Adams, *First American Constitutions*, 66–90. For further consideration of the development of Massachusetts's constitutional regime, see Oscar and Mary Handlin, *The Popular Sources of Political Authority* (Cambridge, MA: Harvard University Press, 1966), and Ronald M. Peters, *The Massachusetts Constitution of 1780: A Social Compact* (Amherst: University of Massachusetts Press, 1978).

44. See Tuck, *Sleeping Sovereign*, 197–198.

45. Larry Kramer, *The People Themselves: Popular Constitutionalism and Judicial Review* (New York: Oxford University Press, 2004).

46. See generally Kramer, 228.

47. Kramer's thesis focuses on the role of judicial review in the American constitutional regime. While this is not the focus of our work, his explication of loci of popular constitutional meaning making is equally useful to an analysis of the development of amendment principles.

48. Kramer, *People Themselves*, 53.

49. See generally Wood, *Creation of the American Republic*, 306–309.

50. South Carolina was an outlier, allowing the state legislature to adopt amendments by simple majority vote and thus endorsing the British approach. See Adams, *First American Constitutions*, 138.

51. Adams, 76.

52. Adams, 137.

53. Mitchell Schmidt, "2020 Election Again Shows Lopsided Republican Legislative Maps," *Wisconsin State Journal*, November 12, 2020, https://madison.com/news/local/govt-and-politics/2020-election-again-shows-lopsided-republican-legislative-maps/article_d0c11425-df16-5d0b-a3e8-4954e7897652.html.

54. Adams, *First American Constitutions*, 138.

Chapter 2: Compromise and Tension

1. Max Farrand, ed., *The Records of the Federal Convention of 1787* (New Haven, CT: Yale University Press, 1937), 1:202–203.

2. This summary of Shays's Rebellion, and the paragraphs that follow, was gathered from a number of historical studies. See generally Leonard L. Richards, *Shays's Rebellion: The American Revolution's Final Battle* (Philadelphia: University of Pennsylvania Press, 2002), 1–5; Michael J. Klarman, *The Framers' Coup: The Making of the United States Constitution* (New York: Oxford University Press, 2016), 73–77; Richard D. Brown, "Shays Rebellion and the Ratification of the Federal Constitution in Massachusetts," in *Beyond Confederation: Origins of the Constitution and American National Identity*, ed. Richard Beeman, Stephen Botein, and Edward C. Carter II (Chapel Hill: Omohundro Institute and University of North Carolina Press, 1987), 15; David P. Szatmary, *Shays' Rebellion: The Making of an Agrarian Insurrection* (Amherst: University of Massachusetts Press, 1980). For another account, arguing that Shays was unjustifiably made into a demagogue by contemporary elites, see Charles U. Zug, "Creating a Demagogue: The Political Origins of Daniel Shays's Erroneous Legacy in American Political History," *American Political Thought* 10, no. 4 (September 1, 2021): 601–628.

3. See generally Richards, *Shays's Rebellion: The American Revolution's Final Battle*, 1–10.

4. "To George Washington from David Humphreys, 9 November 1786," *Founders Online*, National Archives, https://founders.archives.gov/documents/Washington/04-04-02-0313. Original source: *The Papers of George Washington*, Confederation Series, vol. 4, *2 April 1786–31 January 1787*, ed. W. W. Abbot (Charlottesville: University Press of Virginia, 1995), 350–352 (quote edited to modernize grammar, spelling, and syntax).

5. Richards, *Shays's Rebellion: The American Revolution's Final Battle*, 2.

6. Klarman, *Framers' Coup*, 73.

7. See generally Richards, *Shays's Rebellion: The American Revolution's Final Battle*, 27–29.

8. As quoted in Klarman, *Framers' Coup*, 73.

9. Klarman, 73.

10. Klarman, 73.

11. Gordon S. Wood, *The Creation of the American Republic, 1776–1787* (Chapel Hill: University of North Carolina Press, 1969), 354–355.

12. See generally Klarman, *Framers' Coup*, chap. 1.

13. As quoted in Klarman, 12.

14. As quoted in Russell L. Caplan, *Constitutional Brinksmanship: Amending the Constitution by National Convention* (New York: Oxford University Press, 1988), 26 (in original, "shew").

15. As quoted in Klarman, *Framers' Coup*, 25.

16. As quoted in Klarman, 119.

17. As quoted in Caplan, *Constitutional Brinksmanship*, 26 (in original, "legallity").

18. Farrand, *Records of the Federal Convention*, 1:121.

19. John R. Vile, *The Constitutional Amending Process in American Political Thought* (New York: Praeger, 1992), 1.

20. Farrand, *Records of the Federal Convention*, 1:121.

21. Vile, *The Constitution Amending Process in American Political Thought*, 122. See generally Kurt T. Lash, "Rejecting Conventional Wisdom: Federalist Ambivalence in the Framing and Implementation of Article V," *American Journal of Legal History* 38, no. 2 (1994): 202–207.

22. Lash, "Rejecting Conventional Wisdom," 202–203.

23. See Farrand, *Records of the Federal Convention*, 3:120 (noting that under the Pinckney Plan, congressional approval would be required for approval of amendments). See also Lash, "Rejecting Conventional Wisdom," 202n36.

24. Farrand, *Records of the Federal Convention*, 2:468. The inclusion of the two-thirds threshold was likely imported from the Articles' provisions regarding war and coinage. See Caplan, *Constitutional Brinksmanship*, 28.

25. Farrand, *Records of the Federal Convention*, 1:519 ("Mr. Gerry. The world at large expect something from us. If we do nothing, it appears to me we must have war and confusion—for the old confederation would be at an end. Let us see if no concession can be made. Accommodation is absolutely necessary, and defects may be amended by a future convention."). See also Caplan, *Constitutional Brinksmanship*, 28.

26. Farrand, *Records of the Federal Convention*, 2:532.

27. Farrand, 2:558.

28. Farrand, 2:557–558.

29. Farrand, 2:202–203. See also Caplan, *Constitutional Brinksmanship*, 28.

30. Farrand, *Records of the Federal Convention*, 2:558.

31. Farrand, 2:559 (New Hampshire was divided; Delaware voted no).

32. Farrand, 2:559.

33. Farrand, 2:559.

34. James Iredell, *Debate in North Carolina Ratifying Convention* (29 July 1788), *The Debates of the Several State Conventions on the Adoption of the Federal Constitution* (Jonathan Elliot, ed., 1836), 2:432. As quoted in Lash, "Rejecting Conventional Wisdom," 204–205n51.

35. George Mason, *George Mason's Account of Certain Proceedings in Convention*, reprinted in Farrand, *Records of the Federal Convention*, 3:367. As quoted in Lash, 204–205n51.

36. Farrand, *Records of the Federal Convention*, 2:629.

37. Farrand, 2:629.

38. Farrand, 2:630

39. Farrand, 2:631.

40. Farrand, 2:631. For further consideration of Article V's unamendability provisions, see generally George Mader, "Generation Gaps and Ties That Bind: Constitutional Commitments and the Framers' Bequest of Unamendable Provisions," *Howard Law Journal* 60, no. 2 (2017): 483–518; George Mader, "Binding Authority: Unamendability in the United States Constitution—A Textual and Historical Analysis," *Marquette Law Review* 99, no. 4 (2016): 841–892. See also Richard Albert, *Constitutional Amendments: Making, Breaking, and Changing Constitutions* (New York: Oxford University Press, 2019), chap. 4.

41. Farrand, *Records of the Federal Convention*, 2:629.

42. Farrand, 2:629.

43. Farrand, 2:630.

44. Russell Caplan likewise considers Article V's two-track method its "essential compromise." See Caplan, *Constitutional Brinksmanship*, 29.

45. See Lash, "Rejecting Conventional Wisdom," 208–211.

46. "*The Federalist Papers*, No. 39," January 16, 1788, Avalon Project of the Yale Law School Goldman Law Library, https://avalon.law.yale.edu/18th_century/fed39.asp.

47. "*The Federalist Papers*, No. 43," January 23, 1788, Avalon Project of the Yale Law School Goldman Law Library, https://avalon.law.yale.edu/18th_century/fed43.asp.

48. *The Debates of the Several State Conventions on the Adoption of the Federal Constitution* (Jonathan Elliot, ed., 1836), 3:49. As quoted in Lash, "Rejecting Conventional Wisdom," 212.

49. Farrand, *Records of the Federal Convention*, 2:479.

50. The Tenth and Eleventh Amendments are potential, but effectively minor, exceptions to this general claim. The Tenth (ratified in 1791) provides that the federal government only possesses power delegated to it by the Constitution. As interpreted by the courts, the Tenth Amendment forbids the federal government from commandeering state officers and employees and from engaging in excessive coercion of state legislatures. See Printz v. United States, 521 U.S. 898 (1997) (commandeering); NFIB v. Sebelius, 567 U.S. 519 (2012) (theory of excessive coercion). We do not believe the Tenth Amendment, as interpreted, engaged in the kind of curtailing of federal power Mason and the other anti-federalists desired to provide and accomplish through the Article V power. The Eleventh (ratified in 1795) provides that states may not be sued by out-of-state citizens or foreigners and is the primary constitutional hook for the doctrine of state sovereign immunity; while this protects state sovereignty, it does not directly curtail federal power.

51. See, e.g., Michael B. Rappaport, "Reforming Article V: The Problems Created by the National Convention Amendment Method and How to Fix Them," *Virginia Law Review* 96, no. 7 (2010): 1513 ("The congressional amendment method has allowed Congress to promote amendments that accord with its own preferences").

52. See generally Bruce Ackerman, *We the People*, vol. 3, *The Civil Rights Revolution* (Cambridge, MA: Belknap Press of Harvard University Press, 2014).

53. Alexis de Tocqueville, *Democracy in America*, trans. Henry Reeve (New York: G. Adlard, 1839), 94.

54. George Washington to David Humphreys, October 10, 1787, in Farrand, *Records of the Federal Convention*, 3:103–104.

55. Letter of George Washington to Bushrod Washington, November 10, 1787, in *The Origins of the American Constitution: a Documentary History*, ed. Michael Kammen (New York: Penguin, 1986), 83. As quoted in Sanford Levinson, *Our Undemocratic Constitution: Where the Constitution Goes Wrong (and How We the People Can Correct It)* (New York: Oxford University Press, 2006), 21.

56. Klarman, *Framers' Coup*, 596.

57. Farrand, *Records of the Federal Convention*, 1:202–203.

CHAPTER 3: THE ARCHAICS

1. Drew DeSilver, "Congress Has Long Struggled to Pass Spending Bills on Time," *Pew Research Center* (blog), January 16, 2018, https://www.pewresearch.org/fact-tank/2018/01/16/congress-has-long-struggled-to-pass-spending-bills-on-time/.

2. See Sanford Levinson, *Constitutional Faith* (Princeton, NJ: Princeton University Press, 1988).

3. Rather than the noun *archaisms*, we use the term *archaics* as a plural of the adjectival form to place proper emphasis on the habit of perceiving and labeling constitutional provisions as archaic. As we explain, the provisions are never truly archaisms. All constitutional provisions are of the same, equally legitimate stature until they are removed from the Constitution through the Article V mechanism. Rather, it is the public perception of the provisions that changes, requiring a term that appropriately denotes the habit of developing and assigning the archaic moniker.

4. See http://twitter.com/jimamendments/. Some lawyers did seek leave as amicus to argue that the Third Amendment posed a constitutional challenge to the federal eviction moratorium during the COVID-19 pandemic. The court dismissed as moot the group's request to complete full briefing. See Alabama Association of Realtors v. United States Department of Health and Human Services, No 20-cv-3377 (DLF), (D.D.C. Aug. 13, 2021). See also Christian Britschgi, "Is the CDC's Eviction Moratorium a Third Amendment Violation?," *Reason* (blog), August 10, 2021, https://reason.com/2021/08/10/is-the-cdcs-eviction-moratorium-a-third-amendment-violation/.

5. See Griswold v. Connecticut, 381 U.S. 479, 484 (1965) ("The Third Amendment, in its prohibition against the quartering of soldiers 'in any house' in time of peace without the consent of the owner, is another facet of that privacy.").

6. Courts have held some acts of Congress to violate the Constitution's prohibition against bills of attainder. See, e.g., United States v. Brown, 381 U.S. 437 (1965); Foretich, Doris v. United States, 351 F.3d 1198 (D.C. Cir. 2003).

7. The foreign emoluments clause was the subject of litigation during the Trump administration. See Brent Kendall, "Supreme Court Orders Emoluments Lawsuits Against Trump Be Dismissed," *Wall Street Journal*, January 25, 2021, https://www.wsj.com/articles/supreme-court-orders-emoluments-lawsuits-against-trump-be-dismissed-11611592201; Jacob Gershman, "Lawsuit Against Donald Trump Shines Light on Emoluments Clause," *Wall Street Journal*, January 23, 2017, https://www.wsj.com/articles/lawsuit-against-donald-trump-shines-light-on-emoluments-clause-1485204840.

8. See Luther v. Borden, 48 U.S. (7 How.) 1 (1849) (holding that the clause posed nonjusticiable political questions).

9. For a further examination of other "odd clauses," see Jay Wexler, *The Odd Clauses: Understanding the Constitution Through Ten of Its Most Curious Provisions* (Boston: Beacon Press, 2011).

10. 554 U.S. 570 (2008).

11. There are modern state militias—distinct from the National Guard—in some states. They are often volunteer and operate exclusively under state law. See "State Guard Association of the United States," accessed September 20, 2021, https://sgaus.org/states/commanders/.

12. Morris D. Forkosch, *Constitutional Law*, 2nd ed. (Mineola, NY: Foundation Press, 1969), 334, § 332, as quoted in Brannon P. Denning and Glenn H. Reynolds, "Constitutional Incidents: Interpretation in Real Time," *Tennessee Law Review* 70, no. 2 (2003): 282.

13. In this footnote Professor Tribe wrote that "the narrowly limited aim of the amendment [to protect state militias from federal interference was] merely ancillary to other constitutional guarantees of state sovereignty." See Laurence H. Tribe, *American Constitutional Law* (Mineola, NY: Foundation Press, 1978), 226n6.

14. The 1988 edition, which again included only one footnote reference to the amendment, noted that "any invocation of the amendment as a restriction on state or local gun control" was appropriately foreclosed by the amendment's text, history, and over a century of judicial decisions. See Laurence H. Tribe, *American Constitutional Law*, 2nd ed. (Mineola, NY: Foundation Press, 1988), 299n6.

15. Sanford Levinson, "The Embarrassing Second Amendment," *Yale Law Journal* 99, no. 3 (1989): 639–640.

16. L. H. LaRue, "Constitutional Law and Constitutional History," *Buffalo Law Review* 36, no. 2 (1987): 375 (capitalization as in original).

17. Russell D. Feingold, "The Armed Amendment: The Bases and Prospects for the Modern Significance of the Second Amendment to the United States Constitution" (Senior Honors Thesis in Political Science, University of Wisconsin–Madison, 1975), vii, on file with author.

18. Feingold, 3, 6.

19. Feingold, vii.

20. See, e.g., Printz v. United States, 521 U.S. 898, 938 n.2 (1997) (Thomas, concurring) ("Marshaling an impressive array of historical evidence, a growing body of scholarly commentary indicates that the 'right to keep and bear arms' is, as the Amendment's text suggests, a personal right."). For an overview of the development of academic and political resolve regarding a personal right in the Second Amendment, see generally Michael Waldman, *The Second Amendment: A Biography* (New York: Simon & Schuster, 2014), chap. 6.

21. Laurence H. Tribe, *American Constitutional Law*, 3rd ed. (New York: Foundation, 2000), 894–903.

22. 561 U.S. 742 (2010).

23. Some scholars continue to produce important and thought-provoking work on the subject. Professor Sanford Levinson has written widely on the topic. See, e.g., Levinson, *Our Undemocratic Constitution: Where the Constitution Goes Wrong (and How We the People Can Correct It)* (New York: Oxford University Press, 2006); Sanford Levinson, "Accounting for Constitutional Change or, How Many Times Has the United States Constitution Been Amended: A <26; B 26; C >26; D All of the Above," *Constitutional Commentary* 8 (1991): 409–432. Professor Richard Albert has also published insightful pieces on the topic. See, e.g., Richard Albert, *Constitutional Amendments: Making, Breaking, and Changing Constitutions* (New York: Oxford University Press, 2019). So too has Professor Aziz Huq written thought-provoking work on Article V. See, e.g., Aziz Z. Huq, "The Function of Article V," *University of Pennsylvania Law Review* 162, no. 5 (2014): 1165–1236.

24. Garrick B. Pursley, "Defeasible Federalism," *Alabama Law Review* 63, no. 4 (2012): 865 ("There is fairly broad consensus today that Article V's process is too onerous to provide for sufficient adaptability.").

25. Bruce Ackerman, "The Emergency Constitution," *Yale Law Journal* 113, no. 5 (2004): 1077.

26. Sanford Levinson, "Meliorism v. Bomb-Throwing as Techniques of Reform," *Tulsa Law Review* 48, no. 3 (2013): 491.

27. Huq, "The Function of Article V," 1235 (Professor Huq characterizes the common view in this way but argues there are redeeming qualities to Article V that should be considered). For a similar rendition of the common academic approach and a gathering of sources upon which we in part relied, see Richard Albert, "Constitutional Disuse or

Desuetude: The Case of Article V," *Boston University Law Review* 94, no. 3 (2014): 1046–1048.

28. See Zachary Elkins, Tom Ginsburg, and James Melton, *The Endurance of National Constitutions* (Cambridge: Cambridge University Press, 2009), 101. See also Donald S. Lutz, "Toward a Theory of Constitutional Amendment," *The American Political Science Review* 88, no. 2 (1994): 369 (summarizing a study of amendment provisions of thirty-two national constitutions); Richard Albert, "The Structure of Constitutional Amendment Rules," *Wake Forest Law Review* 49, no. 4 (2014): 913–976.

29. The body of scholarship on this topic is too vast to cite fully here. Consider, generally: Erwin Chemerinsky, *We the People: A Progressive Reading of the Constitution for the Twenty-First Century* (New York: Picador, 2018); John O. McGinnis and Michael B. Rappaport, *Originalism and the Good Constitution* (Cambridge, MA: Harvard University Press, 2013); David A. Strauss, "Common Law Constitutional Interpretation," *University of Chicago Law Review* 63, no. 3 (1996): 877–936.

30. See William N. Eskridge and John A. Ferejohn, *A Republic of Statutes: The New American Constitution* (New Haven, CT: Yale University Press, 2010); William N. Eskridge Jr., "America's Statutory Constitution," *U.C. Davis Law Review* 41, no. 1 (2007): 1–44.

31. Bruce Ackerman, "Higher Lawmaking," in *Responding to Imperfection: The Theory and Practice of Constitutional Amendment*, ed. Sanford Levinson (Princeton, NJ: Princeton University Press, 1995), 63. See also Levinson, *Our Undemocratic Constitution*, 23.

32. See generally Bruce Ackerman, *We the People*, vol. 1, *Foundations* (Cambridge, MA: Belknap Press of Harvard University Press, 1991), chap. 10; see also Bruce Ackerman, *We the People*, vol. 2, *Transformations* (Cambridge, MA: Belknap Press of Harvard University Press, 1998), chap. 1; but see Michael W. McConnell, "The Forgotten Constitutional Moment," *Constitutional Commentary* 11, no. 1 (1994): 115–144 (critiquing theory); Randy E. Barnett, "We the People: Each and Every One," *Yale Law Journal* 123, no. 8 (2014): 2576–2615 (same).

33. See generally Ackerman, *We the People*, vol. 2, *Transformations*, chaps. 10, 11.

34. Stephen M. Griffin, "The Nominee Is . . . Article V," *Constitutional Commentary* 12, no. 2 (1995): 172.

35. Most of this change occurs under the rubric of "historical gloss." See generally Curtis A. Bradley and Trevor W. Morrison, "Historical Gloss and the Separation of Powers," *Harvard Law Review* 126, no. 2 (2012): 411–485; Alison L. LaCroix, "Historical Gloss: A Primer," *Harvard Law Review Forum* 126 (2013): 75–85. Regarding war powers, the recent studies of this phenomenon by Professors Michael McConnell and Sai Prakash are particularly insightful. See Michael W. McConnell, *The President Who Would Not Be King: Executive Power Under the Constitution* (Princeton, NJ: Princeton University Press, 2020); Saikrishna Bangalore Prakash, *The Living Presidency: An Originalist Argument Against Its Ever-Expanding Powers* (Cambridge, MA: Belknap Press of Harvard University Press, 2020). Regarding foreign affairs, see generally Curtis A. Bradley, "Treaty Termination and Historical Gloss," *Texas Law Review* 92, no. 4 (2014): 773–836; Harold Koh, "Presidential Power to Terminate International Agreements," *Yale Law Journal Forum* 128 (2018): 432–481.

36. See David A. Strauss, "The Irrelevance of Constitutional Amendments," *Harvard Law Review* 114, no. 5 (2001): 1457–1505. But see Brannon P. Denning and John R.

Vile, "The Relevance of Constitutional Amendments: A Response to David Strauss," *Tulane Law Review* 77, no. 1 (2002): 247–282 (critiquing the irrelevance thesis); Adrian Vermeule, "Constitutional Amendments and the Constitutional Common Law" (University of Chicago Public Law & Legal Theory Working Paper No. 73, 2004) (same); Huq, "The Function of Article V" (arguing that the irrelevance thesis ignores certain stabilizing elements of the Article V regime).

37. Steven G. Calabresi and Livia Fine, "Two Cheers for Professor Balkin's Originalism," *Northwestern University Law Review* 103, no. 2 (2009): 682 ("The U.S. Constitution accomplishes these goals of promoting private ordering because it is so hard to pass laws and because it is almost impossible to amend the Constitution. This is why, in our opinion, we are the freest and most prosperous nation on earth.").

38. We understand that Richard Albert has also taught a course on constitutional amendment at the University of Texas School of Law. See http://law.utexas.edu/courses /class-details/20209/28230/.

39. Jesse Wegman, "Thomas Jefferson Gave the Constitution 19 Years. Look Where We Are Now," *New York Times*, August 4, 2021, https://www.nytimes.com/2021/08/04 /opinion/amend-constitution.html.

40. Jamelle Bouie, "The Constitution Was Made for Us, Not the Other Way Around," *New York Times*, October 29, 2021, https://www.nytimes.com/2021/10/29/opinion /democracy-madison-robert-dahl.html.

41. Per the authors' search at the time of printing. See Wilfred Codrington III, "The Framers Would Have Wanted Us to Change the Constitution," *Atlantic*, September 30, 2021, https://www.theatlantic.com/ideas/archive/2021/09/framers-would-have-wanted -us-change-constitution/620249/; Sanford Levinson, "The Constitution Is the Crisis," *Atlantic*, October 1, 2019, https://www.theatlantic.com/ideas/archive/2019/10/the-constitution-is -the-crisis/598435/.

42. For one example providing an overview of the historical use of the amendment mechanism, see John F. Kowal and Wilfred U. Codrington III, *The People's Constitution: 200 Years, 27 Amendments, and the Promise of a More Perfect Union* (New York: New Press, 2021).

43. See, e.g., Calabresi and Fine, "Two Cheers for Professor Balkin's Originalism."

44. Michael G. Kammen, *A Machine That Would Go of Itself: The Constitution in American Culture* (New York: Knopf, 1986), 142, 148.

45. See generally David E. Kyvig, *Explicit and Authentic Acts: Amending the U.S. Constitution, 1776–2015* (Lawrence: University Press of Kansas, 2016), 188 (and related citations). Kammen, *A Machine That Would Go of Itself*, 142.

46. Woodrow Wilson, *Congressional Government: A Study in American Politics*, 15th ed. (Boston: Houghton, Mifflin, 1901), 242. (This was the fifteenth edition of Wilson's published doctoral dissertation; he originally taught at Bryn Mawr College as an inaugural member of the faculty. See generally August Heckscher, *Woodrow Wilson* [New York: Scribner, 1991].)

47. Herman Vandenburg Ames, *The Proposed Amendments to the Constitution of the United States During the First Century of Its History* (Washington, D.C.: Government Printing Office, 1897), 301.

48. Henry M. Bates, "The American Bar Association's Meeting at Portland," *Michigan Law Review*, 1907, 54.

49. William P. Potter, "Method of Amending the Federal Constitution," *University of Pennsylvania Law Review and American Law Register* 57, no. 9 (1909): 590; Kyvig, *Explicit and Authentic Acts*, 193.

50. Potter, "Method of Amending the Federal Constitution," 593.

51. T. J. Jackson Lears, *Rebirth of a Nation: The Making of Modern America, 1877–1920* (New York: HarperCollins, 2009), 1.

52. See generally Emily J. Zackin, *Looking for Rights in All the Wrong Places: Why State Constitutions Contain America's Positive Rights* (Princeton, NJ: Princeton University Press, 2013).

53. See generally Kyvig, *Explicit and Authentic Acts*, 193–194.

54. As quoted in Russell L. Caplan, *Constitutional Brinksmanship: Amending the Constitution by National Convention* (New York: Oxford University Press, 1988), 64. For discussion of the counting of state convention applications, see Fred P. Graham, "The Role of the States in Proposing Constitutional Amendments," *American Bar Association Journal* 49, no. 12 (1963): 1175–1183.

55. As quoted in Caplan, *Constitutional Brinksmanship*, 64–65.

56. As quoted in Caplan, 64–65.

57. Joseph R. Long, "Tinkering with the Constitution," *Yale Law Journal* 24, no. 7 (1915): 588.

58. Heckscher, *Woodrow Wilson*, 76.

CHAPTER 4: A SLEEPING GIANT

1. John DeWitt, "Essays 1 and 11 (1787)," reprinted in *The Anti-Federalist Papers and the Constitutional Convention Debates*, ed. Ralph Ketcham (New York: New American Library, 2003), 189, 195. As quoted in Richard Albert, "Constitutional Disuse or Desuetude: The Case of Article V," *Boston University Law Review* 94, no. 3 (2014): 1048.

2. Herman Vandenburg Ames, *The Proposed Amendments to the Constitution of the United States During the First Century of Its History* (Washington, DC: Government Printing Office, 1897) 304. See Marbury v. Madison, 5 U.S. (1 Cranch) 137, 177 (1803) ("The constitution is either a superior, paramount law, unchangeable by ordinary means, or it is on a level with ordinary legislative acts, and like other acts, is alterable when the legislature shall please to alter it.")

3. Max Farrand, ed., *The Records of the Federal Convention of 1787* (New Haven, CT: Yale University Press, 1937), 2:558 (in original quote, "supplying defects." *Supplying* in this usage is synonymous with *repair* or *replace*.). See OED Online, s.v. "supply, v.1," last modified March 2022, https://www.oed.com/view/Entry/194666?rskey=dHyIr6&result=2&isAdvanced=false.

4. Farrand, *Records of the Federal Convention*, 2:557–558.

5. Some scholars and commentators have also introduced the notion of amendment as a "sleeping giant." See, e.g., Yaniv Roznai, "Amendment Power, Constituent Power, and Popular Sovereignty," in *The Foundations and Traditions of Constitutional Amendment*, ed. Richard Albert, Xenophon Contiades, and Alkmene Fotiadou (Oxford: Hart, 2017), 31 (and citations therein). Professor Amar has also used the term to describe Article IV's Republican Guarantee Clause. See Akhil Reed Amar, *America's Constitution: A Biography* (New York: Random House, 2005), 281, 380, 609n65 (using phrase and noting historical genesis in congressional debates, respectively).

6. Herbert J. Storing, *What the Anti-Federalists Were For* (Chicago: University of Chicago Press, 1981), 7.

7. David E. Kyvig, *Explicit and Authentic Acts: Amending the U.S. Constitution, 1776–2015* (Lawrence: University Press of Kansas, 2016), 66–67.

8. Storing, *What the Anti-Federalists Were For*, 7.

9. Article VII provides that the Constitution would only be binding on those states that ratified it: "The Ratification of the Conventions of nine States, shall be sufficient for the Establishment of this Constitution between the States so ratifying the Same." But the reality that states that refused ratification would be *functionally* bound by it is clear. What were states to do if they did not ratify? Cast their state governments as new sovereign entities, crafting a foreign policy with the United States with which they used to be bound? The economic impact of such a state of affairs was made plain by the case of Rhode Island.

10. Pauline Maier, *Ratification: The People Debate the Constitution, 1787–1788* (New York: Simon & Schuster, 2011), 223–224.

11. Bruce Ackerman and Neal Katyal, "Our Unconventional Founding," *University of Chicago Law Review* 62, no. 2 (1995): 527 (noting vote and also that many federalists likely boycotted the poll); see also Maier, *Ratification*, 223 (noting boycotts).

12. See Ackerman and Katyal, "Our Unconventional Founding," 538 (noting role of the Senate's proposed embargo on ratification); see also Calvin H. Johnson, *Righteous Anger at the Wicked States: The Meaning of the Founders' Constitution* (Cambridge: Cambridge University Press, 2005), 153–154.

13. As quoted in Ackerman and Katyal, "Our Unconventional Founding," 538.

14. It is important to note Jonathan Gienapp's compelling argument that the idea of constitutionalism was not yet settled in the Founding generation. Nonetheless, concern regarding the legality of the Convention as understood under the Articles' amendability framework remains an important component of the anti-federalist critique. See generally Jonathan Gienapp, *The Second Creation: Fixing the American Constitution in the Founding Era* (Cambridge, MA: Harvard University Press, 2018). Michael Klarman likewise calls the Constitution a "coup." See Michael J. Klarman, *The Framers' Coup: The Making of the United States Constitution* (New York: Oxford University Press, 2016).

15. Kyvig, *Explicit and Authentic Acts*, 68.

16. Kyvig, 68.

17. See Kyvig, 75.

18. Akhil Reed Amar, *The Bill of Rights: Creation and Reconstruction* (New Haven, CT: Yale University Press, 1998), 10–11.

19. See generally Storing, *What the Anti-Federalists Were For*, chap. 6; see also Amar, *Bill of Rights*, 3–19.

20. Storing, *What the Anti-Federalists Were For*, 51.

21. Storing, 15.

22. See generally Storing, chap. 8.

23. Gienapp, *Second Creation*, 51.

24. For a consideration of the history of textual rights guarantees in the early American constitutional imagination, see Gienapp, 50–53.

25. As quoted in Kyvig, *Explicit and Authentic Acts*, 92.

26. "New York Ratifying Convention. Circular Letter to the Governors of the Several States, 26 July 1788," in *The Papers of Alexander Hamilton*, ed. Harold C. Syrett, vol. 5, *June 1788–November 1789* (New York: Columbia University Press, 1962), 196.

27. See generally John P. Kaminski, *George Clinton: Yeoman Politician of the New Republic* (Madison, WI: Madison House, 1993), 166–169.

28. See generally Kaminski, 166–169; Gienapp, *Second Creation*, 168; Klarman, *Framers' Coup*, 439–442, 468–476, 513–514, 554–555.

29. Gienapp, *Second Creation*, 172.

30. The second, concerning apportionment and the size of the House of Representatives, remains active today as one of six unratified amendments. The People could ratify the proposal should they desire, although the road is steep. The proposal would need twenty-seven additional ratifications.

31. Kyvig, *Explicit and Authentic Acts*, 88.

32. See generally Kyvig, chap. 5. Jonathan Gienapp challenges this claim, arguing the concerns with the Constitution had largely subsided after the First Congress was seated. See Gienapp, *Second Creation*, 169–170.

33. See Thomas Jefferson, *A Manual of Parliamentary Practice: For the Use of the Senate of the United States*, with annotations by the author, Senate Document 103–108 (Washington, D.C.: Government Printing Office, 1801).

34. See Ames, *Proposed Amendments to the Constitution*, 19–20.

35. 2 U.S. 419 (1793).

36. See generally Kyvig, *Explicit and Authentic Acts*, 112–114. For a compelling consideration of the history and meaning of the Eleventh Amendment, see generally William Baude and Stephen E. Sachs, "The Misunderstood Eleventh Amendment," *University of Pennsylvania Law Review* 167, no. 3 (2021).

37. Alexander Keyssar, *Why Do We Still Have the Electoral College?* (Boston: Harvard University Press, 2020), 5.

38. See Keyssar, 398n17 (noting discrepancies in different studies on the question and likelihood that the sum is well above 900).

39. Amar, *America's Constitution*, 336.

40. See generally Edward J. Larson, *A Magnificent Catastrophe: The Tumultuous Election of 1800, America's First Presidential Campaign* (New York: Free Press, 2008).

41. See Keyssar, *Why Do We Still Have the Electoral College?*, 47–50.

42. Woodrow Wilson, *Congressional Government: A Study in American Politics*, 15th ed. (Boston: Houghton, Mifflin, 1901), 242.

43. Bruce Ackerman, *We the People*, vol. 2, *Transformations* (Cambridge, MA: Belknap Press of Harvard University Press, 1998), 2:99–119, 207–234.

44. Amar, *America's Constitution*, 364–380.

45. Kyvig, *Explicit and Authentic Acts*, 143–147.

46. Kyvig, 142.

47. Kyvig, 145.

48. Rob Bishop, "H.J.Res.32—116th Congress (2019–2020): Proposing an Amendment to the Constitution of the United States to Give States the Authority to Repeal Federal Rules and Regulations When the Repeal Is Agreed to by the Legislatures of Two-Thirds of the Several States," legislation, January 22, 2019, 32, 2019/2020, https://

www.congress.gov/bill/116th-congress/house-joint-resolution/32. For an overview of contemporary consideration of the nullification question, see generally Sanford Levinson, ed., *Nullification and Secession in Modern Constitutional Thought*, Constitutional Thinking (Lawrence: University Press of Kansas, 2016); James H. Read and Neal Allen, "Living, Dead, and Undead: Nullification Past and Present," *American Political Thought* 1, no. 2 (September 1, 2012): 263–297.

49. Kyvig, *Explicit and Authentic Acts*, 150–151.

50. Virginia (1 Annals of Cong. 258-259 [J. Gales, Sr. ed., 1834] [H.R., May 5, 1789]); New York (H.R. Jour., 1st Cong., 1st Sess. 29-30 [May 6, 1789]); Georgia (S. Jour., 22nd Cong., 2nd sess., 65-66 [Jan. 9, 1833]); South Carolina (H.R. Jour. 22nd Cong., 2nd Sess. 219-220 [Jan. 21, 1833]); Alabama (H.R. Jour., 22nd Cong., 2nd Sess., 361-362 [Feb. 19, 1833]); Kentucky (Cong. Globe, 36th Cong., 2nd Sess. 751 [S., Feb. 5, 1861]); Indiana (Cong. Globe, 37th Cong., Special Sess. 1465-1466 [S., Mar. 18, 1861]); New Jersey (Cong. Globe, 36th Cong., 2nd Sess. 680 [S., Feb. 1, 1861]); Ohio (1861 Ohio Laws 181); Illinois (1861 Ill. Laws 281-282). See also Fred P. Graham, "The Role of the States in Proposing Constitutional Amendments," *American Bar Association Journal* 49, no. 12 (1963): 1179 (reaching same convention application count).

51. Ames, *Proposed Amendments to the Constitution*, 19.

52. Kyvig, *Explicit and Authentic Acts*, 193.

53. Carl S. Smith, *Urban Disorder and the Shape of Belief: The Great Chicago Fire, the Haymarket Bomb, and the Model Town of Pullman* (Chicago: University of Chicago Press, 1995), pt. 2; Robert W. Ozanne, *The Labor Movement in Wisconsin: A History* (Madison, WI: State Historical Society of Wisconsin, 1984), chap. 1; Calvin Schermerhorn, "The Thibodaux Massacre Left 60 African-Americans Dead and Spelled the End of Unionized Farm Labor in the South for Decades," *Smithsonian Magazine*, November 21, 2017, https://beta.smithsonianmag.com/history/thibodaux-massacre-left-60-african-americans-dead-and-spelled-end-unionized-farm-labor-south-decades-180967289/; see also Thomas V. DiBacco, "Recalling 1887, Centennial Year of the Constitution," *Christian Science Monitor*, March 9, 1987, https://www.csmonitor.com/1987/0309/eight.html.

54. Jay S. Bybee, "Ulysses at the Mast: Democracy, Federalism, and the Sirens' Song of the Seventeenth Amendment," *Northwestern University Law Review* 91, no. 2 (1997): 538–539.

55. Bybee, 540.

56. Russell L. Caplan, *Constitutional Brinksmanship: Amending the Constitution by National Convention* (New York: Oxford University Press, 1988), 63. The claims of corruption were not idle talk. From 1857 to 1900, the Senate had investigated several of its members for either taking bribes or bribing state legislators to secure election. State commissions in Alabama, Arkansas, California, Montana, Ohio, Pennsylvania, and Utah had taken up the issue of corruption in legislative selection of senators. As perhaps can be expected when any group investigates its own, however, many of the cases were dismissed for lack of evidence. See Bybee, "Ulysses at the Mast," 539n256. George Henry Haynes, *The Election of Senators* (New York: Henry Holt and Co., 1906), 53–56 (listing Senate investigations); see also Bybee, "Ulysses at the Mast," 539. The *Louisville Courier Journal* put it bluntly in 1897: "To be a Senator is to be a suspect." As quoted in David J. Rothman, *Politics and Power: The United States Senate, 1869–1901* (Cambridge, MA: Harvard University Press, 1966), 243; see also Kyvig, *Explicit and Authentic Acts*, 209.

Despite the lack of widespread investigation or structural change, a few notable exceptions emboldened the claim that the political system was awash with dishonesty and misconduct. In 1900, for example, Senator William Clark of Montana resigned after a Senate investigation found he had bought a majority of the votes in the state legislature necessary for his election. Clark typified the Gilded Age and its excesses. A copper and railroad magnate born in a Pennsylvania log cabin, Clark would later go on to build a 121-room mansion on Fifth Avenue in New York and amass a fortune worth over $3 billion today. Underscoring just how far the Senate had fallen, the Montana legislature reelected him the next year. See Bybee, "Ulysses at the Mast," 539. In response to claims that this second election was as sullied as the first, he famously quipped, "I never bought a man who wasn't for sale." See Matt Schudel, "Huguette Clark, Copper Heiress and Recluse, Dies at 104," *Washington Post*, May 24, 2011, https://www.washingtonpost.com/local /obituaries/huguette-clark-copper-heiress-and-recluse-dies-at-104/2011/05/24/AFxf XrAH_story.html.

57. Steven R. Weisman, *The Great Tax Wars: Lincoln to Wilson: The Fierce Battles over Money and Power That Transformed the Nation* (New York: Simon & Schuster, 2002), chap. 6; see also Michael E. McGerr, *A Fierce Discontent: The Rise and Fall of the Progressive Movement in America, 1870–1920* (New York: Free Press, 2003), 98.

58. See generally, T. J. Jackson Lears, *Rebirth of a Nation: The Making of Modern America, 1877–1920* (New York: HarperCollins, 2009); McGerr, *A Fierce Discontent*.

59. 158 U.S. 564 (1895).

60. As quoted in Kathleen Spaltro, "'I Shall Preserve Inviolate the Integrity of My Soul': Eugene V. Debs as a Prisoner in Woodstock, Illinois," *Illinois Heritage* 19, no. 4 (2016): 11–13.

61. The details of Debs's stay in Woodstock are particularly interesting. With the Supreme Court's unanimous sanction, federal authorities hoped that, jailed in Woodstock, Debs would capitulate and end his quixotic battle against the country's economic and political establishment. But the court had perhaps chosen the wrong jailer. George Eckert, the sheriff of McHenry County, "had read and heard . . . that I was a desperate and dangerous criminal and that I should be treated accordingly," Debs would later recount, "but this did not alter his determination to accord to me the treatment due to any other prisoner in his custody." Eckert allowed Debs to read, study, exchange correspondence, receive visitors, and even use an empty jail cell to print his union publication, the *Railway Times*. Leading labor organizers and Socialists, one of whom provided Debs with his first copy of Karl Marx's *Das Kapital*, became frequent dinner guests at the sheriff's house above the jail on the small town square. See generally Spaltro.

62. See generally Spaltro.

63. See Ernest Freeberg, *Democracy's Prisoner: Eugene V. Debs, the Great War, and the Right to Dissent* (Cambridge, MA: Harvard University Press, 2008), 13.

64. "RADICALS: Eugene V. Debs," *Time*, November 1, 1926, http://content.time .com/time/subscriber/article/0,33009,722648,00.html.

65. Eugene V. Debs, *Writings and Speeches of Eugene V. Debs* (New York: Hermitage Press, 1948), 19–20.

66. See generally Freeberg, *Democracy's Prisoner*, chap. 1.

67. Tim Davenport and David Walters, eds., *The Selected Works of Eugene V. Debs*, vol. 3, electronic resource (Chicago: Haymarket Books, 2020), 74.

68. 1893 Neb. Laws 466-467. See also Graham, "Role of the States," 1179, 1183n1. Robert Caplan, for example, notes that *requests* for a constitutional amendment addressing the direct election question were transmitted to Congress as early as 1874. Yet these were not Article V applications. See Caplan, *Constitutional Brinksmanship*, 63.

69. 33 Cong. Rec. 219 (1899).

70. Caplan, *Constitutional Brinksmanship*, 63.

71. Montana (35 Cong. Rec. 208 [1901]); Pennsylvania (45 Cong. Rec. 7118 [1910]); Michigan (45 Cong. Rec. 7116 [1910]); Idaho (45 Cong. Rec. 7113-7114 [1910]); Colorado (45 Cong. Rec. 7113 [1910]); Arkansas (45 Cong. Rec. 7113 [1910]); Tennessee (35 Cong. Rec. 2344 [1902]); Texas (again) (45 Cong. Rec. 7119 [1910]); Oregon (35 Cong. Rec. 117 [1901]); Nevada (35 Cong. Rec. 112 [1901]); Minnesota (34 Cong. Rec. 2560 [1901]); Washington (1901 WA Laws 333); North Carolina (1901 NC Sess. Laws 1039); Missouri (1901 MO Laws 268); Michigan (35 Cong. Rec. 117 [1901]); Kentucky (45 Cong. Rec. 7115 [1910]).

72. 45 Cong. Rec. 7114 (1910) (noting 1903 application).

73. Caplan, *Constitutional Brinksmanship*, 64.

74. See Jill Lepore, "The Age of Consent: Writing, and Rewriting, Constitutions," *The New Yorker*, March 29, 2021, 79. (Lepore used the term *rewriting* in the past tense: "The U.S. Constitution has been rewritten three times.")

75. Others have noted that Article V has a "prodding" effect. See, e.g., Charles W. Hucker, "Constitutional Convention Poses Questions," *Congressional Quarterly Weekly Report* 37, February 17, 1979, 273–276; see also Roger C. Hartley, *How Failed Attempts to Amend the Constitution Mobilize Political Change* (Nashville, TN: Vanderbilt University Press, 2017); Dwight W. Connely, "Amending the Constitution: Is This Any Way to Call for a Constitutional Convention," *Arizona Law Review* 22, no. 4 (1980): 1016n49 (and citations therein); Thomas H. Neale, "CRS Report R42592; The Article V Convention for Proposing Constitutional Amendments: Historical Perspectives for Congress," October 22, 2012, 9, https://crsreports.congress.gov/product/details?prodcode=R42592.

76. See Caplan, *Constitutional Brinksmanship*, 65 (arguing that a causal link is debated); c.f. Kyvig, *Explicit and Authentic Acts*, 213–215 (putting forth an alternative view).

77. Kyvig, *Explicit and Authentic Acts*, 213.

78. See generally Graham, "Role of the States," 1179–1181.

79. As quoted in Caplan, *Constitutional Brinksmanship*, 64–65.

80. As quoted in Caplan, 64–65.

81. Kenneth D. Rose, *American Women and the Repeal of Prohibition*, The American Social Experience Series 33 (New York: New York University Press, 1996), 71.

82. See generally David E. Kyvig, *Repealing National Prohibition* (Chicago: University of Chicago Press, 1979); David E. Kyvig, ed., *Law, Alcohol, and Order: Perspectives on National Prohibition* (Westport, CT: Greenwood Press, 1985); James H. Timberlake, *Prohibition and the Progressive Movement, 1900–1920* (Cambridge, MA: Harvard University Press, 1963).

83. See Kyvig, *Repealing National Prohibition*, 19.

84. Thomas F. Schaller, "Democracy at Rest: Strategic Ratification of the Twenty-First Amendment," *Publius: The Journal of Federalism* 28, no. 2 (January 1, 1998): 82.

85. 253 U.S. 221, 231 (1920).

86. See generally Jason O. Heflin, "Article V Conventions: Lessons from the Repeal of Prohibition," *Wayne Law Review* 61, no. 2 (2016): 345–360; see also Everett S. Brown, "The Ratification of the Twenty-First Amendment," *The American Political Science Review* 29, no. 6 (1935): 1005–1017.

87. See Kyvig, *Explicit and Authentic Acts*, 367.

88. Robert Blaemire, *Birch Bayh: Making a Difference* (Bloomington: Indiana University Press, 2019), 53–54.

89. See generally Susan Salaz, "The Constitution According to Birch Bayh," *Indianapolis Monthly*, January 20, 2021, https://www.indianapolismonthly.com/news-and -opinion/politics/the-constitution-according-to-birch-bayh; Adam Clymer, "Birch Bayh, 91, Dies; Senator Drove Title IX and 2 Amendments," *New York Times*, March 14, 2019, https://www.nytimes.com/2019/03/14/obituaries/birch-bayh-dead.html; Kyvig, *Explicit and Authentic Acts*, 420–425. Regarding the Equal Rights Amendment, see generally Rebecca DeWolf, *Gendered Citizenship: The Original Conflict over the Equal Rights Amendment, 1920–1963* (Lincoln: University of Nebraska Press, 2021); Julie Chi-hye Suk, *We the Women: The Unstoppable Mothers of the Equal Rights Amendment* (New York: Skyhorse, 2020); June Melby Benowitz, *Challenge and Change: Right-Wing Women, Grassroots Activism, and the Baby Boom Generation* (Gainesville: University Press of Florida, 2015), chap. 6.

90. Among those listed as endorsing the document were the following: a sitting dean of Stanford Law School, a former dean of Berkeley Law (formerly Boalt Hall), multiple former attorneys general of the United States, a former professor and chief judge of the U.S. Court of Appeals for the District of Columbia Circuit, a former president of the American Bar Association, multiple former members of Congress, and many other notable leaders in law, government, and business. See "Great and Extraordinary Occasions: Developing Guidelines for Constitutional Change" (New York: The Century Foundation Press, 1999), xi–xvii.

91. "Great and Extraordinary Occasions," 2, 7.

92. See Kathleen Sullivan, "Constitutional Amendmentitis," *The American Prospect*, October 1, 1995, https://prospect.org/api/content/dcb5168d-fe5f-514c-8c81-35d8dd2d4603/.

93. See Drew DeSilver, "Constitutional Amendments in U.S. Rarely Go Anywhere," *Pew Research Center* (blog), April 12, 2018, https://www.pewresearch.org/fact-tank/2018 /04/12/a-look-at-proposed-constitutional-amendments-and-how-seldom-they-go -anywhere/.

94. See Carl Hulse and John Holusha, "Amendment on Flag Burning Fails by One Vote in Senate," *New York Times*, June 27, 2006, https://www.nytimes.com/2006/06/27 /washington/27cnd-flag.html.

95. "Budget Amendment Sinks in Senate," in *CQ Almanac 1995*, vol. 51, CQ Almanac Online Edition (Washington, D.C.: Congressional Quarterly, 1996), http://library .cqpress.com/cqalmanac/cqal95-1099955.

96. See Steve King, "Proposing an Amendment to the Constitution of the United States to Repeal the Sixteenth Article of Amendment.," H.J.Res.94 (2017), https://www .congress.gov/bill/115th-congress/house-joint-resolution/94.

97. See Ian Swanson, "Senate Republicans Offer Constitutional Amendment to Block Supreme Court Packing," *The Hill*, October 19, 2020, https://thehill.com/homenews /senate/521736-senate-republicans-offer-constitutional-amendment-to-block-supreme -court.

98. See "Rubio Proposes 'Right to Refuse' Constitutional Amendment That Would Invalidate ObamaCare's Mandate Tax," Marco Rubio: U.S. Senator for Florida, June 4, 2013, https://www.rubio.senate.gov/public/index.cfm/2013/6/rubio-proposes-right-to-refuse -constitutional-amendment-that-would-invalidate-obamacare-s-mandate-tax.

99. "US Senator Pushes Amendment to Shift Power Back to States," Associated Press, July 3, 2015, https://apnews.com/article/03da63fcd9bc4113bc8d5e22b872391c.

100. Dusty Johnson, "Proposing an Amendment to the Constitution of the United States to Repeal the Twenty-Third Article of Amendment to the Constitution of the United States," H.J.Res.19 (2021), https://www.congress.gov/bill/117th-congress/house -joint-resolution/19/text.

101. See Kevin Diaz, "Bachmann: No Foreign Currency," *Star Tribune*, March 26, 2009, https://www.startribune.com/bachmann-no-foreign-currency/41919847/; Brian Montopoli, "Bachmann Bill: Don't Replace the Dollar," March 26, 2009, https://www .cbsnews.com/news/bachmann-bill-dont-replace-the-dollar/.

CHAPTER 5: WHAT TRUMP AND THE TEA PARTY COULDN'T DO

1. Ken Stone, "Santorum to ALEC: Convene States to Amend Constitution (but Sidestep Trump)," *Times of San Diego*, December 3, 2021, https://timesofsandiego.com /politics/2021/12/02/santorum-to-alec-convene-states-to-amend-constitution-but -sidestep-trump/.

2. Convention of States Project, "Convention of States Historic Simulation Live-stream," streamed live on September 23, 2016, YouTube video, https://www.youtube.com /watch?v=vqqOVV4oRqI.

3. Nina Easton, "Political Fundamentals," *New York Times*, September 9, 2007, Books, https://www.nytimes.com/2007/09/09/books/review/Easton-t.html; Eric Lipton and Mark Walker, "Christian Conservative Lawyer Had Secretive Role in Bid to Block Election Result," *New York Times*, October 7, 2021, https://www.nytimes .com/2021/10/07/us/politics/religious-conservative-michael-farris-lawsuit-2020 -election.html.

4. Convention of States Project, "Convention of States Historic Simulation Live-stream," 30:09.

5. Convention of States Project, 3:40, 3:42; Rachel Lerman, "Major Trump Backer Rebekah Mercer Orchestrates Parler's Second Act," *Washington Post*, February 24, 2021, https://www.washingtonpost.com/technology/2021/02/24/parler-relaunch-rebekah -mercer/; Jack Nicas, "Parler, a Social Network That Attracted Trump Fans, Returns Online," *New York Times*, February 15, 2021, https://www.nytimes.com/2021/02/15 /technology/parler-back-online.html.

6. Proponents likely import the term *commissioner* from its common usage in some interstate compact bodies. The Great Lakes Basin Compact, for example, is governed by the Great Lakes Commission, the members of which are called commissioners. See, e.g., Minn. Stat. Ann. § 1.21 ("The members of the commission shall serve without compen-sation, but the expenses of each commissioner."). Same with the Atlantic States Marine Fisheries Compact. See Ann. Laws of Mass. ALM Spec L ch. S134, § 1 (using term *commissioner*). Same also with the interstate compact creating the Port of New York District and the Port Authority of New York and New Jersey. See NY CLS Unconsol.,

Ch. 151, § 1 (using term *commissioner*). But the use of the phrase in relation to an Article V convention has little precedent. And to equate an Article V convention with an interstate compact is erroneous as a matter of history and law. Indeed, all states that have codified regulations regarding Article V in their state codes use the term *delegate*. See, e.g., Fla. Stat. Ann. § 11.9345 ("a delegate or alternate delegate"); Tenn. Code Ann. § 3-18-106 (same); Ind. Code § 2-8.2-4-6 (same); Wyo. Stat. Ann. § 9-22-102 (same); S.D. Codified Laws § 2-15-20 (same); Wis. Stat § 13.176 (same); Ga. Code Ann. § 28-6-8 (same); Tex. Gov't Code § 393.001 (same); Tenn. Code Ann. § 3-18-104 (same); Utah Code Ann. § 20A-18-101 ("delegates").

7. Convention of States Project, "Convention of States Historic Simulation Live-stream," 3:35.

8. Convention of States Project, 3:38.

9. Convention of States Project, 3:28.

10. Convention of States Project, 3:23.

11. Sanya Mansoor, "A Tea Party Movement to Overhaul the Constitution Is Quietly Gaining Steam," *Time*, August 1, 2018, https://time.com/5356045/constitutional-convention-tea-party/.

12. Convention of States Project, "Convention of States Historic Simulation Live-stream," 3:23.

13. Convention of States Project, 3:34.

14. Jeremy W. Peters, "Jenna Ellis, a Senior Legal Adviser to the Trump Campaign, Is Not the Type of Lawyer She Plays on TV," *New York Times*, December 3, 2020, https://www.nytimes.com/2020/12/03/us/politics/jenna-ellis-a-senior-legal-adviser-to-the-trump-campaign-is-not-the-type-of-lawyer-she-plays-on-tv.html; Jeremy W. Peters and Alan Feuer, "How Is Trump's Lawyer Jenna Ellis 'Elite Strike Force' Material?," *New York Times*, December 3, 2020, https://www.nytimes.com/2020/12/03/us/politics/jenna-ellis-trump.html; Phillip Bump, "Analysis | Another Lawyer, Another Memo Offering Advice on Stealing the Presidency," *Washington Post*, November 15, 2021, http://www.washingtonpost.com/politics/2021/11/15/another-lawyer-another-memo-offering-advice-stealing-presidency/; Libby Cathey, "Memo from Trump Attorney Outlined How Pence Could Overturn Election, Says New Book," *ABC News*, November 14, 2021, https://abcnews.go.com/Politics/memo-trump-attorney-outlined-pence-overturn-election-book/story?id=81134003.

15. Jenna Ellis and Michael Farris, "A Convention of the States to Amend the Constitution," *National Review*, September 29, 2016, https://www.nationalreview.com/2016/09/constitutional-amendments-states-convention/.

16. Travis Waldron, "A Radical Right-Wing Dream to Rewrite the Constitution Is Close to Coming True," *Huffington Post*, April 27, 2021, https://www.huffpost.com/entry/mark-meckler-article-five-constitutional-convention_n_6086c380e4b09cce6c143b10.

17. Jamiles Lartey, "Conservatives Call for Constitutional Intervention Last Seen 230 Years Ago," *Guardian*, August 11, 2018, https://www.theguardian.com/us-news/2018/aug/11/conservatives-call-for-constitutional-convention-alec.

18. *Robert's Rules of Order* is a manual of parliamentary procedure.

19. John F. Kowal and Wilfred U. Codrington III, *The People's Constitution: 200 Years, 27 Amendments, and the Promise of a More Perfect Union* (New York: New Press, 2021), 258.

20. Whether state legislators are empowered to select convention delegates is an open, unanswered question. The Constitution provides no explicit grant of such authority.

21. Brown v. Board of Education of Topeka, 347 U.S. 483 (1954).

22. Gideon v. Wainwright, 372 U.S. 335 (1963).

23. Baker v. Carr, 369 U.S. 186 (1962); Reynolds v. Sims, 377 U.S. 533 (1964).

24. See Michael W. McConnell, "The Redistricting Cases: Original Mistakes and Current Consequences," *Harvard Journal of Law & Public Policy* 24, no. 1 (2000): 105.

25. Earl Warren, *The Memoirs of Earl Warren* (Doubleday, 1977), 306.

26. Colegrove v. Green, 328 U.S. 549, 556 (1946) (plurality opinion).

27. Kim Isaac Eisler, *A Justice for All: William J. Brennan, Jr., and the Decisions That Transformed America* (New York: Simon & Schuster, 1993), 175.

28. See generally Everett McKinley Dirksen, "The Supreme Court and the People," *Michigan Law Review* 66, no. 5 (1968): 837–874; Arthur Earl Bonfield, "The Dirksen Amendment and the Article V Convention Process," *Michigan Law Review* 66, no. 5 (1968): 949–1000.

29. John R. Vile, *Encyclopedia of Constitutional Amendments, Proposed Amendments, and Amending Issues, 1789–2010* (Santa Barbara, CA: ABC-CLIO, 2010), 17; see also Michael A. Almond, "Amendment by Convention: Our Next Constitutional Crisis," *North Carolina Law Review* 53, no. 3 (1975): 501n53.

30. As quoted in Congressional Record S.10113 (April 19, 1967) (Senator Dirksen, exhibit 1).

31. Fred P. Graham, "Efforts to Amend the Constitution on Districts Gain; One-Man, One-Vote Ruling Spurs First Bid for Charter Convention Since 1787," *New York Times*, March 18, 1967, https://www.nytimes.com/1967/03/18/archives/efforts-to-amend -the-constitution-on-districts-gain-oneman-onevote.html.

32. Graham.

33. See Bonfield, "Dirksen Amendment," 971.

34. Fred P. Graham, "Amendment Drive Meets Challenge; 26 State Petitions Termed Invalid by Two Senators," *New York Times*, March 23, 1967, https://www.nytimes .com/1967/03/23/archives/amendment-drive-meets-challenge-26-state-petitions -termed-invalid.html.

35. 113. Cong. Rec. 10112 (April 19, 1967) (remarks of Senator Proxmire).

36. 113. Cong. Rec. at 10113 (remarks of Senator Proxmire).

37. See Bonfield, "Dirksen Amendment," 950. See also Russell L. Caplan, *Constitutional Brinksmanship: Amending the Constitution by National Convention* (New York: Oxford University Press, 1988), 77. The act was passed by the Senate in 1971 and 1973 but never taken up in the House. Senator Orrin Hatch also introduced legislation to regulate a convention (Caplan, 77).

38. Caplan, 76.

39. Caplan, 76–77.

40. "Wilkie Is Opposed to 'Court of Union,'" *Beloit Daily News (Wis.)*, September 12, 1963.

41. Caplan, *Constitutional Brinksmanship*, 76.

42. As quoted in Caplan, 76.

43. See generally Terry Schwadron and Paul Richter, eds., *California and the American Tax Revolt: Proposition 13 Five Years Later* (Berkeley: University of California Press, 1984), 1–69.

44. As quoted in Caplan, *Constitutional Brinksmanship*, 79.

45. Caplan, 80.

46. Caplan, 81.

47. Caplan, 81.

48. Caplan, 81.

49. 140 Cong. Rec. 14,718 (1994).

50. Louisiana, 2008; Florida, 2010; Louisiana, 2011; North Dakota, 2011; Alabama, 2011; North Dakota, 2012; New Hampshire, 2012; Ohio, 2013; Ohio, 2013; Alabama, 2014; Alaska, 2014; Florida, 2014; Florida, 2014; Florida, 2014; Georgia, 2014; Georgia, 2014; Louisiana, 2014; Michigan, 2014; Tennessee, 2014; Alabama, 2015; North Dakota, 2015; South Dakota, 2015; Utah, 2015; Florida, 2016; Indiana, 2016; Kansas, 2016; New Hampshire, 2016; Oklahoma, 2016; West Virginia, 2016; West Virginia, 2016; Alaska, 2016; Tennessee, 2016; Louisiana, 2016; Arizona, 2017; Arizona, 2017; Missouri, 2017; North Dakota, 2017; Texas, 2017; Wisconsin, 2017; Wyoming, 2017; Missouri, 2017; Alabama, 2018; Utah, 2019; Arkansas, 2019; Mississippi, 2019; Oklahoma, 2021. Data compiled from the Clerk of the House and the Article V Library.

51. Emma Roller and David Weigel, "Give Me Amendments or Give Me Death," *Slate*, December 10, 2013, https://slate.com/news-and-politics/2013/12/chris-kapenga -mark-levin-and-article-v-the-secret-campaign-to-pass-conservative-amendments-in -34-states.html (noting best-seller list placement).

52. Mark R. Levin, *The Liberty Amendments*, reprint ed. (New York: Threshold Editions, 2014).

53. See generally Levin.

54. Isaac Stanley-Becker and Tony Romm, "The Anti-Quarantine Protests Seem Spontaneous. But Behind the Scenes, a Powerful Network Is Helping," *Washington Post*, April 22, 2020, http://www.washingtonpost.com/politics/inside-the-conservative-networks -backing-anti-quarantine-protests/2020/04/22/da75c81e-83fe-11ea-a3eb-e9fc93160703 _story.html; "Right-Wing Users Flock to Parler as Social Media Giants Rein in Misinformation," PBS NewsHour, December 3, 2020, https://www.pbs.org/newshour/nation/right -wing-users-flock-to-parler-as-social-media-giants-rein-in-misinformation.

55. Emma Roller, "Conservatives' Improbable New 'Convention of States' Project," *Slate*, December 4, 2013, https://slate.com/news-and-politics/2013/12/alec-ron-johnson -support-convention-of-states.html; Niraj Chokshi, "Next up for ALEC: Taming the Federal Government," *Washington Post*, December 5, 2013, http://www.washing tonpost.com/blogs/govbeat/wp/2013/12/05/next-up-for-alec-taming-the-federal -government/.

56. Roller and Weigel, "Give Me Amendments."

57. Roller and Weigel.

58. Roller, "Conservatives' Improbable New 'Convention of States' Project."

59. Roller and Weigel, "Give Me Amendments."

60. Josh Keefe, "The Koch Brothers Want a New Constitution—and They're Closer Than You Think," *International Business Times*, June 14, 2017, https://www.ibtimes.com/ political-capital/koch-brothers-want-new-constitution-theyre-closer-you-think-2552039; Fredreka Schouten, "Who Are Mega-Donors Bob and Rebekah Mercer, and Why Are They Influential?," *USA TODAY*, March 7, 2017, https://www.usatoday.com/story/news /politics/2017/03/07/who-are-trump-donors-bob-and-rebekah-mercer/98812284/. For sum of 2018 revenue, see Form 990 reports for Citizens for Self-Governance and Convention of

States Action at, respectively: https://apps.irs.gov/pub/epostcard/cor/271657203_201812_9
90_2020060417174876.pdf, and https://apps.irs.gov/pub/epostcard/cor/472245708_20181
2_990O_2020061117187122.pdf.

61. Convention of States Project, "Endorsements," accessed October 20, 2021,
https://conventionofstates.com/endorsements.

62. Greg Abbott, "The Myths and Realities of Article V," *Texas Review of Law and
Politics* 21, no. 1 (2016): 1–68.

63. "BREAKING: Sen. Rick Santorum Joins Convention of States Project as Senior
Advisor," Convention of States Action, September 27, 2021, https://conventionofstates
.com/news/breaking-sen-rick-santorum-joins-convention-of-states-project-as
-senior-advisor.

64. See generally Alexander Hertel-Fernandez, *State Capture: How Conservative
Activists, Big Businesses, and Wealthy Donors Reshaped the American States—and the Nation*
(New York: Oxford University Press, 2019), chap. introduction.

65. "Balanced Budget Amendment Policy—American Legislative Exchange Council," accessed October 21, 2021, https://www.alec.org/model-policy/balanced-budget
-amendment-policy/.

66. "Application for a Convention of the States Under Article V of the Constitution of
the United States—American Legislative Exchange Council," American Legislative
Exchange Council, September 4, 2015, https://www.alec.org/model-policy/article-v
-convention-of-the-states/.

67. Lisa Nelson et al., "ALEC Coalition Letter to Vice President Mike Pence,"
November 13, 2018, https://letusvoteforbba.org/app/uploads/2018/11/ALEC-Coalition
-Letter-to-Vice-President-Pence.pdf.

68. Lisa Nelson et al., "Your Leadership on a BBA Is Appreciated," April 11, 2018,
https://myemail.constantcontact.com/Your-Leadership-on-a-BBA-is-Appreciated
.html?soid=1102755758952&aid=KEQHpebnHP4.

69. For another overview of the runaway risk and an examination of normative consequences, see Michael B. Rappaport, "Reforming Article V: The Problems Created by the
National Convention Amendment Method and How to Fix Them," *Virginia Law Review*
96, no. 7 (2010): 1528–1531.

70. As quoted in Caplan, *Constitutional Brinksmanship*, 64.

71. For a similar view, see Michael Stokes Paulsen, "A General Theory of Article V:
The Constitutional Lessons of the Twenty-Seventh Amendment," *Yale Law Journal* 103,
no. 3 (1993): 738.

72. For some of these opinions, see Arthur J. Goldberg, "The Proposed Constitutional
Convention," *Hastings Constitutional Law Quarterly* 11, no. 1 (1983): 2; Walter E. Dellinger, "The Recurring Question of the Limited Constitutional Convention," *Yale Law
Journal* 88, no. 8 (1979): 1623–1640. See also Rappaport, "Reforming Article V," 1533n47
(gathering citations).

73. Paulsen, "A General Theory of Article V," 739 (emphasis ours; changed italiciza-
tion from original).

74. Charles L. Black, "Amending the Constitution: A Letter to a Congressman," *Yale
Law Journal* 82, no. 2 (1972): 199.

75. As quoted in Rappaport, "Reforming Article V," 1533n47.

76. See also, generally, Akhil Reed Amar, "Philadelphia Revisited: Amending the Constitution Outside Article V," *University of Chicago Law Review* 55, no. 4 (1988): 1043–1104.

77. Of course both groups of representatives—congresspeople and convention delegates—cannot propose amendments that contravene Article V's own unamendability provisions. As many have argued, it is an open question whether the People could amend Article V itself to remove these provisions.

78. As quoted in Congressional Record S.10104 (April 19, 1967) (remarks of Senator Tydings).

79. Congressional Record S.10112 (April 19, 1967) (remarks of Senator Proxmire and Dirksen).

80. We agree with Professor Paulsen's assertion that the question of whether an application expressing a content limitation is valid must be a separate inquiry from whether a convention can be limited to a specific topic. See Paulsen, "A General Theory of Article V," 742–743.

81. Black, "Amending the Constitution," 199.

82. Dirksen, "Supreme Court and the People," 873.

83. In *Dillon v. Gloss*, the Supreme Court held that Congress had the authority to provide a reasonable time limit to ratification. 256 U.S. 368, 375 (1921). This holding is intuitively correct. But in dicta, the *Dillon* court remarked that the Constitution *requires* a contemporaneity to ratification even absent a time limit in the proposing instrument. See 256 U.S. at 376 ("We conclude that the fair inference or implication from Article V is that the ratification must be within some reasonable time after the proposal."). This logic has been heavily criticized and is arguably wrong. See, e.g., Paulsen, "A General Theory of Article V," 684–704. See also U.S. Constitution, amend. 27 (proposed in 1789 but ratified in 1992). A convention or Congress could reasonably decide to *not* provide a time limit, as with the Twenty-Seventh Amendment.

84. For recent use of the new phrase *convention of states*, see, e.g., S. J. Res. No. 3 (Ark., 2019) ("WHEREAS, it is the solemn duty of the states to protect the liberty of our people, particularly for the generations to come, by proposing amendments to the United States Constitution through a *convention of the states* under Article V of the United States Constitution for the purpose of restraining these and related abuses of power.") (emphasis added); S. J. Res. No 9 (Utah 2019) (using *convention of the states* to refer to a convention held under Article V); S. Conc. Res. No. 596 (Miss. 2019) (same); H. Conc. Res. 2010 (Az. 2017) (same); H. Conc. Res. 3006 (ND 2017) (same); S. Conc. Res. 4 (Mo. 2017) (same); S. J. Res. 67 (Tenn. 2016) (same); S. Conc. Res. 52 (La. 2016) (same); 162 Cong. Rec. S6663 (daily ed. Dec. 1, 2016) (same); 162 Cong. Rec. S6354-6355 (daily ed. Nov. 15, 2016) (same); 161 Cong. Rec. S8601-8602 (daily ed. Dec. 10, 2015) (same); 160 Cong. Rec. S6094-6095 (daily ed. Nov. 18, 2014) (same); 160 Cong. Rec. S4332 (daily ed. July 9, 2014) (same); 160 Cong. Rec. S4332 (daily ed. July 9, 2014) (same).

85. One contemporary commentator has argued that "overwhelming and uncontradicted" evidence substantiates the claim that Article V contemplates a "convention of the states." See Robert G. Natelson, *The Law of Article V: State Initiation of Constitutional Amendments* (Columbia Falls, MT: Apis Books, 2020), 25.

A review of the historical record makes clear that this claim is not accurate. For example, while Virginia's 1788 application did use the *convention of the states* phrase, the application also referred to a gathering held under Article V as a "convention . . . *of deputies from* the several states" (emphasis added). New York's 1789 application did not use the *convention of states* moniker at all, opting for Virginia's invocation of "deputies from." See 1 Annals of Cong. 258-259 (J. Gales, Sr. ed., 1834) (H.R., May 5, 1789) (Virginia) ("We do, therefore, in behalf of our constituents, in the most earnest and solemn manner, make this application to Congress, that a convention be immediately called, of deputies from the several States"); H.R. Jour., 1st Cong., 1st Sess. 29-30 (May 6, 1789) (New York) ("make this application to the Congress, that a Convention of Deputies from the several States be called as early as possible").

The difference between these historic formulations and modern activists' proffered moniker is considerable. How such deputies "from" the states (notably not "deputies *of* the states," a formulation with very different implications) would be selected, and in whose stead those deputies would act, remains undefined. That deputies act in the stead of legislators and not the public at large, as contemporary activists' preferred formulation implies, is not a settled point of law and is unsubstantiated by the historical record. After all, as a leading Founding Era dictionary provides, a deputy "is one that exerciseth an office in another man's right." See Richard Burn and John Burn, *A New Law Dictionary* (London: A. Strahan and W. Woodfall, 1792), 1:276. Surely the right implicated by Article V is the right of the People at large to reform the constitutional arrangement, the most logical assumption in the absence of a distinct constitutional grant of authority otherwise to state legislators. The Constitution put asunder the Articles' state-delegation view of federal governance—a reality made clear by the two documents' preambles, which proclaim the authority with which each drafting body undertook its work. Compare the U.S. Constitution preamble ("We the People") with Articles of Confederation of 1781 preamble ("We the undersigned Delegates of the States").

Far from exhibiting "overwhelming and uncontradicted" use of the *convention of states* term, the other eighteenth- and nineteenth-century applications likewise took varying approaches to naming an Article V convention. Compare H.R. Jour. 22nd Cong., 2nd Sess. 219-220 (Jan. 21, 1833) (South Carolina) (using *convention of states* phrase), and Cong. Globe, 36th Cong., 2nd Sess. 680 (S., Feb. 1, 1861) (New Jersey) (same), and Cong. Globe, 37th Cong., Special Sess. 1465-1466 (S., Mar. 18, 1861) (Indiana) (same), and 1893 Neb. Laws 466-467 (same), with S. Jour., 22nd Cong., 2nd sess., 65-66 (Jan. 9, 1833) (Georgia) (declining to use phrase), and H.R. Jour., 22nd Cong., 2nd Sess., 361-362 (Feb. 19, 1833) (Alabama) (same), and Cong. Globe, 36th Cong., 2nd Sess. 751 (S., Feb. 5, 1861) (Kentucky) (same), and 1861 Ohio Laws 181 (same), and 1861 Ill. Laws 281-282 (same), and H. J. Res. No. 10 (Or. 1864) (Oregon) (same), and 33 Cong. Rec. 219 (1899) (Texas) (same).

This historical use of terms to refer to an Article V convention is mixed, with no single term finding sufficiently universal use to intuit a binding truth regarding the meaning of Article V. The provision's meaning has always been contested.

86. S. Jour., 22nd Cong., 2nd sess., 65-66 (Jan. 9, 1833).

87. Convention of States, "If the Founders showed up in 2022, they'd ask why we haven't called a Convention of States," February 26, 2022, Facebook, https://www.facebook .com/photo/?fbid=263155259323625&set=a.162233932749092.

88. A delegate is defined by the *Oxford English Dictionary* as "a person sent or appointed as deputy or representative for another or others, having the authority to act or

take decisions on their behalf." See "delegate, n," OED Online, Oxford University Press, September 2021, https://www.oed.com/view/Entry/49311?rskey=JqK3BE&result= 1&isAdvanced=false. Founding Era dictionaries and Blackstone's *Commentaries* likewise substantiate such a reading. The Court of Delegates in England was an ecclesial court in which the judges—delegates—exercised the authority of the king with discretion and finality. See William Blackstone, *Commentaries on the Laws of England*, ed. William Carey Jones, vol. 2 (San Francisco, CA: Bancroft-Whitney, 1916), 1582–1583 (*66–67); Burn and Burn, *A New Law Dictionary*, 1:268–269.

89. It is true that some credentials empowering delegates to attend the 1787 Convention used the term *commissioner*. But that use was neither consistent nor universal. Virginia, for example, used this term in its nominating document. But in the very next sentence, that same instrument referred to those persons so nominated as "deputies." See Max Farrand, ed., *The Records of the Federal Convention of 1787* (New Haven, CT: Yale University Press, 1937), 3:560. New Jersey, North Carolina, Delaware, and South Carolina likewise used *commissioner* interchangeably with other terms. See Farrand, 3:563, 567, 569, 571, 574, 581. Pennsylvania, Georgia, and Maryland used only the term *deputies*. See Farrand, 3:565, 577, 586. But other states—New Hampshire, New York, Massachusetts, and Connecticut—used the term *delegate* in their nominating documents. See Farrand, 3:571–572, 579, 584, 585. This variety of approaches in nominating documents makes clear that *commissioner* was not a universally accepted term of art. The inconsistent, passing use of the phrase by some states in their nominating documents cannot reasonably substantiate a method that places dispositive weight on the meaning of the specific term in interpreting the meaning and power of Article V. When considered in the context of what convention members called themselves and their colleagues, the near-universal usage of the term *delegate* by contemporaries to refer to convention members, and the Convention's *own* use of the phrase in relation to state ratifying conventions—a body for which the Convention provided a specific textual grant in Article V—it remains clear that *delegate* is the appropriate term. So too does the 1787 Convention's use of *delegate* in the context of state ratifying conventions—the only consideration by the Convention of terms of art related to future constitutional convenings—lend an additional inference that the term should serve as a useful guide in interpreting the meaning of convention provisions in Article V today. Additionally, as recently as 2017, one contemporary convention advocate himself used the term *delegate* in reference to attendees at the 1787 Convention. See Michael Farris, "Defying Conventional Wisdom: The Constitution Was Not the Product of a Runaway Convention," *Harvard Journal of Law & Public Policy* 40, no. 1 (2017): passim.

90. Farrand, *Records of the Federal Convention*, 1937, 1:xi.

91. See, e.g., Farrand, *Records of the Federal Convention*, 1:6, 190, 257, 264, 411, 494, 574, 580; 2:604.

92. See, e.g., Farrand, *Records of the Federal Convention*, 3:18, 19, 21, 22, 25, 27, 29, 30, 31, 33, 36, 49, 51, 53, 61, 66, 67, 81, 104, 125, 144, 151, 152, 179, 186, 210, 229, 240, 245, 248, 250, 253, 255, 264, 282, 304, 306, 331, 376, 378, 410, 411, 445, 447, 468, 469, 480.

93. There is only one reference to a convention delegate as a "commissioner" in the Farrand appendix of related convention correspondence. See Farrand, 3:67 (Pierce Butler to Weedon Butler, August 1, 1787: "I could not refuse the last Appointment of Acting as One of their Commissioners to the Convention to be held at Philadelphia."). The only

other reference, in a document of Madison's hand entitled "Preface to Debates in the Convention of 1787," uses the term in the context of an interstate gathering regarding borders. See Farrand, 3:544 ("It happened also that Commissioners who had been appointed by Virga. & Maryd. to settle the jusisdiction [*sic*] on waters dividing the two States had, apart from their official reports, recomended [*sic*] a uniformity in the regulations of the States on several subjects & particularly on those having relation to foreign trade.")

94. Farrand, *Records of the Federal Convention*, 2:604, 665 (using term *delegates*).

95. See previous notes detailing Founding Era use of the terms *deputy* and *delegate*.

96. See previous note detailing use of phrase *delegate* in state codes.

97. "The Jefferson Statement" (Convention of States Action, September 11, 2014), 1, https://conventionofstates.com/files/the-jefferson-statement.

98. See Michael S. Schmidt and Maggie Haberman, "The Lawyer Behind the Memo on How Trump Could Stay in Office," *New York Times*, October 2, 2021, https://www .nytimes.com/2021/10/02/us/politics/john-eastman-trump-memo.html; Josh Dawsey, Jacqueline Alemany, Jon Swaine, and Emma Brown, "During Jan. 6 Riot, Trump Attorney Told Pence Team the Vice President's Inaction Caused Attack on Capitol," *Washington Post*, October 29, 2021, http://www.washingtonpost.com/investigations/eastman-pence -email-riot-trump/2021/10/29/59373016-38c1-11ec-91dc-551d44733e2d_story.html; Aaron Blake, "The Most Shocking New Revelation About John Eastman," *Washington Post*, October 30, 2021, http://www.washingtonpost.com/politics/2021/10/30/most -shocking-new-revelation-about-john-eastman/.

99. Lipton and Walker, "Christian Conservative Lawyer."

100. David Olson, "Constitutional Convention Risky? No, but Necessary," *Grand Island Independent*, April 7, 2021, https://theindependent.com/opinion/letters/constitutional -convention-risky-no-but-necessary/article_5da0ab4e-9724-11eb-b615-d7ede2434e81 .html.

101. "Article V: A Handbook for State Lawmakers," accessed April 13, 2021, https://www.alec.org/app/uploads/2016/06/2016-Article-V_FINAL_WEB.pdf.

102. Robert Natelson, "Article V: A Handbook for State Lawmakers," June 23, 2016, v, https://www.alec.org/publication/article-v-a-handbook-for-state-lawmakers/.

103. Natelson, 15. For a general overview of the academic debate, see Black, "Amending the Constitution," 198 (arguing that applications purporting to limit a convention are invalid); Paulsen, "A General Theory of Article V," 738; Dellinger, "Recurring Question," 1624; Goldberg, "Proposed Constitutional Convention," 2; Robert M. Rhodes, "A Limited Federal Constitutional Convention," *University of Florida Law Review* 26, no. 1 (1973): 1–18; "Problems Relating to State Applications for a Convention to Propose Constitutional Limitations on Federal Tax Rates: Staff Report to the Committee on the Judiciary, House of Representatives" (Washington, D.C.: Government Printing Office, 1952); William Van Alstyne, "Does Article V Restrict the States to Calling Unlimited Conventions Only—a Letter to a Colleague," *Duke Law Journal* 1978, no. 6 (1978): 1295–1306; Gerald Gunther, "Constitutional Brinksmanship: Stumbling Toward a Convention," *American Bar Association Journal* 65, no. 7 (1979): 1046–1049; Laurence H. Tribe, "Issues Raised by Requesting Congress to Call a Constitutional Convention to Propose a Balanced Budget Amendment," *Pacific Law Journal* 10, no. 2 (1979): 627–640; William W. Van Alstyne, "The Limited Constitutional Convention—the Recurring Answer," *Duke*

Law Journal 1979, no. 4 (1979): 985–998; Grover Rees III, "Constitutional Conventions and Constitutional Arguments: Some Thoughts About Limits Symposium on Federalism," *Harvard Journal of Law and Public Policy* 6, no. 1 (1982): 79–92; Rappaport, "Reforming Article V"; Michael Stern, "Reopening the Constitutional Road to Reform: Toward a Safeguarded Article V Convention," *Tennessee Law Review* 78, no. 3 (2011): 765–788; Michael Stokes Paulsen, "How to Count to Thirty-Four: The Constitutional Case for a Constitutional Convention," *Harvard Journal of Law & Public Policy* 34, no. 3 (2011): 837–872; Michael B. Rappaport, "The Constitutionality of a Limited Convention: An Originalist Analysis," *Constitutional Commentary* 28, no. 1 (2012): 53–110; Ruth Bader Ginsburg, "On Amending the Constitution: A Plea for Patience," *University of Arkansas at Little Rock Law Journal* 12, no. 4 (1989): 677–694; Abner J. Mikva, "Government, Society, and Anarchy," *Mercer Law Review* 38, no. 3 (1987): 753–766.

104.   Natelson, "Article V," 17. Natelson's assertions regarding the political nature of convention delegates are beside the point. The runaway question is not whether the political environment would preclude it. The question is about foundational constitutional authorities. And on that count, the *Handbook* makes no settled claims. It is also a major concern that the *legislatures* of twenty-six states would support the change in convention mandate, a scenario for which Natelson's approach does not account.

105.   Natelson, 17.

106.   Natelson, 42–43nn25–27, 35.

107.   For example, Professor Michael Paulsen's 1993 article clearly argues that conventions cannot be limited. Paulsen, "A General Theory of Article V," 737–743.

108.   Phyllis Schafly, "CON CON: Playing Russian Roulette with the Constitution," *Phyllis Schlafly Report* 18, no. 5 (December 1984), posted on Eagle Forum, accessed April 2, 2022, http://eagleforum.org/psr/1984/dec84/psrdec84.html.

109.   Debra Cassens Weiss, "How Scalia and Ginsburg Would Amend the Constitution," *ABA Journal*, April 21, 2014, https://www.abajournal.com/news/article/how_scalia_and_ginsburg_would_amend_the_constitution.

110.   Natelson, "Article V," 15.

111.   Fla. Stat. Ann. § 11.9345.

112.   Tenn. Code Ann. § 3-18-106; Ind. Code Ann. § 2-8.2-4-6; Utah Code Ann. § 20A-18-101.

113.   Wyo. Stat. Ann. § 9-22-102.

114.   S.D. Codified Laws § 2-15-20 ("is subject to a civil fine of not more than five thousand dollars to be levied by the secretary of state and deposited in the state general fund").

115.   "Senate Bill 332" (2021), http://www.wvlegislature.gov/Bill_Text_HTML/2021_SESSIONS/RS/bills/SB332%20SUB1.pdf; "Bill Status—Complete Bill History," accessed October 23, 2021, https://www.wvlegislature.gov/bill_status/bills_history.cfm?INPUT=332&year=2021&sessiontype=RS.

116.   Wis. Stat. Ann. § 13.176.

117.   It is an unsettled, open question whether a convention held under Article V would adhere to a one-state-one-vote model. We do not take a position on this question. For a general overview of the issues involved, see Thomas H. Neale, "CRS Report R42589, 'The Article V Convention to Propose Constitutional Amendments: Contemporary Issues for Congress,'" 2016, https://crsreports.congress.gov/product/details?prodcode=R42589.

118. Natelson, "Article V," 17.

119. Natelson, 2.

120. Natelson, 20.

121. See Deepa Seetharaman, "Facebook, Rushing into Live Video, Wasn't Ready for Its Dark Side," *Wall Street Journal*, March 6, 2017, https://www.wsj.com/articles/in-rush-to-live-video-facebook-moved-fast-and-broke-things-1488821247 (noting Facebook slogan and use in corporate headquarters).

122. See, e.g., Jeffrey Collins, "SC House Panel Calls for US Constitutional Convention," Associated Press, April 20, 2021, https://apnews.com/article/constitutions-voting-rights-slavery-south-carolina-gun-politics-fb8465e7391a84095660732e7f-24fbbd ("Rep. Cezar McKnight, a Kingstree Democrat, said that as a Black man, he could not approve of a process that could 'change the very fabric of the United States of America' 'What are we to do' if the protections against slavery were removed, McKnight asked. 'Find good white folks to buy us who won't work us so hard?'").

123. For an overview of proposals to draft entirely new constitutions, see John R. Vile, *Re-Framers: 170 Eccentric, Visionary, and Patriotic Proposals to Rewrite the U.S. Constitution* (Santa Barbara: ABC-CLIO, 2014). Five states passed six applications between 1943 and 1949 seeking a convention to propose amendments allowing the United States to join a world federal governing regime. See, 89 Cong. Rec. 5690 (1943) (Florida); 95 Cong. Rec. 4568-4569 (1949) (California); 95 Cong. Rec. 7689 (1949) (Connecticut); 95 Cong. Rec. 7000 (1949) (Florida); 95 Cong. Rec. 4348 (1949) (Maine); 95 Cong. Rec. 4571 (1949) (New Jersey); 95 Cong. Rec. 6587-6588 (1949) (North Carolina). For international law, see proposal of Samuel Moyn in "We the People Have a Few Ideas for the Constitution," *New York Times*, August 4, 2021, https://www.nytimes.com/interactive/2021/08/04/opinion/us-constitution-amendments.html ("In order to promote world peace, and consenting to such limitations on sovereign powers as required, the American people declare that international law is part of our law, directly creating rights and duties for citizens. Acts tending to and undertaken with intent to disturb the peaceful relations among nations shall be unconstitutional and be made a criminal offense. The inviolable and inalienable rights of persons are the basis of peace and justice within and beyond U.S. territory."). For "distributist and monarchical constitution," see Vile, *Re-Framers*, 224–225.

124. Convention of States Action, "Third Time's the Charm: A Convention of States Can Do What the Tea Party and Trump Couldn't," March 10, 2021, https://conventionofstates.com/news/third-time-s-the-charm-a-convention-of-states-can-do-what-the-tea-party-and-trump-couldn-t.

125. Mark Meckler, "A Convention of States Could Block Court Packing Schemes," *Newsmax*, April 19, 2021, https://www.newsmax.com/markmeckler/supreme-court-scotus-court-packing-convention-of-states/2021/04/19/id/1018140/.

CHAPTER 6: COUNTING TO THIRTY-FOUR

1. "Workshop—Four Paths to a State Drafted Voter Ratified US Balance Budget Amendment," American Legislative Exchange Council (ALEC), July 23, 2020, video, 21:56, https://www.youtube.com/watch?v=33WxxZ6gdDQ (*sic—balanced* misspelled in original).

2. Note that the legislature was bicameral at this time. See 1893 Neb. Laws 466-467.

3. David E. Kyvig, *Explicit and Authentic Acts: Amending the U.S. Constitution, 1776–2015* (Lawrence: University Press of Kansas, 2016), 210.

4. Don Walton, "Convention of the States Proposal Gains Second Life in Nebraska Legislature," *Lincoln Journal Star*, May 27, 2021, https://journalstar.com/news/state-and-regional/govt-and-politics/convention-of-the-states-proposal-gains-second-life-in-nebraska-legislature/article_b9343b5b-861b-52a3-9c12-af3ec71f84f7.html; "Nebraska Will Not Join Others in Calling for Convention of States to Amend U.S. Constitution," *Omaha World-Herald*, April 24, 2021, https://norfolkdailynews.com/news/nebraska-will-not-join-others-in-calling-for-convention-of-states-to-amend-u-s/article_80c1571a-a505-11eb-9028-afb995a3736b.html.

5. Sam Wilson, "Fiery Constitutional Debate Splits Senate Republicans," *Helena Independent Record*, February 11, 2021, https://helenair.com/news/state-and-regional/govt-and-politics/fiery-constitutional-debate-splits-senate-republicans/article_8ad20c76-e8c5-55af-aeb4-6a7f80859eb4.html.

6. See Montana State Senate Live Broadcast, http://sg001-harmony.sliq.net/00309/Harmony/en/PowerBrowser/PowerBrowserV2/20210210/-1/41112, 13:59:00.

7. See "Budget Hawks Hatch Plan to Force Constitutional Convention," Associated Press, July 31, 2020, https://apnews.com/article/wisconsin-constitutions-scott-walker-politics-business-0079f922a810f82336a64b4ac6a3a214.

8. American Legislative Exchange Council (ALEC), *Workshop—Four Paths*, 21:56.

9. American Legislative Exchange Council (ALEC), 20:20.

10. For a general overview of ALEC, see Alexander Hertel-Fernandez, *State Capture: How Conservative Activists, Big Businesses, and Wealthy Donors Reshaped the American States—and the Nation* (New York: Oxford University Press, 2019).

11. See, e.g., Olivia Ward, "America's Secret Political Power," *Toronto Star*, December 17, 2011, https://www.thestar.com/news/world/2011/12/17/americas_secret_political_power.html.

12. "Budget Hawks Hatch Plan."

13. So too could Illinois, New York, and others rescind their so-called plenary applications, setting the count back like Colorado's rescission.

14. Jeffrey Collins, "SC House Panel Calls for US Constitutional Convention," Associated Press, April 20, 2021, https://apnews.com/article/constitutions-voting-rights-slavery-south-carolina-gun-politics-fb8465e7391a84095660732e7f24fbbd; "34-States v. Congress," *Let Us Vote for a Balanced Budget Amendment* (blog), accessed October 17, 2021, https://letusvoteforbba.org/34-states-v-congress/; "South Carolina Legislature—S 141 Session 124 (2021–2022)," accessed October 17, 2021, https://www.scstatehouse.gov/query.php?search=DOC&searchtext=balanced%20budget&category=LEGISLATION&session=124&conid=36873617&result_pos=0&keyval=1240141&numrows=10. For statehouse consideration, see Jeffrey Collins, "South Carolina House OKs Constitutional Convention Call," Associated Press, May 11, 2021, https://apnews.com/article/south-carolina-constitutions-election-2020-government-and-politics-838a4832a434822d09dae4c0469ff163.

15. Louisiana, 2008; Florida, 2010; Louisiana, 2011; North Dakota, 2011; Alabama, 2011; North Dakota, 2012; New Hampshire, 2012; Ohio, 2013; Ohio, 2013; Alabama, 2014; Alaska, 2014; Florida, 2014; Florida, 2014; Florida, 2014; Georgia, 2014; Georgia, 2014; Louisiana, 2014; Michigan, 2014; Tennessee, 2014; Alabama, 2015; North

Dakota, 2015; South Dakota, 2015; Utah, 2015; Florida, 2016; Indiana, 2016; Kansas, 2016; New Hampshire, 2016; Oklahoma, 2016; West Virginia, 2016; West Virginia, 2016; Alaska, 2016; Tennessee, 2016; Louisiana, 2016; Arizona, 2017; Arizona, 2017; Missouri, 2017; North Dakota, 2017; Texas, 2017; Wisconsin, 2017; Wyoming, 2017; Missouri, 2017; Alabama, 2018; Utah, 2019; Arkansas, 2019; Mississippi, 2019; Oklahoma, 2021. Data compiled from the Clerk of the House and the Article V Library.

Five states have also made applications calling for more liberal policies, namely, overturning the Supreme Court's decision in *Citizens United*. California, 2014 (160 Cong. Rec. S5507 [daily ed. Sep. 10, 2014]); Illinois, 2014 (162 Cong. Rec. S71 [daily ed. Jan 12, 2016]); Vermont, 2014 (160 Cong. Rec. S4331 [daily ed. July 9, 2014]); New Jersey, 2015 (161 Cong. Rec. H9205 [daily ed. Dec. 9, 2015]); Rhode Island, 2017 (162 Cong. Rec. S5276 [daily ed. Sep. 6, 2016]).

16. See Robert G. Natelson, "Proposing Constitutional Amendments by Convention: Rules Governing the Process," *Tennessee Law Review* 78, no. 3 (2011): 712–714; see generally Robert G. Natelson, "Counting to Two Thirds: How Close Are We to a Convention for Proposing Amendments to the Constitution?," *The Federalist Society Review* 19 (2018): 11.

17. 1861 Ill. Laws 281-282 (Mar. 14, 1861).

18. Ky. H. Res. 1 (Jan. 25, 1861).

19. H.R. Jour., 1st Cong., 1st Sess. 29-30 (May 6, 1789).

20. H.R. Jour., 1st Cong., 1st Sess. 29-30 (May 6, 1789); see also http://article5library .org/gettext.php?doc=1256.

21. Professor David Super has also written convincingly on this topic. See generally David Super, "A Dangerous Adventure: No Safeguards Would Protect Basic Liberties from an Article V Convention," American Constitution Society, October 2021, https:// www.acslaw.org/wp-content/uploads/2021/10/Super-IB-Final3615.pdf.

22. So too do convention proponents' attempts to search for legally operative text prove erroneous, with their standards shifting depending on the application in question. See Natelson, "Counting to Two Thirds," 56 (compare consideration of New York's application, which discarded some language following "resolved," to that of New Jersey's, which considered text following "resolved" as legally controlling over preambulatory clauses to the contrary).

23. Natelson, 55.

24. Applications have no binding force beyond their constitutionally prescribed purposes. While some states do put applications through the presentment process (requiring gubernatorial assent), this is not required. While their closest legislative analogue is a nonbinding resolution, even this form of legislative instrument is unique in form to an application under Article V.

25. H. Jour., 1st Cong., 1st Sess. 28-29 (May 5, 1789).

26. The New York application is but one example of proponents' disparate approaches to determining legally operative language. Contemporary convention advocates have no consistent approach for determining which element of an application is considered "operative." In some, they rely on "resolved" as the legally significant demarcation between so-called prefatory and operative text, but in others—when purposes follow "resolved"— they adopt a contextual approach. Even if one believes Article V applications can have prefatory and operative language (we believe applications cannot), the method for determining such legally operative text must at the very least be consistent.

27. If one is disinclined to think of applications like letters or petitions, then reading them like a contract, a legal frame in which the Founding generation often conceived of constitutions, is equally appropriate. The applications thus communicate a state's assent to an agreement between the People to begin a process of constitutional reformation. In this frame, there must be a manifestation of mutual assent between those who passed the application and those to whom they would be bound, the other states. See, e.g., Michael J. Klarman, *The Framers' Coup: The Making of the United States Constitution* (New York: Oxford University Press, 2016), 188 (remarks of William Paterson: "When independent societies confederate for mutual defense, they do so in their collective capacity; and then each state for those purposes must be considered as one of the contracting parties."); see also Tom Ginsburg, "Constitutions as Contract, Constitutions as Charters," in *Social and Political Foundations of Constitutions*, ed. D. J. Galligan and Mila Versteeg, Comparative Constitutional Law and Policy (Cambridge: Cambridge University Press, 2013), 182–204.

If there is not reasonable contemporaneity and subject-matter agreement between the various applications (manifestations of assent), the instruments cannot form the necessary legal bond. Without a meeting of the minds, there can be no valid application. And as in the case of any court interpreting a contract, the determination of such mutual assent would require at the very least a consideration of all text in the document to determine the true extent of the parties' intentions, not only a narrow glance at the so-called operative provision. Indeed, such an inquiry might even require evidence *outside* the document, which courts often consider when ambiguities arise regarding parties' intentions. Under this theory, applications must be considered *in toto* even under the narrow four-corners conception of the Parol Evidence Rule. Under the more permissive extrinsic evidence rule, a decision maker would look to any relevant information—even information outside the textual instrument itself, including legislative debates and contemporary reporting regarding the application, among other possible acceptable sources of meaning. See, e.g., 6 Corbin on Contracts § 25.5 (Charlottesville, VA: Lexis Law, 2021) (detailing the Restatement [Second] of Contracts' consideration of the Parol Evidence Rule).

Our point here is limited to the issue of Article V applications. Some have raised critiques of contract approaches to amendment ratification, which we do not engage here. The difference between Article V applications and amendment ratification is made plain by the legal act's purpose: an application is akin to an offer to deal, which can form a legally binding manifestation of assent. Applying the contract model to ratification questions is, as many have argued, inapt. Ratification is a legal act with certain consequences, consummating a process. An application begins a process and has no independent power. See, e.g., Michael Stokes Paulsen, "A General Theory of Article V: The Constitutional Lessons of the Twenty-Seventh Amendment," *Yale Law Journal* 103, no. 3 (1993): 705–706. Some have also raised insightful critiques of the constitution-as-contract view in the broader frame of constitutional interpretative theory. We do not engage that issue here. See, e.g., Randy E. Barnett, "The Misconceived Assumption About Constitutional Assumptions," *Northwestern University Law Review* 103, no. 2 (2009): 615–662; Edward A. Fallone, "Charters, Compacts, and Tea Parties: The Decline and Resurrection of a Delegation View of the Constitution," *Wake Forest Law Review* 45, no. 4 (2010): 1067–1124.

28. For the explication of the theory that preambulatory text should be ignored, see Natelson, "Counting to Two Thirds: How Close Are We to a Convention for Proposing Amendments to the Constitution?," 55.

29. William Blackstone, *Commentaries on the Laws of England*, ed. William Carey Jones, vol. 1 (San Francisco, CA: Bancroft-Whitney, 1915), 1:102 (*61).

30. Fortunatus Dwarris, *A General Treatise on Statutes: Their Rules of Construction, and the Proper Boundaries of Legislation and of Judicial Interpretation*, ed. Platt Potter (Albany, NY: W. Gould & Sons, 1871), 269 (emphasis added). For Supreme Court usage of treatise, see District of Columbia v. Heller, 554 U.S. 570, 578 (2008); see also *Heller*, 554 U.S. at 643 n.7 (Stevens, J., dissenting).

31. See, e.g., J. G. Sutherland, *Statutes and Statutory Construction*, ed. Norman J. Singer, 5th rev. ed. (Deerfield, IL: Clark Boardman Callaghan, 1992), sec. 47.04 ("The settled principle of law is that the preamble cannot control the enacting part of the statute *in cases where the enacting part is expressed in clear, unambiguous terms*.") (emphasis added).

32. See United States v. Priestman, 4 U.S. (4 Dall.) 29 (1800) (per curiam); see also United States v. Fisher, 6 U.S. (2 Cranch) 358 (1805).

33. See William N. Eskridge Jr., James J. Brudney, Josh Chafetz, Philip P. Frickey, and Elizabeth Garrett, *Cases and Materials on Legislation and Regulation, Statutes and the Creation of Public Policy*, 6th ed. (St. Paul, MN: West Academic, 2021), 712; see also, generally, Jacob Scott, "Codified Canons and the Common Law of Interpretation," *Georgetown Law Journal* 98, no. 2 (2010): 341–432.

34. See Scott, "Codified Canons," 431.

35. New York has also mandated such an approach. See Scott, 428.

36. Michael Paulsen argues that the interpretive question is necessarily one of *federal* law and thus Congress should not look to state-level interpretive doctrine. While this claim might make some sense in a vacuum, it is wholly inappropriate to bind state legislators to an interpretive regime to which they had no notice when they transmitted the application instrument. The essential inquiry in application validity is the ambit of the *state's* desire. That cannot be properly assessed without looking to how the state legislature itself would cause its own enactments to be interpreted, or in the case of a contract view of applications, the broad textual and nontextual context of the enactment. See Paulsen, "A General Theory of Article V," 1993, 743n224.

37. See Robert Natelson, "Are Recent 'Rescissions' of Article V Applications Valid?," *Independence Institute* (blog), August 14, 2018, https://i2i.org/are-recent-rescissions-of -article-v-applications-valid/. Among such supposed "material mistakes" is a legislature's belief that a convention is uncontrollable, a very legitimate concern shared by many for centuries. Another supposed fatal error that would allow Congress to ignore legislatures' democratic acts is the use of the phrase *constitutional convention*, which Natelson asserts is an inapt and inaccurate name for a convention held under Article V. He insists the term that legislatures must use to appropriately rescind applications is *a convention for proposing amendments*. Never mind that the phrase *constitutional convention* has been the common phrase used by scholars, judges, lawyers, and public policy professionals for well over a century to refer to such a convening. For just a small sampling of scholarship referring to a convention held under Article V as a "constitutional convention," see Herman Vandenburg Ames, *The Proposed Amendments to the Constitution of the United States during the First Century of Its History* (Washington, D.C.: Government Printing Office, 1897), 196, 257; John Charles Daly, Paul Bator, and Gerald Gunther, eds., *A Constitutional Convention, How Well Would It Work?*, American Enterprise Institute 31 (Washington, D.C.: The Institute, 1979); *Constitutional Convention Procedures: Hearing Before the Subcommittee on*

the Constitution of the Committee on the Judiciary, United States Senate, Ninety-Sixth Congress, First Session, on S. 3, S. 520 and S. 1710 . . . November 29, 1979 (Washington, D.C.: Government Printing Office, 1980); Wilbur Edel, *A Constitutional Convention: Threat or Challenge?* (New York: Praeger, 1981); American Enterprise Institute for Public Policy Research, ed., *Proposed Procedures for a Limited Constitutional Convention: 1984, 98th Congress, 2d Session,* AEI Legislative Analyses, no. 46, 98th Congress (Sept. 1984) (Washington, D.C.: American Enterprise Institute for Public Policy Research, 1984); James Edward Bond, David E. Engdahl, and Henry N. Butler, *The Constitutional Convention: How Is It Formed? How Is It Run? What Are the Guidelines? What Happens Now?* (Washington, D.C.: National Legal Center for the Public Interest, 1987); Roger Sherman Hoar, *Constitutional Conventions: Their Nature, Powers, and Limitations* (Littleton, CO: F. B. Rothman, 1987); Paul J. Weber and Barbara A. Perry, *Unfounded Fears: Myths and Realities of a Constitutional Convention,* Contributions in Legal Studies, no. 55 (New York: Greenwood Press, 1989); Malcolm Richard Wilkey, Walter Berns, and Roger Clegg, *Is It Time for a Second Constitutional Convention?* (Washington, D.C.: National Legal Center for the Public Interest, 1995); Richard E. Labunski, *The Second Constitutional Convention: How the American People Can Take Back Their Government* (Versailles, KY: Marley and Beck Press, 2000); "Problems Relating to State Applications for a Convention to Propose Constitutional Limitations on Federal Tax Rates," (using phrase *constitutional convention* on nearly every page); Ralph M. Carson, "Disadvantages of a Federal Constitutional Convention," *Michigan Law Review* 66, no. 5 (1968): 921–930; Robert M. Rhodes, "A Limited Federal Constitutional Convention," *University of Florida Law Review* 26, no. 1 (1973); Walter E. Dellinger, "The Recurring Question of the Limited Constitutional Convention," *Yale Law Journal* 88, no. 8 (1979); Neal S. Manne, "Good Intentions, New Inventions, and Article V Constitutional Conventions Note," *Texas Law Review* 58, no. 1 (1979): 131–170; Laurence H. Tribe, "Issues Raised by Requesting Congress to Call a Constitutional Convention to Propose a Balanced Budget Amendment," *Pacific Law Journal* 10, no. 2 (1979); William W. Van Alstyne, "The Limited Constitutional Convention—the Recurring Answer," *Duke Law Journal* 1979, no. 4 (1979).

38. Natelson, "Are Recent 'Rescissions' of Article V Applications Valid?"

39. For example, in the contemporary resurgence of textualist approaches to statutory instruments, one animating argument is that Congress and other legislative bodies are on notice about the prevailing statutory interpretive canons. There is a common understanding between drafter and interpreter that guides the work of legal texts at all stages of life. In many states, the legislature has codified interpretive canons. The further one goes back in time, the less purchase such an argument can claim. Approaches to interpretive theory have radically changed. See, for example, the historical discussion in Eskridge Jr. et al., *Cases and Materials,* 405–424.

40. Russell L. Caplan, *Constitutional Brinksmanship: Amending the Constitution by National Convention* (New York: Oxford University Press, 1988), 76.

41. For theory on application staleness, see Natelson, "Proposing Constitutional Amendments," 712–715. For theory regarding rescission, see Natelson, "Are Recent 'Rescissions' of Article V Applications Valid?"

42. See generally "Problems Relating to State Applications"; Paulsen, "A General Theory of Article V," 1993; Michael Stokes Paulsen, "How to Count to Thirty-Four: The Constitutional Case for a Constitutional Convention," *Harvard Journal of Law & Public*

Policy 34, no. 3 (2011): 837–872; Thomas H. Neale, "CRS Report R42592; The Article V Convention for Proposing Constitutional Amendments: Historical Perspectives for Congress," March 29, 2016, https://crsreports.congress.gov/product/details?prodcode =R42592; James Stasny, "The Constitutional Convention Provision of Article V: Historical Perspective," *Cooley Law Review* 1, no. 1 (1982): 101–108.

43. Caplan, *Constitutional Brinksmanship*, 159.

44. The Constitution provides no guidance on how a convention would set its rules or establish voting thresholds (i.e., adopting a one-state, one-vote paradigm or a proportional model like the Electoral College). We take no position on the question.

45. Colby Itkowitz, "Sen. Graham: 'Not Trying to Pretend to Be a Fair Juror,'" *Washington Post*, December 14, 2019, http://www.washingtonpost.com/politics/lindsey-graham -not-trying-to-pretend-to-be-a-fair-juror-here/2019/12/14/dcaad02c-1ea8-11ea-b4c1 -fd0d91b60d9e_story.html; Ledyard King and Maureen Groppe, "Can Senators Who Have Already Voiced Opinions Do 'Impartial Justice' at Trump Impeachment Trial?," *USA TODAY*, January 16, 2020, https://www.usatoday.com/story/news/politics /2020/01/16/impeachment-senators-pledge-impartial-justice-trump-trial /4488539002/; for another take on congressional oaths, see Russ Feingold, "Upholding an Oath to the Constitution: A Legislator's Responsibilities," *Wisconsin Law Review* 2006, no. 1 (2006).

46. Michael B. Rappaport, "Reforming Article V: The Problems Created by the National Convention Amendment Method and How to Fix Them," *Virginia Law Review* 96, no. 7 (2010): 1513.

47. Activists have also used the theory to prod some states to help their cause. In a November 13, 2019, letter to the then governor-elect Tate Reeves of Mississippi, David Biddulph, a proponent of an Article V convention, argued that—with application aggregation—the country was one state away from a successful call. David Biddulph, "Would You Consider Supporting an Effort to Amend Mississippi's Existing Article V Balanced Budget Amendment Application in Order to Lead the Country Back to Fiscal Policies Like Those Achieved Under Your Administration as Lieutenant Governor?," November 13, 2019, http://letusvoteforbba.org/app/uploads/2020/02/Governor-elect -Reeves-Letter-with-Natelson-Article-and-Applications-1.pdf; Steve Wilson, "Will Mississippi Join Call for Convention of States?," Mississippi Center for Public Policy, March 4, 2019, https://mspolicy.org/will-mississippi-join-call-for-convention-of-the-states/.

48. Compare Laurence H. Tribe, "A Constitution We Are Amending: In Defense of a Restrained Judicial Role," *Harvard Law Review* 97, no. 2 (1983): 433–445, with Walter E. Dellinger, "The Legitimacy of Constitutional Change: Rethinking the Amendment Process," *Harvard Law Review* 97, no. 2 (1983): 386–432; see also, Paulsen, "A General Theory of Article V," 1993.

49. Coleman v. Miller, 307 U.S. 433, 450 (1938).

50. See Coleman, 307 U.S. at 459 (Black, J., concurring) (plurality opinion) (Congress enjoys "sole and complete control over the amending process, subject to no judicial review").

51. See also Erwin Chemerinsky, *Constitutional Law: Principles and Policies*, 6th ed., Aspen Treatise Series (New York: Wolters Kluwer, 2019), 158–159.

52. Mary Margaret Penrose, "Conventional Wisdom: Acknowledging Uncertainty in the Unknown," *Tennessee Law Review* 78, no. 3 (2011): 789–806 (arguing that the justiciability question is more opaque than *Coleman* provides); David Castro,

"A Constitutional Convention: Scouting Article Five's Undiscovered Country Comment," *University of Pennsylvania Law Review* 134, no. 4 (1986): 939–966; Paulsen, "A General Theory of Article V," 1993 (arguing that *Coleman* is "bad law" and that Article V does present justiciable questions); Dellinger, "The Legitimacy of Constitutional Change."

53. Lester B. Orfield, *The Amending of the Federal Constitution*, electronic resource, Michigan Legal Studies (Ann Arbor: University of Michigan Press, Chicago: Callaghan & Co, 1942), 36, http://0-heinonline.org.libus.csd.mu.edu/HOL/Index?index=beal/zacw&collection=beal.

54. Paulsen, "A General Theory of Article V," 713.

55. Some district courts have determined that amendment-related questions were justiciable. See, e.g., Dyer v. Blair, 390 F. Supp. 1291 (N.D.Ill., 1975) (three-judge court); Idaho v. Freeman, 529 F. Supp. 1107 (D. Idaho, 1981), vacated and remanded to dismiss, 459 U.S. 809 (1982) (on mootness grounds). Of particular importance, the *Dyer* court distinguished *Coleman* by citing Article V cases like *Hawke* and *Dillon v. Gloss* that predated *Coleman*. The *Dyer* court notably did not consider the question of whether *Coleman* overruled *Hawke* or *Dillon* on the justiciability question.

56. See Rucho v. Common Cause, 139 S. Ct. 2484, 2494 (2019) ("Among the political question cases the Court has identified are those that lack 'judicially discoverable and manageable standards for resolving [them].'" (quoting Baker v. Carr, 369 U. S. 186, 217 (1962))).

57. Chemerinsky, *Constitutional Law*, 140.

58. Chemerinsky, 140.

59. Some scholars disagree. See, e.g., Penrose, "Conventional Wisdom."

60. See Francis H. Heller, "Article V: Changing Dimensions in Constitutional Change," *University of Michigan Journal of Law Reform* 7, no. 1 (1973): 81; see also Arthur Earl Bonfield, "Proposing Constitutional Amendments by Convention: Some Problems," *Notre Dame Lawyer* 39, no. 6 (1964): 672–673 (noting resurgence of view during the Dirksen years).

61. See, e.g., Arthur Earl Bonfield, "The Dirksen Amendment and the Article V Convention Process," *Michigan Law Review* 66, no. 5 (1968): 981–982; note, "Proposed Legislation on the Convention Method of Amending the United States Constitution," *Harvard Law Review* 85, no. 8 (1972): 1643–1644.

62. Scott Walker and others argue that a court could issue a writ of mandamus ordering Congress to issue a call. But this theory misstates the very premise of mandamus jurisdiction. The writ, as constructed under both the English common law and as imported to the United States, functions as a directive from a court to an executive or judicial officer to undertake a ministerial function, or to a noncoequal body, like a *state* legislature, to redress a constitutional grievance. Here, proponents would entreat a court to issue the writ against a *legislative body* of coequal station in the federal constitutional system, an application wholly inconsistent with the historical foundation of the writ and a brazen afront against the separation of powers. See Blackstone, *Commentaries on the Laws of England*, 2:1633–1664 (*110–111) (outlining a variety of situations in which mandamus may issue against executive officials under the English common law, including ordering the opening of government buildings for certain uses). Unlike *Coleman*, which was heard at the Supreme Court on certiorari to the Kansas Supreme Court on a question involving mandamus jurisdiction, the issue as Walker presents it would be seeking the writ to issue

from a *federal* court to the Congress. 307 U.S. 433 (1939). This would trigger separation of powers concerns not raised in *Coleman*. So too does this state-federal distinction make the common role of mandamus in apportionment cases inapt as applied to Article V issues. There, federal courts order *state* legislatures to undertake reapportionment. No separation of powers issues are raised in such a scenario. See, e.g., Baker v. Carr. 369 U.S. 186 (1962). For a more detailed examination of mandamus jurisdiction in the Article V context, see David Super, "Gov. Scott Walker's Proposed Mandamus to Compel Congress to Call an Article V Convention," *Balkinization* (blog), July 31, 2020, https://balkin.blogspot.com/2020/07/gov-scott-walkers-proposed-mandamus-to.html.

63. Some might argue that Congress cannot limit how future Congresses undertake their ministerial act. This might be true (we take no position on the question), but at the very least congressional action would set clear expectations that could exert a powerful normative force on legislators undertaking the ministerial duty.

CHAPTER 7: "WE THE PEOPLE" IN PERILOUS TIMES

1. "Washington's Farewell Address (1796)," Avalon Project of the Lillian Goldman Law Library, Yale Law School, accessed November 19, 2021, https://avalon.law.yale.edu/18th_century/washing.asp.

2. Karen Yourish, Larry Buchanan, and Denise Lu, "The 147 Republicans Who Voted to Overturn Election Results," *New York Times*, January 7, 2021, https://www.nytimes.com/interactive/2021/01/07/us/elections/electoral-college-biden-objectors.html.

3. Logan Dancey and Geoffrey Sheagley, "Partisanship and Perceptions of Party-Line Voting in Congress," *Political Research Quarterly* 71, no. 1 (2018): 33.

4. "*The Federalist Papers*, No. 10," November 23, 1787, Avalon Project of the Yale Law School Goldman Law Library, https://avalon.law.yale.edu/18th_century/fed10.asp.

5. "Washington's Farewell Address (1796)."

6. "From John Adams to Jonathan Jackson, 2 October 1780," *Founders Online*, National Archives, https://founders.archives.gov/documents/Adams/06-10-02-0113. Original source: *The Adams Papers*, Papers of John Adams, vol. 10, *July 1780–December 1780*, ed. Gregg L. Lint and Richard Alan Ryerson (Cambridge, MA: Harvard University Press, 1996), 192–193 (punctuation as in original).

7. Michael Wines, "In the War Against Gerrymandering, an Army of Voters Meets a Dug-in Foe," *New York Times*, August 15, 2019, https://www.nytimes.com/2019/08/15/us/gerrymandering-redistricting-wisconsin.html.

8. Mitchell Schmidt, "2020 Election Again Shows Lopsided Republican Legislative Maps," *Wisconsin State Journal*, November 12, 2020, https://madison.com/news/local/govt-and-politics/2020-election-again-shows-lopsided-republican-legislative-maps/article_d0c11425-df16-5d0b-a3e8-4954e7897652.html.

9. Schmidt.

10. Sam Levine, "Wisconsin: The State Where American Democracy Went to Die," *Guardian*, April 10, 2020, https://www.theguardian.com/us-news/2020/apr/10/wisconsin-voter-restrictions-democracy-coronavirus-primary.

11. David Daley, "Inside the Republican Plot for Permanent Minority Rule," *New Republic*, October 15, 2020, https://newrepublic.com/article/159755/republican-voter-suppression-2020-election.

12. Vann R. Newkirk, "How Redistricting Became a Technological Arms Race," *Atlantic*, October 28, 2017, https://www.theatlantic.com/politics/archive/2017/10/gerry mandering-technology-redmap-2020/543888/.

13. Newkirk.

14. Nebraska's unicameral legislature is, by law, nonpartisan. But it is dominated by Republican-affiliated legislators. Compiled from the National Conference of State Legislatures, https://www.ncsl.org/research/about-state-legislatures/partisan-composition.aspx.

15. See Rucho v. Common Cause, 139 S. Ct. 2484 (2019).

16. Reid J. Epstein, "Wisconsin Republicans Push to Take Over the State's Elections," *New York Times*, November 19, 2021, https://www.nytimes.com/2021/11/19/us /politics/wisconsin-republicans-decertify-election.html.

17. Epstein.

18. Molly Beck, "Wisconsin Senate Republicans Block Resolution Condemning U.S. Capitol Assault and Affirming Biden Victory," *Milwaukee Journal Sentinel*, January 12, 2021, https://www.jsonline.com/story/news/politics/2021/01/12/wisconsin-senate-gop -blocks-resolution-condemning-u-s-capitol-riot/6646635002/.

19. Epstein, "Wisconsin Republicans Push"; Molly Beck, "A Wisconsin Republican Drew Praise from Trump for His Call to Decertify the 2020 Vote. Here's Why That Won't Happen," *Milwaukee Journal Sentinel*, November 19, 2021, https://www.jsonline .com/story/news/politics/elections/2021/11/19/wisconsin-gop-leader-rejects -trump-backed-call-decertify-election/8668447002/.

20. Clara Hendrickson and Dave Boucher, "Michigan Senate Republicans Overhaul Voter ID Bill to Include New Restrictions," *Detroit Free Press*, October 6, 2021, https:// www.freep.com/story/news/politics/2021/10/06/michigan-senate-republicans -voter-id-bill/7794844002/.

21. Igor Derysh, "Election Clerks 'Panic' over Michigan GOP Voting Scheme That Could Eliminate 20% of Polling Sites," *Salon*, November 17, 2021, https://www.salon .com/2021/11/17/michigan-gops-latest-vote-crushing-scheme-could-eliminate -20-of-polling-sites/.

22. See "Roll Call Vote, Utah Senate Joint Resolution 9, 2019 General Session," Legiscan, accessed November 20, 2021, https://legiscan.com/UT/rollcall/SJR009/id /814215.

23. Max Farrand, ed., *The Records of the Federal Convention of 1787* (New Haven, CT: Yale University Press, 1937), 2:630.

24. We do not take a position here on whether the ERA has been successfully ratified. The consideration here refers to the changes in judicial doctrine preceding contemporary claims of successful ratification.

CHAPTER 8: THE CONSTITUTION IN JEOPARDY

1. For one article summarizing and supporting this change in the Republican Party, see "Against the Dead Consensus," *First Things*, March 21, 2019, https://www.firstthings .com/web-exclusives/2019/03/against-the-dead-consensus ("Yet more than two years later, we speak with one voice: There is no returning to the pre-Trump conservative consensus that collapsed in 2016. Any attempt to revive the failed conservative consensus that preceded Trump would be misguided and harmful to the right.").

2. Willi Paul Adams, *The First American Constitutions: Republican Ideology and the Making of the State Constitutions in the Revolutionary Era* (Lanham, MD: Rowman & Littlefield, 2001), 137–138.

3. As quoted in Adams, 137–138.

4. As quoted in Adams, 137–138.

5. See Blake Hounshell and Leah Askarinam, "'Daddy, What's an Originalist?,'" *New York Times*, February 3, 2022, https://www.nytimes.com/2022/02/02/us/politics /bethany-mandel-conservative-childrens-books.html.

6. See generally Maggie Astor, "How the Supreme Court Quietly Undercut Roe v. Wade," *New York Times*, September 2, 2021, https://www.nytimes.com/2021/09/02 /us/politics/roe-v-wade-supreme-court.html; Jamelle Bouie, "In the Dead of Night, the Supreme Court Proved It Has Too Much Power," *New York Times*, September 3, 2021, https://www.nytimes.com/2021/09/03/opinion/texas-roe-supreme-court.html; David Leonhardt, "Rulings Without Explanations," *New York Times*, September 3, 2021, https://www.nytimes.com/2021/09/03/briefing/scotus-shadow-docket-texas-abortion -law.html; Charlie Savage, "Texas Abortion Case Highlights Concern Over Supreme Court's 'Shadow Docket,'" *New York Times*, September 2, 2021, https://www.nytimes. com/2021/09/02/us/politics/supreme-court-shadow-docket-texas-abortion.html.

7. Scholars note the Supreme Court's holding in *Oregon v. Mitchell* as instigating consideration of the Twenty-Sixth Amendment. 400 U.S. 112 (1970). The amendment did not *overturn* the Court, however, but rather required the rule that the Court declined to establish in *Oregon*. See David E. Kyvig, *Explicit and Authentic Acts: Amending the U.S. Constitution, 1776–2015* (Lawrence: University Press of Kansas, 2016), 367.

8. See generally G. Edward White, *The Constitution and the New Deal* (Cambridge, MA: Harvard University Press, 2000); Marian C. McKenna, *Franklin Roosevelt and the Great Constitutional War: The Court-Packing Crisis of 1937* (New York: Fordham University Press, 2002); see also Bruce Ackerman, *We the People*, vol. 2, *Transformations* (Cambridge, MA: Belknap Press of Harvard University Press, 1998), vol. 2, pt. 3.

9. Thomas Jefferson, "Letter to Abigail Adams, September 11, 1804," in *The Writings of Thomas Jefferson*, ed. Paul Leicester Ford, vol. 8 (New York: G. P. Putnam's Sons, 1897), 310.

10. For a survey of scholarly consideration of changing popular perspectives of the Court, see Daniel Hemel, "Can Structural Changes Fix the Supreme Court?," *Journal of Economic Perspectives* 35, no. 1 (February 1, 2021): 119–142. Regarding court reform, see generally Daniel Epps and Ganesh Sitaraman, "How to Save the Supreme Court," *Yale Law Journal* 129, no. 1 (2019): 148–207; Bruce Ackerman, "Trust in the Justices of the Supreme Court Is Waning. Here Are Three Ways to Fortify the Court," *Los Angeles Times*, December 20, 2018, https://www.latimes.com/opinion/op-ed/la-oe-ackerman-supreme -court-reconstruction-20181220-story.html.

11. United States v. Carolene Products Co., 304 U.S. 144, 155 n.4 (1938).

12. 140 S. Ct. 1731 (2020). For scholarly consideration of the decision and its malcontents, see Andrew Koppelman, "Bostock, LGBT Discrimination, and the Subtractive Moves," *Minnesota Law Review* 105, no. 1 (2020): 1–41; Tara Leigh Grove, "Which Textualism?," *Harvard Law Review* 134, no. 1 (2020): 265–307.

13. Burgess Everett, "Hawley on LGBTQ Ruling: Conservative Legal Movement Is Over," *POLITICO*, June 16, 2020, https://www.politico.com/news/2020/06/16/josh -hawley-lgbt-supreme-court-conservatives-323254.

14. Harvard Law School, "The Antonin Scalia Lecture Series: A Dialogue with Justice Elena Kagan on the Reading of Statutes," YouTube video, November 25, 2015, https://www.youtube.com/watch?v=dpEtszFT0Tg.

15. See Adrian Vermeule, "Beyond Originalism," *Atlantic*, March 31, 2020, https://www.theatlantic.com/ideas/archive/2020/03/common-good-constitutionalism/609037/; Conor Casey and Adrian Vermeule, "Myths of Common-Good Constitutionalism," *Ius & Iustitium* (blog), September 9, 2021, https://iusetiustitium.com/myths-of-common-good-constitutionalism/; Dan McLaughlin, "Explaining Common-Good Originalism Does Not Help Its Case," *National Review*, August 19, 2021, https://www.nationalreview.com/2021/08/explaining-common-good-originalism-does-not-help-its-case/.

16. 505 U.S. 833 (1992).

17. Vermeule, "Beyond Originalism."

18. Hadley Arkes, Josh Hammer, Matthew Peterson, and Garrett Snedeker, "A Better Originalism," *American Mind*, March 18, 2021, https://americanmind.org/features/a-new-conservatism-must-emerge/a-better-originalism/. Vermeule made a similar claim, likewise conflating constitutional and statutory interpretation. See Adrian Vermeule, "Gnostic Constitutional Theory," *Ius & Iustitium* (blog), November 15, 2021, https://iusetiustitium.com/gnostic-constitutional-theory/ ("When Justice Gorsuch wrote the explicitly originalist opinion for the Court in *Bostock*, a number of originalist critics tried to defend the theory by condemning the man, saying that Gorsuch had simply done originalism wrong. But if a Marshall Scholar and John Finnis student who wrote a whole book on originalism can't do it right, it's time to start wondering whether the fault lies in the theory.").

19. See, among many others, William Pryor Jr., "Politics and the Rule of Law; the 14th Annual Joseph Story Lecture," The Heritage Foundation, October 20, 2021, https://www.heritage.org/the-constitution/lecture/politics-and-the-rule-law; Randy E. Barnett, "Common-Good Constitutionalism Reveals the Dangers of Any Non-Originalist Approach to the Constitution," *Atlantic*, April 3, 2020, https://www.theatlantic.com/ideas/archive/2020/04/dangers-any-non-originalist-approach-constitution/609382/; Garrett Epps, "Common-Good Constitutionalism Is an Idea as Dangerous as They Come," *Atlantic*, April 3, 2020, https://www.theatlantic.com/ideas/archive/2020/04/common-good-constitutionalism-dangerous-idea/609385/; David B. Rivkin Jr. and Andrew M. Grossman, "The Temptation of Judging for 'Common Good,'" *Wall Street Journal*, July 23, 2021, https://www.wsj.com/articles/supreme-court-conservative-liberal-originalist-vermeule-11627046671.

20. Our short consideration of judicial review here does not convey our complete views on the complex and nuanced questions involved. We have sketched with a broad brush (undoubtedly missing important nuance due to its brevity) what many see as the contemporary state of affairs to help consider the state of Article V in the contemporary context. A robust theory of judicial review could, and arguably should, coexist alongside a reformed amendment mechanism. Whether and how to conceptualize that theory is not our topic here.

21. See John Hart Ely, *Democracy and Distrust: A Theory of Judicial Review* (Cambridge, MA: Harvard University Press, 1980). For a critique of Ely's theory, see Richard A. Posner, "Democracy and Distrust Revisited," *Virginia Law Review* 77, no. 4 (1991): 641–652. For a consideration of the modern state of Ely's theory, see Jane S. Schacter, "Ely at the Altar: Political Process Theory Through the Lens of the Marriage Debate," *Michigan Law Review* 109, no. 8 (2011): 1363–1412.

CHAPTER 9: REVOLUTION, REVISITED

1. Thomas Jefferson, "Letter to Samuel Kercheval, July 12, 1816," in *The Portable Thomas Jefferson*, ed. Merrill Peterson (New York: Viking, 1975), 552, 560.

2. "An Electoral Surprise in Chile May Produce a Left-Wing Constitution," *Economist*, May 27, 2021, https://www.economist.com/the-americas/2021/05/27/an-electoral -surprise-in-chile-may-produce-a-left-wing-constitution.

3. "A Constitutional Convention in Chile Could Forge a New Social Contract," *Economist*, March 18, 2021, https://www.economist.com/the-americas/2021/03/18/a-constitutional -convention-in-chile-could-forge-a-new-social-contract.

4. "An Electoral Surprise in Chile."

5. Katy Watson, "Jubilation as Chile Votes to Rewrite Constitution," *BBC News*, October 26, 2020, https://www.bbc.com/news/world-latin-america-54687090.

6. Mandalit del Barco, "The Story of 'No' Is the Story of Modern Chile," NPR, February 14, 2013, https://www.npr.org/2013/02/15/172040656/the-story-of-no-is-the -story-of-modern-chile.

7. "An Electoral Surprise in Chile."

8. Watson, "Jubilation as Chile Votes."

9. Watson.

10. "An Electoral Surprise in Chile."

11. Many countries, like Ecuador, use the phrase *constituent assembly*. For clarity, we sum all such assemblies under the moniker *constitutional convention*.

12. "Constitution Rankings," Comparative Constitutions Project, updated April 8, 2016, https://comparativeconstitutionsproject.org/ccp-rankings/.

13. Articles 30, 33, 52, respectively. See "Ecuador 2008 (Rev. 2021) Constitution," accessed November 1, 2021, https://www.constituteproject.org/constitution/Ecuador _2021?lang=en.

14. "Constitution Rankings."

15. For a scholarly consideration of these phenomena, see generally Adam S. Chilton and Mila Versteeg, *How Constitutional Rights Matter* (New York: Oxford University Press, 2020). For consideration of some of these phenomena in the context of new constitutions, see generally Tom Ginsburg and Aziz Z. Huq, eds., *From Parchment to Practice: Implementing New Constitutions*, Comparative Constitutional Law and Policy (Cambridge: Cambridge University Press, 2020).

16. "Can Chile's Constitutional Convention Defuse People's Discontent?," *Economist*, October 2, 2021, https://www.economist.com/the-americas/2021/10/02/can-chiles-constitutional -convention-defuse-peoples-discontent.

17. "A Constitutional Convention in Chile."

18. For a general overview of the Chilean process, see "A Constitutional Convention in Chile"; "An Electoral Surprise in Chile"; "Can Chile's Constitutional Convention Defuse People's Discontent?"; Watson, "Jubilation as Chile Votes"; Dave Sherwood, Fabian Cambero, and Aislinn Laing, "Chile's Govt in Shock Loss as Voters Pick Independents to Draft Constitution," Reuters, May 17, 2021, https://www.reuters.com/world/americas/chile -ruling-coalition-heading-disappointment-constitutional-delegates-vote-2021-05-17/; Will Freeman and Lucas Perelló, "Chilean Voters Have Turned Their Backs on Traditional

Coalitions. What's Next?," *Foreign Policy*, accessed November 1, 2021, https://foreignpolicy.com/2021/05/17/chile-elections-independents-to-write-new-constitution/.

19. For another take, see Sanford Levinson, "The Constitution Is the Crisis," *Atlantic*, October 1, 2019, https://www.theatlantic.com/ideas/archive/2019/10/the-constitution-is-the-crisis/598435/.

20. John R. Vile, *The Constitutional Amending Process in American Political Thought* (New York: Praeger, 1992), 1.

21. As discussed in the introduction, Professor Mary Sarah Bilder's scholarship has demonstrated the inconsistency of Madison's notes. It is possible, but of course cannot be proved, that Madison's comment that there were insufficient "constitutional regulations" to make Article V's convention route function properly was in reality a backward-looking assessment added after the Convention rather than a contemporaneous account. See Mary Sarah Bilder, *Madison's Hand: Revising the Constitutional Convention* (Cambridge, MA: Harvard University Press, 2015).

22. For discussion of this general theme, see Donald S. Lutz, "Toward a Theory of Constitutional Amendment," *American Political Science Review* 88, no. 2 (1994); see also Vincent Ostrom and Barbara Allen, *The Political Theory of a Compound Republic: Designing the American Experiment* (Lanham, MD: Lexington Books, 2008).

23. Letter of George Washington to Bushrod Washington, November 10, 1787, in *The Origins of the American Constitution: A Documentary History*, ed. Michael Kammen (New York: Penguin, 1986), 83. As quoted in Sanford Levinson, *Our Undemocratic Constitution: Where the Constitution Goes Wrong (and How We the People Can Correct It)* (New York: Oxford University Press, 2006), 21.

24. As argued by the Roxbury Town Delegates in 1778. As quoted in Willi Paul Adams, *The First American Constitutions: Republican Ideology and the Making of the State Constitutions in the Revolutionary Era* (Lanham, MD: Rowman & Littlefield, 2001), 137–138.

25. Adams, 82; see also Gordon S. Wood, *The Creation of the American Republic, 1776–1787* (Chapel Hill: University of North Carolina Press, 1969), 308.

26. In their comparative analysis of state constitutions and foreign national constitutions, Professors Versteeg and Zackin reach a similar conclusion regarding the multifaceted nature of American constitutionalism, arguing that the conception of "American constitutional exceptionalism" as defined by the federal constitutional regime should be reconsidered. See Mila Versteeg and Emily Zackin, "American Constitutional Exceptionalism Revisited," *University of Chicago Law Review* 81, no. 4 (2014): 1641–1707.

27. For an overview of varying approaches to amending mechanisms in the states, including the use of conventions, see John J. Dinan, *The American State Constitutional Tradition* (Lawrence: University Press of Kansas, 2006), chaps. 1, 2. For another consideration on this theme, see Jeffrey S. Sutton, *51 Imperfect Solutions: States and the Making of American Constitutional Law* (New York: Oxford University Press, 2018).

28. Richard Tuck, *The Sleeping Sovereign: The Invention of Modern Democracy* (Cambridge, MA: Cambridge University Press, 2015), 197n20.

29. Massachusetts (1778); New Hampshire (1779); Mississippi (1817), Connecticut (1818), Maine (1819), New York (1821), Rhode Island (1824), Alabama (1828), Virginia (1830), Tennessee (1834), North Carolina (1835), Michigan (1835), Pennsylvania (1838), New Jersey (1844), Iowa (1844), Louisiana (1845), Texas (1845), Missouri (1845),

Wisconsin (1846), Illinois (1848), Ohio (1851), Kansas (1855), Oregon (1857), Minnesota (1857), Kansas, (1859), Georgia (1861), Arkansas (1864), Nevada (1864), South Carolina and Florida (1868), Vermont (introduced in 1870, although original 1793 Constitution—still in force—did not provide for plebiscite), West Virginia (1872), Colorado (1876). See Tuck, 197n20. See also Francis Newton Thorpe, ed., *The Federal and State Constitutions: Colonial Charters, and Other Organic Laws of the States, Territories, and Colonies, Now or Heretofore Forming the United States of America* (Washington, D.C.: Government Printing Office, 1909).

30. John J. Dinan, *State Constitutional Politics: Governing by Amendment in the American States* (Chicago: University of Chicago Press, 2018), 13.

31. See P.R. Const., art. VII; Am. Sam. Rev. Const., art. V, § 3; N. Mar. I. Const. art. XVIII; D.C. Code, § 1–203.03. The United States Virgin Islands and Guam do not have constitutions but are rather governed by acts of Congress, namely, the Revised Organic Act of the Virgin Islands of 1954 and the Guam Organic Act of 1950.

32. See Ill. Const., art. XIV, § 2, pt. (b); see also, art. XIV, § 3 (same standard for citizen-initiated amendment).

33. John J. Dinan, *State Constitutional Politics*, 16.

34. See also Steven L. Piott, *Giving Voters a Voice: The Origins of the Initiative and Referendum in America* (Columbia: University of Missouri Press, 2003); see also Tuck, *Sleeping Sovereign*; Thomas E. Cronin, *Direct Democracy: The Politics of Initiative, Referendum, and Recall* (Cambridge, MA: Harvard University Press, 1989); Thomas Goebel, *A Government by the People: Direct Democracy in America, 1890–1940* (Chapel Hill: University of North Carolina Press, 2002).

35. Dinan, *State Constitutional Politics*, 12.

36. See N.Y. Const., art. XIX, § 2.

37. Levinson, *Our Undemocratic Constitution*, 12.

38. Jesse McKinley, "New York Voters Reject a Constitutional Convention," *New York Times*, November 8, 2017, https://www.nytimes.com/2017/11/07/nyregion/new-york-state-constitutional-convention.html; Jesse McKinley, "Fear vs. Hope: Battle Lines Drawn Over a Constitutional Convention," *New York Times*, October 26, 2017, https://www.nytimes.com/2017/10/26/nyregion/fear-vs-hope-battle-lines-drawn-over-a-constitutional-convention.html. For detailed election results, see "NYS Board of Elections Proposal Election Returns," November 7, 2017, https://www.elections.ny.gov/NYSBOE/elections/2017/general/2017GeneralElectionProp1.pdf. See also Gerald Benjamin, "The Amending Clause in the New York Constitution and Conventionphobia," *Pace Law Review* 38, no. 1 (2017): 14–27.

39. John Dinan, "The Political Dynamics of Mandatory State Constitutional Convention Referendums: Lessons from the 2000s Regarding Obstacles and Pathways to Their Passage," *Montana Law Review* 71, no. 2 (2010): 418.

40. Dinan, 396.

41. The interplay between mid-to-late-twentieth-century Article V debates and state constitutional law is particularly interesting in Illinois. The 1970 Illinois Constitution, drafted by convention, provides specific constitutional procedures for how the legislature is to handle federal Article V matters. Such specific procedures were likely a response to the efforts of Illinois' own Everett Dirksen on the question, which occurred while the Illinois convention undertook its work. See Ill. Const., art. XIV, § 4. For an overview of

the history of that convention, see Ann M. Lousin, "Why Did Illinois Call a Constitutional Convention in 1968?," *Rutgers University Law Review* 72, no. 4 (2020): 1021–1044. For an insightful reflection on that convention and the work of state constitutional change, see Ann M. Lousin, "How to Hold a State Constitutional Convention in the Twenty-First Century," *Loyola of Los Angeles Law Review* 44, no. 2 (2011): 603–622.

42. John J. Dinan, "State Constitutions and American Political Development," in *Constitutional Dynamics in Federal Systems: Sub-National Perspectives*, ed. Michael Burgess and G. Alan Tarr (Montreal: McGill-Queen's University Press, 2012), 46 (number of conventions); Mila Versteeg and Emily Zackin, "American Constitutional Exceptionalism Revisited," *University of Chicago Law Review* 81, no. 4 (2014), 1672, 1705 (number of state constitutions and amendments, respectively).

43. Dinan, *State Constitutional Politics*, 26.

44. Kyvig, *Explicit and Authentic Acts Amending the U.S. Constitution, 1776–2015*, 249–253; David P. Thelen, *Robert M. La Follette and the Insurgent Spirit* (Boston: Little, Brown, 1976), 172–173, 180; Nancy C. Unger, *Fighting Bob La Follette: The Righteous Reformer* (Chapel Hill: University of North Carolina Press, 2000), 191, 194, 214, 289.

45. 50 Cong. Rec. 239 (1913).

46. See Lester B. Orfield, "The Reform of the Federal Amending Power," *North Carolina Law Review* 10, no. 1 (1931): 16–55; Lester B. Orfield, "The Reform of the Federal Amending Power," *Nebraska Law Bulletin* 10, no. 3 (1932): 350–396.

47. Orfield, "Reform of the Federal Amending Power," 1931, 25–27.

48. Orfield, 38.

49. Michael B. Rappaport, "Reforming Article V: The Problems Created by the National Convention Amendment Method and How to Fix Them," *Virginia Law Review* 96, no. 7 (2010).

50. See, e.g., Wisc. Const., art. XII (requiring both houses to approve a proposed amendment in two consecutive sessions before referral to voters). For academic consideration of this mechanism, see Lutz, "Toward a Theory of Constitutional Amendment," 361.

51. Reforming Article V's procedures has long been the subject of Article V convention applications. See 60 Cong. Rec. 31 (1920) (Louisiana); 99 Cong. Rec. 9864 (1953) (Illinois); 99 Cong. Rec. 9180-81 (1953) (South Dakota); 101 Cong. Rec. 2770-71 (1955) (Texas); 101 Cong. Rec. 6744-45 (1955) (Georgia); 102 Cong. Rec. 7240-41 (1956) (Michigan); 103 Cong. Rec. 4831-32 (1957) (Idaho); 103 Cong. Rec. 6471-72 (1957) (Indiana); 109 Cong. Rec. 2768 (1963) (Arkansas); 109 Cong. Rec. 2072 (1963) (Florida); 109 Cong. Rec. 2769 (1963) (Kansas); 109 Cong. Rec. 5868 (1963) (Missouri); 109 Cong. Rec. 1172 (1963) (Oklahoma); 109 Cong. Rec. 10,441-42 (1963) (South Carolina); 109 Cong. Rec. 4779 (1963) (Wyoming); 111 Cong. Rec. 880 (1965) (Virginia); 158 Cong. Rec. H3805 (daily ed. May 31, 2011) (North Dakota).

52. See Sue Halpern, "Why the Right Keeps Saying That the United States Isn't a Democracy," *New Yorker*, October 15, 2020, https://www.newyorker.com/news/daily-comment/why-republicans-keep-saying-that-the-united-states-isnt-a-democracy.

53. See, e.g., Mark V. Tushnet, *Taking the Constitution Away from the Courts* (Princeton, NJ: Princeton University Press, 1999), chap. 8 (summarizing critique).

54. This provision arose as part of Alabama's local amendment mechanism, which puts amendments relating to local issues to those local voters alone. But in this particular circumstance, the question was posed to the entire state due to the "no" vote of a

legislator. See "Alabama Voters Approve Gun Proposal for Franklin County," Associated Press, November 4, 2020, https://www.usnews.com/news/best-states/alabama/articles/2020-11-03/senate-race-between-jones-tuberville-tops-alabama-ballot.

55. Sue Bell Cobb and Elizabeth H. Bowles, "The Call for Reform," *New England Law Review* 45, no. 4 (2011): 813.

56. Jessica Levinson, "California Constitution, Altered Over 500 Times; U.S. Constitution, Only 27," *KCET*, September 3, 2012, https://www.kcet.org/socal-focus/california-constitution-altered-over-500-times-u-s-constitution-only-27.

57. John M. Allswang, *The Initiative and Referendum in California, 1898–1998* (Stanford, CA: Stanford University Press, 2000); see also Debra Bowen, "The California Initiative Process at Its Centennial," *California Western Law Review* 47, no. 2 (2011): 253–258; Glenn Smith and Brendan Bailey, "Legislative Reform of California's Direct Democracy: A Field Guide to Recent Efforts," *California Western Law Review* 47, no. 2 (2011): 259–300; Nick Brestoff, "The California Initiative Process: A Suggestion for Reform," *Southern California Law Review* 48, no. 4 (1975): 922–958; John Diaz, "California Initiative Process Is Out of Control," *San Francisco Chronicle*, September 7, 2018, https://www.sfchronicle.com/opinion/diaz/article/California-initiative-process-is-out-of-control-13213651.php; John Myers, "Powerful, Wealthy Interest Groups Keep Tight Grip on California Proposition System," *Los Angeles Times*, November 5, 2020, https://www.latimes.com/california/story/2020-11-05/analysis-ballot-initiatives-system-california-spending.

58. See previous note gathering sources regarding reform efforts.

59. Jim Miller, "Three Californias? Calexit Effort Joined by New State-Splitting Plan," *Sacramento Bee*, August 18, 2017, http://www.sacbee.com/news/politics-government/capitol-alert/article168118272.html; Andrea Diaz, "3 Californias? The Initiative to Break up the State May Be on the Ballot in November," CNN, April 13, 2018, https://www.cnn.com/2018/04/13/us/california-closer-to-split-into-three-states-trnd/index.html.

60. Bob Egelko, "Splitting up California: State Supreme Court Takes Initiative off Ballot," *San Francisco Chronicle*, July 19, 2018, https://www.sfchronicle.com/politics/article/Splitting-up-Calif-State-Supreme-Court-takes-13085880.php; Maura Dolan, "Measure to Split California into Three States Removed from Ballot by the State Supreme Court," *Los Angeles Times*, July 18, 2018, https://www.latimes.com/local/lanow/la-me-ln-three-state-court-20180718-story.html. For an insightful assessment of the role of referenda in state constitutional meaning making, and state court assessment of "referendum sovereignty," see Jonathan L. Marshfield, "Forgotten Limits on the Power to Amend State Constitutions," *Northwestern University Law Review* 114, no. 1 (2019): 65–148.

61. Regarding racial discrimination, see Marshfield, "Forgotten Limits on the Power to Amend State Constitutions," 67n2 (gathering citations to racially discriminatory state constitutional amendments). Regarding religious discrimination, see, e.g., Pierce v. Society of Sisters, 268 U.S. 510 (1925) (holding voter-approved referendum that denied right of parents to send children to private schools—a provision supported by the KKK and other anti-Catholic actors—unconstitutional under the Fourteenth Amendment); Espinoza v. Montana Department of Revenue, 140 S. Ct. 2246 (2020) (holding voter-approved state constitutional provision prohibiting distribution of public funds to religious institutions unconstitutional). Regarding sexual minority discrimination, see, e.g., Romer v. Evans, 517 U.S. 620 (1996) (holding as unconstitutional a Colorado voter-approved

amendment to the state constitution that banned anti-discrimination laws protecting gay, lesbian, or bisexual people); Hollingsworth v. Perry, 570 U.S. 693 (2013) (holding that litigants did not have standing to challenge district court finding that California voter-approved constitutional amendment defining marriage was unconstitutional); Obergefell v. Hodges, 576 U.S. 644 (2015) (holding as unconstitutional many voter-approved, state constitutional amendments defining marriage).

62. See, e.g., Espinoza, 140 S. Ct. (2020) (state constitutional provision); Romer, 517 U.S. (1996) (same); Obergefell, 576 U.S. (2015) (same). In *Obergefell*, the Court specifically considered constitutional provisions in Kentucky, Michigan, and Tennessee; Ohio's contested provision was a state statute. See Obergefell, 576 U.S. at 653 (gathering citations to constitutional and statutory provisions). For the canonical consideration of the countermajoritarian nature of the Supreme Court's power of judicial review, see Alexander M. Bickel, *The Least Dangerous Branch: The Supreme Court at the Bar of Politics*, 2nd ed. (New Haven, CT: Yale University Press, 1986).

63. "*The Federalist Papers*, No. 49," February 5, 1788, Avalon Project of the Yale Law School Goldman Law Library, https://avalon.law.yale.edu/18th_century/fed49.asp.

64. Julian P. Boyd, ed., "Letter from Thomas Jefferson to James Madison (Sept 6, 1789)," in *The Papers of Thomas Jefferson* (Princeton, NJ: Princeton University Press, 1958), 392–396.

65. *Washington's Farewell Address: And the Constitution of the United States* (Middlebury, VT: Washington Benevolent Society, 1812), 13, 17–18.

EPILOGUE

1. "Farewell Address at Springfield, Illinois; February 11, 1861," in *Collected Works of Abraham Lincoln*, vol. 4 (New Brunswick, NJ: Rutgers University Press, 1953), 190–191.

2. Understanding of this plot was drawn from leaked proceedings of a select committee of the House. See "The Revolution," *New York Daily Herald*, January 28, 1861, Morning ed., 1.

3. See Michael J. Kline, *The Baltimore Plot: The First Conspiracy to Assassinate Abraham Lincoln* (Hyattsville, MD: Westholme, 2013), 363.

4. William E. Gienapp, *Abraham Lincoln and Civil War America: A Biography* (New York: Oxford University Press, 2002), 77.

5. Gienapp, 77–78.

6. "First Inaugural Address—Final Text; March 4, 1861," in *Collected Works of Abraham Lincoln*, vol. 4 (New Brunswick, NJ: Rutgers University Press, 1953), 269–270. In original, "I can not be ignorant. . . ."

7. Mark V. Tushnet, *Taking the Constitution Away from the Courts* (Princeton, NJ: Princeton University Press, 1999), 181.

INDEX

As a lawmaker, diplomat, attorney, and professor, **Russ Feingold** has devoted his career to protecting the Constitution's bedrock guarantees. Serving nearly two decades in the United States Senate, Feingold was the only senator to vote against the Patriot Act, citing civil liberty concerns, and cosponsored the Bipartisan Campaign Reform Act (McCain-Feingold Act), the most important campaign finance reform in decades. He sat on the Senate Judiciary Committee and chaired its Subcommittee on the Constitution.

Feingold has also served as a U.S. special envoy and taught at Stanford, Harvard, Yale, and Marquette Law Schools. He is now president of the American Constitution Society, the nation's leading progressive legal organization, and is an affiliate at the Stanford Constitutional Law Center. He is a recipient of the John F. Kennedy Profile in Courage Award. His previous book, *While America Sleeps: A Wake-up Call for the Post-9/11 Era*, was a *New York Times* best seller.

Peter Prindiville is a nonresident fellow at the Stanford Constitutional Law Center and an attorney based in Washington, D.C. He previously was a fellow on the Senate Judiciary Committee and a high school history and civics teacher. Prindiville earned a law degree from Stanford; master's degrees from Notre Dame and University College Cork, Ireland, where he was a Mitchell Scholar; and an undergraduate degree from Georgetown.

PublicAffairs is a publishing house founded in 1997. It is a tribute to the standards, values, and flair of three persons who have served as mentors to countless reporters, writers, editors, and book people of all kinds, including me.

I. F. STONE, proprietor of *I. F. Stone's Weekly*, combined a commitment to the First Amendment with entrepreneurial zeal and reporting skill and became one of the great independent journalists in American history. At the age of eighty, Izzy published *The Trial of Socrates*, which was a national bestseller. He wrote the book after he taught himself ancient Greek.

BENJAMIN C. BRADLEE was for nearly thirty years the charismatic editorial leader of *The Washington Post*. It was Ben who gave the *Post* the range and courage to pursue such historic issues as Watergate. He supported his reporters with a tenacity that made them fearless and it is no accident that so many became authors of influential, best-selling books.

ROBERT L. BERNSTEIN, the chief executive of Random House for more than a quarter century, guided one of the nation's premier publishing houses. Bob was personally responsible for many books of political dissent and argument that challenged tyranny around the globe. He is also the founder and longtime chair of Human Rights Watch, one of the most respected human rights organizations in the world.

·   ·   ·

For fifty years, the banner of Public Affairs Press was carried by its owner Morris B. Schnapper, who published Gandhi, Nasser, Toynbee, Truman, and about 1,500 other authors. In 1983, Schnapper was described by *The Washington Post* as "a redoubtable gadfly." His legacy will endure in the books to come.

Peter Osnos, *Founder*